PRAISE FO[R]

The Naked [Brewer]

"This is a perfect book for anyone who is a fan of artisanal beer and homebrewing. I personally am a huge fan of the Honey Chamomile Blonde beer that these two incredibly talented ladies have developed, and now I can learn to brew it myself at home. Their philosophy of using fresh and local ingredients to create delicious recipes is perfect for the artisanal craft movement evolving today."

—Shiva Rose, actress and founder/writer of www.thelocalrose.com

"The Beer Chicks' unique approach to homebrewing is a breath of fresh air. They make it simple, accessible, and fun—as beer and brewing should be."

—Joel Elliott, co-owner and brewmaster at Strand Brewing Company

"It is almost impossible not to have fun when you're hanging out with the Beer Chicks. Leave it to Hallie and Christina to take the intimidation out of the brewing process and inject that sense of mischievous adventure that seems to follow them everywhere. Whether you're a curious newbie or a stone-cold veteran brewer, you will find it almost impossible not to have fun with this book."

—Jeremy Raub, cofounder and head brewer at Eagle Rock Brewery

"As with cooking, learning to make great homebrew requires finding mentors whose palates you can trust. Christina and Hallie know beer and know how to help you find your own palate and turn your desires into a frothy beverage you can be proud to serve as your own. How fantastic that their zest for sharing a passion for the world's most accessible drink now reaches into your own kitchen!"

—Evan Kleiman, host of KCRW's "Good Food"

THE
NAKED BREWER

FEARLESS HOMEBREWING,
TIPS, TRICKS &
RULE-BREAKING RECIPES

Christina Perozzi & Hallie Beaune

A PERIGEE BOOK

A PERIGEE BOOK
Published by the Penguin Group
Penguin Group (USA) Inc.
375 Hudson Street, New York, New York 10014, USA
Penguin Group (Canada), 90 Eglinton Avenue East, Suite 700, Toronto, Ontario M4P 2Y3, Canada
(a division of Pearson Penguin Canada Inc.) • Penguin Books Ltd., 80 Strand, London WC2R 0RL,
England • Penguin Group Ireland, 25 St. Stephen's Green, Dublin 2, Ireland (a division of Penguin
Books Ltd.) • Penguin Group (Australia), 250 Camberwell Road, Camberwell, Victoria 3124, Australia
(a division of Pearson Australia Group Pty. Ltd.) • Penguin Books India Pvt. Ltd., 11 Community
Centre, Panchsheel Park, New Delhi—110 017, India • Penguin Group (NZ), 67 Apollo Drive,
Rosedale, Auckland 0632, New Zealand (a division of Pearson New Zealand Ltd.) • Penguin Books
(South Africa) (Pty.) Ltd., 24 Sturdee Avenue, Rosebank, Johannesburg 2196, South Africa

Penguin Books Ltd., Registered Offices: 80 Strand, London WC2R 0RL, England

While the author has made every effort to provide accurate telephone numbers, Internet addresses, and
other contact information at the time of publication, neither the publisher nor the author assumes any
responsibility for errors, or for changes that occur after publication. Further, the publisher does not have
any control over and does not assume any responsibility for author or third-party websites or their content.

THE NAKED BREWER

First edition: October 2012

ISBN: 978-0-399-53768-4

An application to catalog this book has been submitted to the Library of Congress.

PRINTED IN THE UNITED STATES OF AMERICA

10   9   8   7   6   5   4   3   2   1

The recipes contained in this book are to be followed exactly as written. The publisher is
not responsible for your specific health or allergy needs that may require medical supervision.
The publisher is not responsible for any adverse reactions to the recipes contained in this book.

Most Perigee books are available at special quantity discounts for bulk purchases for
sales promotions, premiums, fund-raising, or educational use. Special books, or book
excerpts, can also be created to fit specific needs. For details, write: Special Markets,
Penguin Group (USA) Inc., 375 Hudson Street, New York, New York 10014.

ALWAYS LEARNING   PEARSON

For Matthew and Kirill.
The men behind the chicks, behind the beer.
Your love and support made this book possible.

ACKNOWLEDGMENTS

Christina and Hallie would like to thank all of the brewers, beer experts, beer lovers, homebrewers, and beer drinkers who contributed to this book and to their general beer-loving life: Rob Tod, Patrick Rue, Victor Novak, Greg Koch, Sam Calagione, Brian Thompson, Jonathan Porter, Kevin Watson, Mark Hegedus, Angela Jasus, Eric Kremer, Joe Corona, Kevin Day, Ting Su, Steve Raub, Lisa Morrison, Cyrena Nouzille, Steve Grossman, Jonathan Porter, Meg Gill, Skipp Shelly, Rich Rush, Tom Kelley, and the Brewers Association.

We'd also like to thank local beer friends, who supported us in our hometown of Los Angeles. Although once considered a wasteland, craft beer in L.A. has finally found a strong and innovative foothold. Thank you to Cedd Moses, Skyler Reeves, Scotty Mitchell, Lauren Wong, Stephen Dorame and everyone at 213 Nightlife, Karen Kurzbuch, Felicity "Fee" Doyle, Alea Bell, Josh Lurie and Sean Inman at Food GPS, the Yeastside Brewers, Jane and Russell Adams, Johnnie "the Scot" Mundell, Tomm Carroll, Ryan Sweeney, Maury Morgan, Jenn Garbee, Dave Stickel, Jason Bernstein, and Mila and Martin Daraz.

A special shout-out to:

Greg Beron and everyone at Culver City and Eagle Rock Homebrewing Supply and

Sean O'Malley and everyone at O'Malley Productions.

A very special thank-you to:

Erin Tarasi—Your intelligence, sense of humor, cooking ability, and attention to detail are a wicked combination.

Chantel Fiedler—Your penchant and talent for all things beer and fantastic research skills were an enormous help.

Mark Jilg (Craftsman Brewing Company)—You have always been an inspiration, mentor, and great help to us throughout our beer life. Thanks for your pointed guidance with this book and throughout our beer journey.

Jeremy Raub (Eagle Rock Brewery)—We can't thank you enough for checking out our recipes and the countless times you and your brewery (and your beer) have helped us out.

Joel Elliott (Strand Brewing Company)—Brewing with you was a great education! Thanks for vetting our recipes and encouraging us to brew outside the box!

Christina would especially like to thank: My awesomely hip parents, Bill and Claudia, and my super supportive siblings, Dan Perozzi and Danté Cox. My dear friends—the core group—who were always willing to meet me at the pub for a pint. And Kirill, who stalwartly endured my endless beer geekery along with other stunts and still has my back. Mad props again to HB!

Hallie would especially like to thank: Matthew, my beer-loving husband; my loving parents, Catherine and Roy; my sisters Christine, Holly, and Wendy, who are always up for a beer with me; cute Karter and Kennedy; my grandmothers, Eleanor and Betty, who remember when everyone used to homebrew; Mike, Carol, Marlisse, and Lexi, the wonderful new additions to my family; Stacey, Rachael, and Erin, my trio of longtime supportive girlfriends; all of my dear friends, you know who you are; Thunder, who always keeps me company when I brew; and, of course, CP!

Last, but not least, we would like to again thank our literary agent Michelle Brower and everyone at Folio Literary Management. A special thank-you to our editor, Maria Gagliano, and also to our publicist, Heather Conner, two bona fide beer chicks. Thank you also to everyone at Perigee and the Penguin Group.

Beer Is Good.

CONTENTS

Appendixes

THE
NAKED BREWER

You Don't Have to Be a Pro, You Just Have to Relax

The shadow that hovers over homebrewing is the idea that you need an entire room for the operation. People consider taking up the hobby and immediately think they'll need a cavernous basement that can serve as a speakeasy of sorts. While that would be *really awesome* to have, most of us already struggle to find a place for all of our stuff in our modest homes or tiny apartments. Those who have a spare garage or room for a mini brew house are few and far between. We won't lie, you *will* need to buy some equipment to make beer fairly well and to make brewing easier on yourself. And you may need to clear out a shelf for your carboy, but relax, you don't have to alter your lifestyle. And anyway, you made space for that bread maker you never use and the banana hook your mom gave you. Much better to make room for equipment that enables you to make your own artfully crafted beer, don't you think?

Let's get this out of the way too. To begin to homebrew you do not need to have the following: advanced knowledge of beer, a manly way about you, a beer belly, a beard, suspenders and a mustache, or a penchant for hops. You *may* have those things in any combination of course, but you don't *have* to. You just need to want to drink beer. That you made. Oh yeah, and it also helps if you like to cook.

We're not chefs, but we love to cook. In the beginning, we made use of the tips we learned from our mothers, mostly by watching them repeat family recipes borne of good, solid Midwestern cooking. When our foodie selves emerged in our adulthood, we cracked the cookbooks, read edgy food blogs, and began to attempt to follow more challenging recipes. At first, recipes with 15 steps seemed like just too much work, but as we learned the difference between sweating and sautéing onions—that is, some of the basics—those more-involved recipes came into focus and seemed fairly simple.

Homebrewing is like cooking. You hear this comparison all the time from homebrewers, and brewmasters at professional breweries are much like chefs in a restaurant. Most of the process is boiling and simmering ingredients in a big pot. The soup analogy is obvious. Adding hops feels like spicing a dish. Some recipes call for spices straight from your spice rack or for seasonal fruit. When you learn to cook or to homebrew, you learn the tools of the trade, define the ingredients in a way that makes sense for you, begin to follow recipes with simple steps, then attack more complicated dishes (maybe even bake), and finally, get creative and build your own recipes. With this comparison, we hope to help you understand that homebrewing is not *easy* per se, but it's not that difficult. Certainly it's difficult to become an award-winning homebrewer, and eventually a professional brewer, but to make a nice tasty brew in the comfort of your own home that you would be proud to share with your friends is not an impossible feat.

The hardest thing about homebrewing is actually the waiting. Homebrewed beer is not an instant-gratification exercise (like opening and drinking a beer is), and in our society, that can seem quite unappealing. Most beers take 7 to 10 days to ferment and become beer and another 2 weeks to carbonate. This kind of sucks. When cooking, you season the game hen, you roast the ramps and oyster mushrooms, and in an hour or two you can eat it. You can immediately enjoy and share your creation, judge and make note of successes and failures. Homebrewing requires a bit more patience. That is why the most important part of homebrewing, in our opinion, is having a generous supply of craft beer to drink *while* brewing. This takes the edge off any brewing mishaps and makes the waiting seem like a small pain to bear. Snacks don't hurt either. . . . So stock your fridge and start with a simple recipe. Don't worry, as author and general beer guru Charlie Papazian said in the *Complete Joy of Homebrewing*, "Relax, Don't Worry, Have a Homebrew" (RDWHAHB for you Twitter-users out there).

Our First Foray into Homebrewing

Perhaps Voltaire said it best in his 1764 *Dictionnaire Philosophique* when he wrote, "*Le mieux est l'ennemi du bien*," which translates to "The perfect is the enemy of the good." This couldn't be truer than with beginning homebrewing. If the goal in your homebrewing is to immediately make the biggest, strangest, weirdest, hoppiest, highest alcohol, and bestest beer in the world, you will be sorely disappointed—as we were initially—until we learned this very important lesson: The singular goal of our homebrewing is to get inside of our love of beer. And the recipes and methods in this book are meant to help anyone off the street make solid, good-tasting, even *really* good-tasting, nay even *delicious*, beer at home.

But here's what happens when you aim for perfect right away.

THE CHAI TEA PORTER INCIDENT

Very early on in our brewing experience, maybe even our second batch, we decided that we were going to make the greatest Porter ever made. It was going to be a chai tea Porter. We spent many hours researching chai tea and what chai spices were. We went to a specialty spice store to put together our own specialty blend of chai, with the perfect amounts of cardamom, clove, cinnamon, and fennel, plus whatever other "secret" spices (which were actually pretty basic spices) we could find.

We researched which malts we thought would be toasty and nutty enough for a Porter but would still be complemented by chai flavors in an understated way. We studied different hop strains and read about their properties and their alpha acid levels and decided when to add them to the boil. We were geniuses! This chai tea Porter was going to blow our beer-loving friends' minds! Yay us!

What can we say, we were new to homebrewing. We didn't realize that adding these particular spices and herbs early in the boil could create some really bitter, acrid, bile-like off-flavors. We didn't realize that some additions can leave an oily residue that can float on the top of your beer and kill the head. We didn't have experience with how the extremely different hops can behave if added for 60 minutes or for just 5 minutes at the end of the boil. We didn't strain enough. We didn't sanitize enough. We may have drunk the beer way too young. What we ended up with was a cloudy, hazy, muddy beer that smelled like poop and tasted like, oh what's the word . . . oh yeah, *vomit*. So much for our genius.

Needless to say, we were totally discouraged. We had put in so much time and effort and energy into what was arguably the *worst* beer ever made in the history of homebrewing. We should have just made some damn chai tea instead. We felt a little better after talking to a few homebrewing friends who assured us that this overreaching is a very common occurrence. We homebrewers, who are most often craft beer connoisseurs first, have delusions of grandeur and become overly ambitious believing that, after having very little practice, we're going to make a beer as good as a Duvel Golden Ale or Pliny the Elder, or Westmalle Tripel, beers that are made professionally in breweries that have been refining their approach and their recipes for many, many years.

We're not saying that some great beer isn't brewed at home. And since the CTPI (chai tea Porter incident), we've brewed some delicious beers. What we're saying is that truly great beer is usually made by brewers with years and years of experience and know-how. What we want our recipes to do is help everyone gain the ability to make really good beer using easy methods that allow for shortcuts where they can be afforded and that provide the most efficient brewing methods in terms of time, effort, and setup. We hope to teach you the techniques we use to mitigate some very common beginning homebrewer mistakes. Some of our methods are controversial to the purists, but we ask you to reserve your judgment and give the beer a taste. It's all about the self-satisfaction of brewing your very own tasty brew.

After we shook off the pain and embarrassment of the CTPI, we tried to brew a chai tea Porter again. Humbled, and far more careful, this time we used a solid tried-and-true recipe from friends at our local homebrew store for a medium-bodied Porter made with extract and steeped specialty grains. For the chai, we simply added some organic chai tea bags that we bought at the local health food store when there was 15 minutes left in the boil. After a 3-week fermentation period, we kegged the beer, put it under pressure, and let it rest in the fridge for another 2 weeks. What we ended up with was a really, really good chai tea Porter. It wasn't the fantastical overreaching concoction that we came up with in our own minds. It was better. Because it was delicious, and it was ours, and we made it.

We are not telling you this story to discourage you from creativity. We love risk taking and just going for it. But even the greatest artists need to learn the techniques before they can let all of that go and let their creativity fly. You need not be afraid to fail, the bumps along the way are what bond us to our fellow homebrewers. We just want you to get a little experience under your belt first, learning some beginning techniques by using the recipes and methods in this book, so that you can learn from our mistakes and our successes alike. So, based on our own early mishaps, here's a little advice to consider before you get started:

- Beer needs time. Meditate on this.
- There's usually an easier and better way to do things.
- No, there's no way around sanitizing.
- Don't cry over spilled wort.
- Smack your yeast pack early!
- An ice bath cools down 2½ gallons pretty damn quick.
- Get the order of your brew steps in your head before you start. Think, mise en place.
- It's hard to lift 5 gallons by yourself, so get help or brew small.
- Secondary helps make better beers.
- Ask for help from other homebrewers and professional brewmasters
- If you make a mistake, reward yourself with a store-bought beer and try again another day.

How to Use This Book

Our book is organized by month. We offer you three homebrew recipes per month that we think are appropriate for that time of year. We chose the beers that we'd like you to drink *during* the month in which they are listed. Because beer takes time, you may want to brew them a month or two before you want to drink them, depending on how long the beer takes to ferment and sit in a secondary vessel. So if you want to make Stupid Cupid's Bittersweet Chocolate Stout for someone special in time for Valentine's Day, you'll need to get started in January. If you're not a planner, then screw it, brew whatever whenever.

Some recipes we chose are appropriate for the holiday(s) of that month (see Christmas Spiced Porter in December). Others incorporate an ingredient or two that is in season at that time (like the rosemary in April's Rosemary Laurel Savory Saison). Sometimes we chose recipes that pair well with the weather, food, and general spirit of the month (see the Honey Chamomile Blonde in August). But there are no rules really, open the book and brew whatever beer inspires you. Follow your taste preferences and please your own palate.

Each recipe provides the style of brewing (extract, extract with specialty grains, partial mash, all-grain) and the difficulty level, so you know what you're getting yourself into. We are using terms from our previous book, *The Naked Pint*, to denote the difficulty level as we see it. These refer to your level as a brewer or perhaps as a beer connoisseur. In order, from easiest to most difficult, they are as follows: Neophyte (newbie), Sophomore (moving up), Devout (really into it), Promiscuous (up for anything). We also offer the following stats for each beer: estimated Original Gravity (OG), estimated Final Gravity (FG), Alcohol by Volume (ABV), and International Bitterness Units (IBUs).

Don't freak out if your brew doesn't hit the mark right off the bat. In fact, don't ever freak out about homebrew. It's not worth it, it's supposed to be a fun endeavor, so keep that in mind. We all miss our Final Gravities now and then. This is one of the more difficult things to master in homebrewing. Before you throw out your batch because you didn't hit the right ABV, ask yourself if you *like* your beer, if you think it tastes good, what flavors you want to enhance or change. Don't get depressed if your beer is a bit too low in alcohol or bitterness. All of this will improve with experience and more careful brewing practices. Think of the stats as just a general guideline for the recipe and style of beer.

We've written our beer recipes much like one would a cooking recipe. All of the steps are explained and laid out in sequential order. We hope this helps make it easier to brew. When we started, we wished someone had done this for us. A list of ingredients without a step-by-step procedure can be quite daunting.

These recipes have made tasty beer in our households and some of our friends' homes, but you may need to tweak them here and there based on your setup and flavor profile preferences. Every brew house (and home) is different, and efficiency varies from system to system, so when you begin to understand the ingredients better, alter the recipes as you see fit. You may prefer more or less of a spice or herb, or perhaps you're finding the beers too hoppy or not bitter enough, so start experimenting and adjusting amounts so that your homebrew becomes unique to you and your palate.

At the end of each recipe we have Rule Breakers and Tips. These are shortcuts and helpful hints that allow you to skip some of the hard stuff, use different ingredients, or improve the brewing and fermenting process. They're not for purists, but should help you out if you need it.

We suggest letting most beers rest in secondary vessels after the primary fermentation of your beer. This is not required, but we've found that it helped our homebrews improve significantly.

Finally, we have a food recipe in each month that uses a homebrew as an ingredient. Beer is not just our favorite pairing drink but also our favorite cooking ingredient. We started cooking with beer before we even started homebrewing. There's so much to be done with it in the culinary world. Chefs everywhere are incorporating it in a variety of dishes, sometimes in traditional ways, sometimes in innovative, unusual ways. Using beer in a food recipe is cool, but using your own homebrewed beer in a recipe and then pairing it with that same homebrew on the dinner table will floor your dinner companions. Anyway, you need something to eat after all that homebrewing, right?

Are you ready to brew now?

STOP! Skip the Next Two Chapters!

 If you are ready to brew up some beer, skip the next two chapters. You can jump into June and make some delicious homebrew without knowing the details of the brewing process or the intricacies of the ingredients. Just buy the following from your local homebrew supply store or from an online site:

- One 5-gallon brew pot
- Two 3- to 5-gallon plastic buckets with lids (with stopper holes drilled)
- One airlock and rubber stopper
- A strainer
- A long spoon

Add the ingredients listed in the recipe, and then, hit the kitchen!

Back when we first brewed, we started with a pretty good knowledge of beer but no real knowledge of brewing. It helps, of course, to have those things, but sometimes you just want to get started on a project and read the instructions later. The nuts and bolts may be a little loose, but you have the damn shelves up!

So feel free to choose your own adventure and start in on a recipe. Come back to "Beer Refresher Course" and "Become the Brewer" while you're waiting for your first beer to ferment.

Beer Refresher Course

If you're going to be brewing beer, you'd best know what it is and what it's made of. In *The Naked Pint*, we wrote, "Beer in its most basic form is a carbonated alcoholic beverage made from fermented grains. It is primarily made up of four key ingredients: malt, hops, water and yeast." Boom. Done. Now you know more than most people on the street. During the fermentation process, yeast eats the sugars from the malt and the natural byproduct is alcohol and carbon dioxide (CO_2). This is what makes beer bubbly and alcoholic instead of just malty, hoppy water. The art of beer making is how these ingredients work and harmonize together to create a delectable experience for your senses. Here's a slightly more detailed description of the ingredients:

- **Malt:** Malted grains, typically barley, sometimes wheat or other grains; they provide the fermentable sugars in beer, any color that you see in the beer, and flavor.
- **Hops:** Delicate, green flowering cones that grow on a vine; they provide all of the bitterness and/or dryness in beer, act as a preservative, and offer flavor and aromatics.

- **Yeast:** Classified as fungi, yeasts are single-celled organisms that eat the sugar during fermentation and create alcohol and CO_2; they can also provide flavor and aromatics.
- **Water:** The type of water used in brewing is an important part of the process; water can be soft or hard and may contain chemicals or excess minerals.

It's all coming back to you, right? You don't need to know everything about these ingredients to start brewing, but it certainly helps if you have a solid understanding of how the ingredients affect beer. Otherwise it's a bit like brewing with a blindfold on: You may make a yummy beer, but you won't understand why or how you did it. So let's get a deeper understanding of these ingredients.

You'd Be Nothing Without Me: Malt

In the simplest explanation, malts are cereal grains (usually barley) that have gone through the malting process. During the malting process, the grain is encouraged to germinate and sprout by being soaked in water and is then dried to halt the germination process. This process renders the starch that exists in the seed usable as a fermentable sugar. The grain is then kilned, roasted, smoked, baked, and so on to different degrees and to every shade of gold and brown imaginable—from the lightest beige biscuit malts to the darkest black patent malt. The flavor these different malts impart depends on many factors: How long they were roasted, at what temperature they were kilned, or if they were roasted *and* kilned. Malts are steeped and/or boiled during the brewing process to extract the fermentable sugars, flavor, and color from the grains.

WHAT DOES MALT CONTRIBUTE TO BEER?

- **Color:** The degree to which the malt has been roasted, and the combination of the colors of the malts used in the brewing of a beer are the sole factors responsible for the color of that beer. Neither water, hops, nor yeast (save for some cloudy effects in some styles) has an effect on the color of a beer.
- **Alcohol and CO_2:** The amount of malt used, in conjunction with the amount of yeast used, is solely responsible for the alcohol content of that beer. CO_2 and alcohol are created as a byproduct of the yeast eating the sugars in the malt.
- **Flavor and aromatics:** Depending on the malting process used, malted grains can impart many different flavors. Here are some flavors you can expect from different malts: bread, biscuit, toast, nuts, honey, caramel, toffee, coffee, chocolate, and ash. Hops and yeast tend to dominate in the aroma category, but you may smell a toasty or coffee character from the malt.

A Word to Know: *Wort*

Wort is a word you definitely want to be able to throw around when talking about brewing. First off, you need to know that it's pronounced "wert." Yeah we know, it's weird, but pronouncing it wrong is a dead giveaway that you are a newbie in the craft beer world. It derives from the Old English *wyrt*. Wort is the liquid that you end up with after the mash. Basically this is the beer before it is fermented. Wort is a sweet and strange-tasting liquid, but as you become a seasoned homebrewer, you will grow to love tasting the wort and guessing at how the beer will change after fermentation. So say it loud, say it proud, say it right, WORT!

- **Sweetness and mouthfeel:** Many people describe sweet beers as "malty." What they are tasting are the residual sugars and additional alcohol content that can remain in a beer from an especially large amount of malt. This results in a prominent sweetness of flavor and a viscosity, heat, and fullness in the mouthfeel of the beer. They may also be noting an absence of dryness or bitterness, and this is the result of a low hop character in a beer, not necessarily because of a lot of malt character.

HOW TO USE MALT IN YOUR HOMEBREW

When you're homebrewing beer you are brewing in one of four ways: extract only, extract with specialty grains, partial mash, or all-grain. Note that all of the malt (except for flaked malts) has to be milled (or crushed) before use. The definition of these terms differs among homebrewers, but here is the basic idea behind each style of brewing. (The recipes in this book each use one of the methods listed below. Although each recipe can technically be adapted to any of these methods, our recipes record the method we used to brew each beer.)

- **Extract only:** These brewing recipes use only malt extract as the malt and sugar source of your beer. Malt extract is basically a wort that has been reduced for you and comes either in a syrup form or a dry powder form. When brewing extract only or partial-mash recipes, you will use malt extract as a large part of your recipe. The extract replaces the mashing of the base malt in all-grain or partial-mash brewing. It is basically a nice, easy shortcut for homebrewers.
- **Extract with specialty grains:** This is brewing with recipes that use mostly malt extract as the base malt but that also call for a small amount of specialty malts to be steeped like tea. These malts primarily provide flavor and color to your brew.

- **Partial mash:** This is basically the half step between extract brewing and all-grain brewing. With partial mash, you use some malt extract as your fermentable sugar source and some base malt and specialty malts as your fermentable sugar source. The extra step here is mashing the grains, which means that instead of steeping for about 30 minutes, you will keep the grains in water for a longer amount of time, usually an hour, at a constant temperature. This allows the malt to undergo the conversion of starch to fermentable sugars. The liquid from the mashing process is then added to malt extract during the boil. Using this method is a bit more advanced but allows you some more control over the flavor and quality of your beer.
- **All-grain:** This is what professional brewers in a brewery do. They use only grain, no extract. All-grain brewing requires a lot more time, space, water, and patience than the other methods. That's why it can be challenging to do in a homebrew situation. With all-grain you are mashing all of your malt, there is no extract involved.

I'm Not Jaded, I'm Bitter: Hops

Oh, *Humulus lupulus* (Latin name for hops), wolf among the weeds (translation of the Latin name), how important you are to beer! Hops may be just the small female flowering cones of a vining plant, but these delicate, tiny green pine-cone-looking things pack a powerful punch. Basically, hops are what add the balance to what would otherwise be a cloyingly sweet, potentially moonshine-like concoction instead of a mélange of sweet and dry, sometimes even bitter, flavors. Many people don't realize that hops are totally invisible in a finished beer. Hops are used in beer in the boil, during which the hops' qualities are extracted, and the actual hop cones are strained out of the beer. You can detect hops, however, by tasting and smelling the beer. This means you can't look at a beer and know how bitter it is. Let that sink in a minute. . . . Neophyte beer drinkers often think the color tells you something about the bitterness, but that's just not true. You have to smell and taste a beer, whether light or dark or amber in color, to be able to describe it as dry or bitter.

WHAT HOPS CONTRIBUTE TO BEER

- **Bitterness:** The most important quality that hops provide in beer is bitterness. This is due to something called alpha acids that exist in the resin glands of hops. Different hop varietals have different alpha acid levels and different qualities. Some are better for bittering, some are better for flavoring, and some are better suited for aromatics, others are great for all three. The longer the hops are boiled, the more bitterness you'll get out of them; the less they're boiled, the more aromatics you'll get out of them.
- **Perceived dryness:** Hops contain a chemical compound called tannins that contribute to the puckery or cottony mouthfeel that we perceive as dry (true dryness being the actual lack of sugar versus the feeling of dryness on your tongue). Tannins exist in other places in the food world. They exist in the skins and stems of grapes, contributing dryness to wine. They exist in tea leaves and in wood and in many fruits. Tannins also exist in malt—so hops aren't the sole provider of dryness in beer, but they are the main contributor.
- **Aromatics and flavor:** Hops can provide subtle to smack-you-in-the-face aromatics in beer and, at times, some hops are added only to provide aromatics. Hops can be spicy, earthy, herbal, or grassy. They can taste and smell like grapefruit rind, pine tree, rosemary, citrus, and pot (no you can't smoke hops, but they are related to cannabis).
- **Preservatives:** Early in brewing history, brewers discovered that hops have an antibacterial/antimicrobial quality that can act as a preservative in beer. This allowed for more stability, which

provided longer storage time and the ability for beer to travel farther. It was this discovery that led to the famously aggressively hopped beers like the India Pale Ale and the Russian Imperial Stout. More hops were added to help keep the beers from going bad on the journey from England to India, and from England to Russia, respectively.

HOW TO ADD HOPS TO YOUR HOMEBREW

Hops are added to beer at different increments when you are boiling the wort. These are called "hop additions." Some beers require only one hop addition, others may have three, four, five, or more. Typically hops are always added at the beginning of the boil. These hops function as bittering hops. They provide the bitterness, balance, and/or dryness for your beer. A second addition can provide bitterness and flavor, and these often function as flavoring hops. If another addition is added toward the end of the boil or at the very end, these hops primarily provide aroma and are referred to as aroma hops.

The combinations of types of hops, number of hop additions, and amount of hops used are endless. Every recipe is slightly different, and it's easy to get carried away with hop additions. We've tried to restrain ourselves with the recipes in this book, but you'll get to use different types of hops and a variety of combinations.

You will see hops for sale online or at the homebrew supply store in the following forms: pellets, fresh cones, and plugs. We use pellets (with a few exceptions) in our recipes because they are extremely efficient and easy to get ahold of. Here's a rundown of the different options:

- **Pellets:** These little things look like cat food, but certainly don't taste like it. They are actually whole hops that have been ground and pressed into a mold. This is our generally preferred version of hops for homebrewing and for many professional brewers.

They are extremely efficient in evenly distributing the flavor and bitterness in hops.

- **Fresh cones:** These are fresh, pretty-looking dried hop cones. They resemble a bunch of green dried flowers. Some professional breweries, like Sierra Nevada Brewing Company in Chico, California, use only fresh hops in their beer. For many professional breweries, fresh cones can be hard to come by in the quantity they need, so they often use pellets instead.

- **Plugs:** These are whole-hop cones that are shredded and compressed into plugs. Each plug weighs about a half an ounce. They are used mostly for aroma and dry hopping. They're a bit more rare than the previous options.

- **Aged:** These hops are just what they sound like. They are hops that have been aged, sometimes for years. They can come in pellets or cones and can be any varietal. Aged hops are used in beers when you want absolutely no bitterness from the hops but are still looking for some drying qualities. Sour beers like Lambics most frequently use aged hops.

Where the Action Is: Yeast

 Known in the days of yore as "God Is Good," yeast has for eons been considered the magical mechanism that creates fermentation. All hail yeast! Yeasts are living organisms, which form colonies of single, simple cells. Officially, scientists call this organism a fungus. Yeasts are hungry, and yeasts can be furious! They can be lazy and they can die. How much food (sugar) there is for the yeast to eat in your brew, at what temperature the yeasts are allowed to eat, and how healthy the yeasts are create conditions responsible for how much alcohol and CO_2 you will ultimately have in your beer. This yeast that we're talking about is not the bread yeast you've had in your cabinet for 2 years, or the brewer's yeast that you got at the health food store for the vitamin B_{12}. This yeast is known as *Saccharomyces cerevisiae* and it's specifically cultured for the fermentation of beer.

WHAT DOES YEAST CONTRIBUTE TO BEER?

- **Alcohol:** Obviously, without yeast, we would have no fermentation and thus no alcohol. And then we would be sad.
- **Esters:** Esters are chemical compounds that yeast emits in beer and our brains perceive as pleasant flavors and aromas. There are many different yeast strains that contribute different flavors and aromatics. They mimic many things. For example, esters can be fruity like pears, strawberries, and dark cherries; they can be spicy like cloves and white pepper; they can be flowery like rose petals and jasmine; and they can be herbaceous like sage and lavender.
- **Mouthfeel:** Yeast can contribute greatly to a beer's mouthfeel through the carbonation of the beer. In the process of creating alcohol, yeast also creates the CO_2 that exists in beer. If the yeast strain has produced a lot of carbonation, it will create a prickly feeling on the tongue that makes the beer feel lighter and more crisp. Also, if the beer style is unfiltered, the yeast will remain suspended in the beer, providing a fuller, rounder, thicker mouthfeel.
- **Style:** Specific yeast strains create certain flavors and aromatics that are quintessential to a certain style of beer. For instance, Bavarian wheat yeast contributes esters that impart the banana and clove and bubble gum characteristics that Bavarian Hefeweizen is known for. Saison yeast gives that style of beer its spicy, peppery, citrusy qualities.

When you hit the homebrew supply store for the first time, you may be surprised to see what yeast actually looks like. Examine a typical vial of yeast and you'll see immediately it's not the prettiest ingredient in beer. Yeast looks like light brown sludge, kind of gross but also kind of cool. It makes you feel like you're about to perform a science experiment, which is exactly what you're doing. Here are the types of yeast you'll use for homebrewing:

- **White Labs brand tubes (liquid yeast):** These are vials of liquid yeast from one of the major yeast-producing companies. They need to be refrigerated until three to six hours before you brew. Then take them out of the fridge and let them come to room temperature. When you're ready to add the vials to your brew, shake them up and dump the yeast in.

- **Wyeast Laboratories brand Smack-packs (liquid yeast):** These are large plastic packages that contain liquid yeast and a tiny pack inside that you'll smack open to get the yeast activated and working. Once you've smacked them, they'll usually swell up, which is exactly what you want. (If the package doesn't swell, don't worry, this happens sometimes.) These packs need to be refrigerated until one day or at least three hours before you brew. When you are ready, take them out of the fridge, smack the pack, and let the package come to room temperature.

- **Dry yeast:** Until pretty recently if you were brewing beer, you were most likely using dried yeast. Now more people prefer brewing with the liquid version, but dry yeast does have its advantages. It has a longer shelf life and can keep for months. It also has a high cell count and starts fermenting very quickly. The downside is that dry yeast strains are not kept sterile, so there's always the chance for contamination. You should rehydrate your dry yeast before you add it to the beer. For best results, rehydrate your packet of dry yeast in 95° to 100°F water and then proof the yeast by adding a bit of sugar to see if the little buggers are still alive after being dried and stored. (Look for rehydration instructions on the packets.)

- **Yeast starter:** Many brewers recommend doing something called a yeast starter to help the yeasts get a head start before they are pitched into the beer, but the yeasts we recommend you use have very high cell counts, so you don't need to make a starter. Ready-to-pitch yeasts, and the larger 175-milliliter Smack-packs do not need a starter, especially if they're fresh. Make sure to look at the use-by dates on the packaging.

During fermentation, the yeast is going to eat the sugars in your wort and create alcohol and CO_2 as byproducts. Each style of beer and yeast has an ideal fermentation temperature. Some even work better if the temperature changes during fermentation. For example, Saison yeasts do well when the beer is heated up during fermentation to 80° to 90°F. In each recipe we have provided an *ideal* temperature at which to ferment your brew. Most of us don't live in an ideal brewing situation, so we understand that you may not be able to maintain this temperature. Don't worry too much, your beer will still be tasty. But if you live in a hot or cold climate, you may want to protect your beer by keeping it in a cool or warm spot in your abode.

Water, You've Heard of It

Because beer is made up mostly of water, the water is an important ingredient in the brewing process. That being said, we hesitate to talk about water chemistry and its makeup in beer because this is where a beginning brewer (we know because it happened to us) can start to get bogged down in chemistry and water table charts and pH levels and parts per millions and calcium sulfate and mineral content, spending hours trying to decide about adding gypsum salts or other things to adjust your water one way or the other to get the perfect brew. We also know—from experience—that you can brew perfectly delicious beer without knowing much about water chemistry.

It is true that famous beer styles brewed around the world use local water sources that have different mineral components, different pH levels, and so on. As a result, different regions are better suited to making certain types of beer. However, you do not have to duplicate Dublin water to make a great Irish Stout.

Your water source is definitely something to have a peripheral understanding about, but unless you have an Erin Brockovich–type situation happening with your water, you can probably use your tap water to make perfectly good beer. We do. Some styles may turn out better than others. For instance (though this is a bit of a generalization), nuanced Pilsners and other light-colored styles usually do better with low-alkaline water or softer water, whereas a rich Irish Dry Stout and other dark-colored styles generally do better with high-alkaline or hard water. Once again, we brew both of these styles in our home kitchens using our tap water, and we must say they've turned out pretty damn good. And we're using good old Los Angeles municipal water.

All Beer Is an Ale or a Lager

All beers in the world fall into one of two categories: Ales or Lagers. We find that most people, men and women alike, don't know the difference between the two. They use the words interchangeably, guessing at the meaning, so we're going to break it down for you here (please pass the information along to your friends).

WHAT'S AN ALE?

An Ale is a beer that uses yeast that has been cultured to ferment at the top of the fermentation vessel and at relatively high temperatures (60° to 75°F), resulting in a quick fermentation period (seven to eight days, or even less). Ale yeasts are generally known to produce fairly big flavors (there are exceptions.) You'll often get a lot of aromatics from the whiff of an Ale. Ales tend to have more residual sugar, meaning sugar that has not been consumed by the yeast during the fermentation process.

WHAT'S A LAGER?

The word *Lager* comes from a German word meaning "to store." A Lager is a beer that is brewed using yeast strains that are cultured to ferment at the bottom of the fermenting vessel and at relatively low temperatures (34° to 50°F), resulting in a long fermentation time (weeks to months). Lager yeasts produce fewer byproduct characters than do Ale yeasts, creating a cleaner, crisper taste (again, there are exceptions).

What's Your Type? Beer Styles

So what is a beer style? Well, basically, it is a name given to a beer based on its general flavor profile and/or its origin and history. The first thing you usually know about a beer is its style, as this is often on the label; therefore, it is helpful to understand the attributes of these styles.

We explained earlier that all beers are either Ales or Lagers. In addition, Ales and Lagers are broken down into styles. For instance, a Pilsner is a style of Lager, a Doppelbock is a style of Lager, a Porter is a style of Ale, a Stout is a style of Ale, an India Pale Ale is, obviously, an Ale.

Beers are categorized both on the basis of historical tradition and on sensory characteristics. Flavors that are most important to a beer style are type and strength of malt, yeast strain, strength of bitterness, and the type and strength of hops. Aromatics that are most important to a beer style include strength and type of malt aroma, strength and type of hop aroma, and yeast ester aroma. The feel of a beer in the mouth, both from thickness of the liquid and the amount of prickliness from the carbonation, is also an important factor in determining a beer style. The visual characteristics that are most important to a beer style are color, clarity, and the nature of the head (for example, the thickness).

Whether the beer is dubbed Bavarian Hefeweizen or Russian Imperial Stout, the name hints at what the aromatics are like, how strong it is, what sort of body it has, how it was brewed, and even its history. There are many, many variations of each particular style, and each brewer makes his or her own version of specific styles, but knowing a beer's style gives you an idea of what to expect.

TWO

Become the Brewer

Brewing Beer in the Real World

When we first conceived of this book, we said, "Let's write a book so that people can see how easy homebrewing can really be." But, here's the thing . . . brewing ain't *that* easy. *Drinking* beer is easy, but *making* beer is a bit of a process. Now, it certainly isn't that hard, but in our day and age, when the definition of *easy* in the food world means peeling back the corner of the package and heating on high for 2 minutes, homebrewing is definitely a labor of love (but not as hard as child labor, so there's that).

There's a lot of careful consideration and patience required in homebrewing. There are ingredients to understand, temperatures to check, and boiling times to watch. There is some special equipment you'll have to buy (unless you're really into blowing your own glass). You need to keep most of your equipment clean and sanitized. And sanitizing isn't much fun. So there's a lot going on here. We have, however, throughout our homebrewing journey, come to learn a few tricks of the trade and have been given some very good advice, including some rule-breaking shortcuts and tips that have resulted in homebrews that taste great and are relatively easy to make. We hope these methods are helpful and useful and will save you a lot of time and/or anguish.

The bottom line (and what inspires our homebrewing), is that *it's totally worth it!* Drinking beer that you brewed yourself is so, so gratifying. It's like growing your own vegetables or baking your own bread or pickling your own cucumbers. It takes a while, but when you finally consume your own homebrew, your chest swells with pride at the thought that "you did this all yourself!" Oh, and also that it's beer, and you love beer. And the process of brewing that beer elevates your appreciation of beer to an entirely new level. If beer is your favorite drink, and statistics show that it is, then you will learn more about beer brewing than you could drinking all of the beers in the world. You will birth beer (too much?), and you will fall in love with beer all over again.

Why We Brew Smaller

The recipes in this book are for 2½ gallons of beer, which makes approximately 24 (12-ounce) bottles. Why such a small batch? We started out making 5 gallons, which is what most people do when they start because most of the recipes out there are for 5 gallons. The common feeling being, if you're going to spend a few hours brewing something and then many weeks fermenting and conditioning, you might as well make as much of it as you possibly can. That argument does make a lot of sense. It's great to get a lot of beer out of the ingredients and the process. However, we don't throw a party *every* weekend, and we're urban dwellers with relatively small living spaces and pretty tiny kitchens. One 5-gallon batch makes about 48 (12-ounce) bottles of beer. If you're brewing this size consistently, the amount of beer that you end up with (even after drinking as much as possible) seems endless. The bottles, kegs, and fermenters will start to spill out of your fridge, closets, and basement. In fact, one day one of us couldn't take a shower because of the fermenting buckets occupying the bathtub. We started to wonder if this qualified as hoarding. It was time to take it down a notch.

Upon doing so, we found that there were many other advantages to smaller batches than just saving space. Smaller batches are, in general, much easier to deal with. You can get a smaller amount of liquid to come to a boil faster. Inversely, it's easier to cool down a smaller batch of beer, an essential step that needs to happen quickly in home-brewing. You don't need as much stove power, which is very helpful, especially with cranky or electric stovetops. Another plus is that small batches are so much easier for us to lift, transfer, and generally maneuver, especially when we're brewing alone. We aren't giant dudes, so working with a size that we can lift is important to us.

The other great thing about small batches is the feeling that if you screw it up, you don't have 5 gallons of shitty beer to drink. You have half that, and you can drink, dump, or cook with it without feeling too pathetic or wasteful. With small batches, we feel free to experiment and try, try again without too much hassle. Having said all that, if you *are* having a party and want to brew 5 gallons, our recipes can easily be doubled for a larger batch. It's a good idea to check the numbers in a beer software program, like BeerSmith or BeerTools (see "Homebrew Resources" on page 289), when doubling a batch, so that you get the beer stats you desire.

So, How Is It Done?

BASIC STEPS

The following list makes up the bare-bones basic steps to making beer, in order of when they are done and our honest feelings about performing them:

1. Steeping/mashing the grains (unless brewing all-extract) (cool!)
2. Boiling the wort (comforting)
3. Adding the hops (smells good)
4. Cooling the wort (kind of boring)
5. Sanitizing (sucks)
6. Pitching the yeast (exciting!)
7. Waiting for fermentation (sucks)
8. Bottling or kegging (both exciting and annoying)
9. Waiting for bubbles (blows)
10. Drinking! (euphoric!)

OK, so that's the basic truth of it. See, it's not easy, but it's not hard, and in the end we promise you'll feel that euphoria we feel. Here's an in-depth look at each step:

1. Steeping/mashing the grains. You will not need this step if you are making a beer entirely from extract. This is for recipes that use (1) extract with specialty grains that steep like tea and are added to your brew to lend it color and flavor; (2) recipes that use the partial-mash method, in which the grains are steeped and kept at a controlled temperature long enough to extract flavor, color, and fermentable sugars before they are added to the boil with extract; and (3) all-grain recipes that use no extract. This book has mostly extract and specialty grain recipes, although there are a few partial-mash and all-grain recipes. Specific instructions are included with each recipe.

Steeping grains means placing the specialty grains called for in the recipe into a grain bag, closing up the bag, and placing it in a pot of water that has been heated up to 160°F. You'll cover the pot and let the grains steep for 30–60 minutes for most recipes. Then you'll carefully open the top of the grain bag and pour a specific amount of 170°F water over the grains to make sure you're getting most of the good flavors. This act of pouring the hot water is called "sparging." Sparging is not crucial when you're simply steeping grains; most of the flavor has already been extracted during the steeping time in the pot. But sparging is very important in partial-mash and all-grain brewing. The colorful, flavorful liquid that remains from the steeping will be added to the boil.

If the recipe calls for a partial mash or all grain, you'll need to do a mash at the temperatures and times listed in the recipes. For partial-mash recipes, in which most of the fermentable sugars are coming from the extract and we are mostly getting flavor, color, and texture from the specialty grains, we usually mash for 30 minutes. For all-grain recipes, in which we are getting all of the fermentable sugars from the actual grains, we will mash for anywhere from 30 to 90 minutes.

2. Boiling the wort. This is the time when the wort is brought to a boil and hops are added to extract their flavors. Boiling also, among other things, helps many of the proteins (which can be harmful to the beer) clump together and drop to the bottom of the brew kettle. This is known as the "hot break." Achieving a hot break helps remove the worst of these proteins, which can cause instability or off-flavors in the beer. This is very important for partial-mash and all-grain recipes. Boiling for an hour is less important in all-extract brewing, in which the majority of harmful proteins have already come to a break during the process that produces the extract. Boiling the wort is crucial for achieving hop characteristics; the longer you boil hops, the more bitterness you extract.

3. Adding the hops. As we've mentioned, hops are responsible for any bitterness and dryness you detect in beer. They also balance the beer, which would be very sweet and cloying if there were no hops in the recipe. Hops can also add flavor and aroma, depending on the beer. They have the added bonus of being a natural preservative. There is usually at least one hop addition, meaning a point during the boil when you add the hops, but sometimes there are many more. So for example, you may add hops at the beginning of your boil that lasts 60 minutes, then you might add more hops at 30 minutes, and then yet more at 5 minutes. Multiple additions affect the bitterness, measured in International Bitterness Units (IBUs), as well as the flavor and aroma of your beer. There are many different kinds of hops, and each impart different IBUs and flavors to the beer (see "Hop Chart" on page 293).

4. **Cooling the wort.** Before adding your yeast to the brew, you have to get your just-boiled wort down to about 70°F. This, and sanitizing, is one of the most annoying parts of brewing. It takes a bit of patience to cool down a large amount of liquid. This is part of why we like to brew in small batches, it's quicker to cool 2½ gallons than 5 gallons. We like to use our sink or a large bucket (plastic or metal) and fill it with cool water, ice, and ice packs. We then put the brew pot in this cold bath and use a sanitized floating thermometer to check on the temperature until the liquid is ready for the yeast. If your sink is too small, you can invest in the large bucket. If you don't want a bucket lying around (though it comes in handy as an ice vessel for cooling bottles and cans of beer when you throw a party) and your sink is too small, you can use a bathtub. If you don't use an ice bath and let your wort cool down by just leaving it at room temperature, it will take a long time and you increase the chances that bacteria will fall into your wort, which can spoil your beer and affect the yeast.

5. **Sanitizing.** OK we admit it, this is the most pain-in-the-ass part of homebrewing. Who really likes to clean and sanitize? Not us (we're not exactly Susie Homemaker types), but sanitizing is one of the most important steps of the homebrew process. If you brew with equipment that is dirty or holds bacteria, your homebrew can become funky, infected, and taste off. Trust us, treat this step with reverence. There's nothing more aggravating than going through the process of home-

brewing only to find you've spoiled your work by poor sanitation procedures. Having said that, we're not super OCD about cleaning and we don't go crazy, *but* we do what is suggested and do our best. We don't sterilize like a surgeon but sanitize to keep our beer relatively safe. Remember you need to clean the pieces of your brew kit before you sanitize them, you can't just throw the sanitizer into a bucket that contains beer or yeast residue and hope for the best. So clean your brewing equipment first, rinse the soap, and then sanitize.

Sanitation is not just cleaning your brewing equipment, you need to use a sanitizer to get rid of all the bad stuff you can't see with your naked eye. So you'll need to buy a sanitizer. We use iodophor, which is an iodine-based product. You drop a few drops into water and it will sanitize your equipment. You can use bleach if you are very careful to wash it away afterward because it can make you sick or ruin your beer otherwise. It's very important to use the proper amount of sanitizer for the appropriate amount of time, as advised on the bottle. If you don't use enough, it will not kill any bacteria, if you use too much, the residual amount left on your equipment could affect you and your beer. Cool to room-temperature water is ideal for sanitizing and agitating may help. You typically want to sanitize all of your equipment that will come into contact with your freshly made wort. In other words, everything that will go into the boil will be sanitized by the boiling water, but anything that touches your wort *after the boil* must be sanitized. This is the point at which bacteria can get into your beer and do nasty things.

Here are some sanitizing options:

- **Star San**—Works in 5 minutes and foams up, which is supposed to help it get into cracks. Leaves a bit of a film on the equipment, which is OK for food use and doesn't affect the smell or taste of the beer. As stated by the company, this product is environmentally friendly and biodegradable. Use 1 ounce in 5 gallons of water. You do not need to rinse.

- **Iodophor**—Iodine based, but not harmful to the beer. The drawback is the color; it can stain things, turning them orange, so you don't want to be messy with it. Your plastic bucket may look mildly orange after using this sanitizer. If you get some on your hands, put a little vodka on there to get it off. Doesn't leave much residue. It is said that you don't have to rinse this away after sanitizing, but you can rinse with clean water. Should be in contact for 2 to 5 minutes. Use 1 ounce in 5 gallons of water. You can use test strips to make sure your amounts are correct.

- **Boiling water**—This is not as efficient as the other choices and may melt some of your equipment (racking cane), so be careful what you put in the boiling water. But in a pinch, if this is all you have, you can go this route to sanitize.

Pills Are Good . . .

WHIRLFLOC TABLETS

A Whirlfloc tablet is what we call in the homebrewing world a "clarifier," which means it helps coagulate and settle proteins and beta-glucans that exist in your wort. In layman's terms, Whirlfloc tablets help refine your beer. We love these tablets and use them in any beer for which we want a really sparkly clear finish. Now before you get all upset about putting additives in your homebrew, know that this quick-dissolving tablet is a blend of Irish moss (carrageenan), which is a species of red algae that grows naturally along the Atlantic coast of Europe and North America. When we use the tablet, we add it right at the very end of our boil with just 5 minutes remaining. According to the manufacturer, if Whirlfloc is in the boil for any longer than 10 minutes, the active ingredients become denatured and therefore will not do their job.

6. **Pitching the yeast.** Once your wort is chilled down to 70°F or below, you can transfer the wort by pouring it through a sanitized strainer into a plastic bucket or through a sanitized strainer and funnel into a glass carboy. Then pitch the yeast, which basically means dumping the yeast into the cool wort. Technically, the person who pitches the yeast is the actual brewer of the beer. So take a moment and be proud of yourself at this point, you are about to begin the fermentation process! Remember to sanitize the outside of the yeast vessel by dipping it into your sanitizing solution. This will get rid of any bacteria hanging out on the package that may find its way into the beer. A couple of important things to remember so that your pitching is effective:

- **Smack it!**—If you are using the awesome Smack-pack yeast from Wyeast, you will have to smack, aka break, the tiny starter pack inside the packet to activate the yeast. You need to do this at least three hours before you pitch the yeast, but you can do it a day before you brew as well. It will most likely swell up after you've smacked the packet. This is a good sign.

- **Let it sit**—Whether you're using the Wyeast Smack-pack or the White Labs tube of yeast, you need to let the product come up to room temperature, so that it isn't shocked when it is thrown into the cooled-down wort. If it goes from the fridge to your wort, the temperature change will affect the yeast, which might not work effectively in your beer. For long-term storage, however, the yeast needs to be refrigerated.

Let It All Out: Airlock and Blow-Off Tube

 When you transfer your cooled-down wort into your fermentation vessel, you will need to cover it, so that bacteria, flies, and other things don't get in and ruin your beer. But you also need to make sure that some air can get out because CO_2 is a natural byproduct of the fermentation process. The answer is an airlock and stopper or a blow-off tube. An airlock is a plastic deal that has one narrow end that sticks into the hole in a plastic bucket lid or plastic stopper that is placed into the top of a carboy. The airlock is filled halfway with vodka or a similar alcohol to protect the beer and covered with its plastic cap, which has tiny holes in the top. It sounds complicated, but it's not at all.

The other option is to use a blow-off tube. We use this method when (1) we think that we're going to have a huge fermentation that could clog or blow off our airlock and possibly contaminate our beer or blow up our fermenter or (2) we don't have enough headspace in the fermenter, which could result in clogging or blowing off our airlock and possibly contaminate our beer. Making a blow-off tube is simple. First, get 3 feet of ⅜-inch vinyl tubing from your local homebrew shop and fit it through the hole in the rubber stopper that you use for your airlock. The other end of the tubing should go in a bucket or pitcher of water. You'll start seeing the CO_2 bubbles in the bucket or pitcher of water, and you're good to go without threat of contamination or personal injury.

7. Waiting for fermentation. The hardest part, no doubt, is waiting for fermentation. Beer needs time for the yeast to eat the sugar from the malt and create the byproducts of alcohol and CO_2. At the least, beers need about 5 days to ferment, but we recommend giving it seven to ten days. You just have to be patient and let your beer be. Beer should ferment out of the sun in a fairly constant-temperature part of your home. We recommend using your large bucket, filling it with a bit of room-temperature water and setting your fermentation vessel in that. The water helps keep the beer at a constant temperature. Some beer styles take longer than others to ferment. You will know fermentation has started when you see bubbles coming up in your airlock or through your blow-off tube. We typically recommend a second period of waiting called "secondary." This is when you move the beer to another vessel to take it off of the yeast and let it sit for a bit longer. This usually makes a better beer. You are taking the beer off of yeast that is dying and thus can produce off-flavors in your beer. To make it through fermentation without whining, you'll need plenty of beer on hand to drink.

8. Bottling or kegging. Once your beer is fermented, it's time to put it into a bottle. This is where the beer will gain a bit more carbonation. If you taste it out of the fermenter (and you should), it will be a bit flat. This is the natural state of the beer, but most beers that you drink at the pub or from a bottle you bought at the store, have been force-carbonated. This means that CO_2 has been added, so that the beer is nice and sparkly. To do that at home, you have to add priming sugar.

9. Waiting. Even harder than waiting for the beer to ferment is waiting for the beer in the bottle to carbonate. Usually this takes anywhere from 7 days to 2 weeks. It usually helps to pop one open to test it when you can't stand waiting any longer. If you hear that familiar *fssst* sound, you know you're on the right track.

10. Drinking. Self-explanatory.

How to Bottle (So You Can Drink Your Beer)

Before you bottle, it's best to make sure your fermentation is done. If you bottle your beer too early, you could have some exploding bottles on your hands or simply overcarbonation. Carefully take a sample from your beer and check the specific gravity with your hydrometer. It's best to check again in two days to make sure the number is the same. This will verify that fermentation is finished.

STEP BY STEP

1. Sanitize everything; and by *everything* we mean:

    Your bottles
    Bottle caps
    Tube siphon
    Bottle filler
    Bottling bucket (3- to 5-gallon plastic fermenting bucket)

    The easiest way to do this is to wash them all first, and then fill your bottling bucket with water and the appropriate amount of sanitizer based on the directions on the sanitizing bottle. Then soak everything in the sanitizing solution. Remove everything and place on paper towels. Empty the bucket and use it as your bottling bucket.

2. You will also need to have the following on hand:

Bottle capper
Priming sugar (corn sugar or white table sugar)

3. Set your bottles upside down on paper towels or better yet on a bottling rack (something else to buy) to drain, taking care not to contaminate them.

4. In general for a 2½-gallon batch of beer, boil 1 cup of water, take it off of the heat and then add either 2 ounces of corn sugar or ⅓ cup of white sugar and let the mix cool. If you want to get the carbonation just right for the style of beer you are brewing, you can use the handy priming solution calculator available at TastyBrew (www.tastybrew.com/calculators).

5. Gently pour the priming solution into your bottling bucket. Now you need to transfer your beer into the bottling bucket, taking it off of unwanted yeast sediment, and mix it with the priming solution. To do that, use your sanitized tube siphon, and gently, ever so gently, transfer the beer into the sanitized bottling bucket. You do not want the beer to splash or to aerate at this point. Make sure to leave the sediment from the fermenter behind.

6. Once you've transferred all your beer into the bottling bucket, and the priming solution is evenly distributed into the beer, it's time to bottle. Attach your bottle filler to the tube end of your tube siphon, place the bottle filler into a bottle, carefully siphon your primed beer

into the bottle. Fill the bottle by pressing down on the bottle filler on the bottom of the inside of the bottle to let the beer flow. Simply lift the bottle filler to stop the flow of beer and move on to the next bottle. Fill the bottles to just below the top, leaving about an inch gap.

7. Once your bottles are filled, cap them with crown seals as quickly as you can with your hand capper.

8. Store the beer at the temperature (or room temperature) and time listed in the recipe.

9. Now you wait for the bubbles. While the rest of the yeast in the beer eats the tasty priming sugar in your beer and farts out CO_2 bubbles, you have to be patient once again. You'll have to let your bottles sit at room temperature away from sunlight. You can taste the beer along the way to see how it's coming, but you really should wait at least 2 weeks for the beer to be at its best. Then you can refrigerate and move on to the last step.

10. Congratulations! You made beer! Now drink it! Be sure to get a nice well-made glass and take notes on your first tasting. Note the color of the beer, the head retention, OG, FG, carbonation, ABV, flavor, hop character, yeast character, and everything you smell and taste in your beer. It's very important that you take note of where you went right and what may be off about your brew. Next time you make the recipe you can compare and contrast to these notes, and this, more than anything else, will improve your homebrewing. Be sure to share your beer with your friends; we love the look of pride on a homebrewer's face when she brings a homebrew over to share with us. Homebrewed beer really is the most impressive beverage you can bring to a party, so be sure to share and get the praise you deserve.

Beer Stats: ABVs, IBUs, OGs, FGs, Ls, and SRMs

There are a few abbreviations that you need to know for brewing. These will pop up in our recipes and most other recipes you come across. You can just nod and smile when a fellow homebrewer asks if you hit your OG with your homebrew and are happy with your SRM and ABV, but it's much better to know what the hell that person is talking about.

ABV (Alcohol by Volume). This directly relates to how drunk you are going to get. If all you've had are the mass-produced Lagers, the beers that you've been drinking are probably between 3% and 5% Alcohol by Volume. When you start getting into craft beers, the ABVs can range from what you are used to (3% to 5%) to big beers (anywhere from 6% to 20%; watch out!). If you're going to drink a beer, or a few, you'd better know your ABVs. Believe us when we tell you that there is a *huge* difference between a 5% beer and an 8% beer. A 5% beer can make you friendly; an 8% beer can make you French-kiss a tree. Of course this all depends on how well you can hold your liquor. Can you handle your martinis or do you get sauced after half a glass of Pinot Gris? It's critical, especially for women, to be vigilant about how much alcohol we are actually consuming. Know your ABVs and you, your neighbor, and the tree in her garden will thank us.

IBU (International Bitterness Units). The IBU scale provides a way to measure the bitterness of a beer. The number on the bitterness scale is a result of some complicated empirical formula using something called a spectrophotometer and solvent extraction. We don't pretend to understand that, and the good thing is that you don't have to understand it either. The bottom line is that this scale was based on tasted beer samples and correlating the perceived bitterness to a measured value on a scale of 1 to 100. On this scale, the higher the number, the higher the concentration of bitter compounds in the beer. For example, a mass-produced American Lager might have an IBU of 5, whereas a Double IPA might be somewhere around 90 IBUs. Some brewers are starting to put this number on bottle labels, but more often than not, this number is not shown on the actual beer. If you're worried about bitterness, it will help to know the general range of IBUs for each beer style. We encourage you to use your own palate to determine bitterness, as the IBU scale can be a bit confusing for newer craft beer drinkers. Some of the more advanced drinkers, and those who are adept at brewing, may begin to pay closer attention to these numbers. You can generally find the IBU number for a beer on the brewery's website. For an IBU range for beer styles, check out the Beer Judge Certification Program's website (www.bjcp.org/index.php).

OG (Original Gravity). No, not that OG; this OG is a measurement of the weight of your wort compared to the weight of the water. This is measured before fermentation and will help you determine the strength of your beer after fermentation.

FG (Final Gravity). This is the same measurement as OG, but taken after fermentation. Using the OG and FG, you can figure out the alcohol by volume of the beer.

L (Lovibond). This is a measurement of the roast level or color of a particular malt and/or the color of a beer. For example, one Caramel/Crystal malt may have an L of 60, whereas another may have an L of 120, the 120 being a darker level of color. This is important when you're trying to produce a certain color in your beer.

SRM (standard reference method). This is a measurement of beer color much like Lovibond. It is a newer measurement than Lovibond but is similar. Each beer has a general guideline for color, you don't have to be strict with this, but it is nice to make sure, for example, that your amber won't be too dark. The SRM in recipes and recipe-calculating software will help you find the color you want in a particular beer.

Calculating Alcohol

 We've actually done quite a bit of brewing in the past not knowing what our alcohol content was, just having faith and being content with knowing that there was some alcohol in there somewhere. Now, however, we're a little obsessed with knowing how we did. You never really *have* to do this (you can find out how alcoholic it is using other empirical data, like how tipsy you get), but if you want to find out exactly how much alcohol is in your beer, you need to take some readings with a hydrometer or a refractometer. We've provided target numbers for you to hit for each recipe. Here's how you figure out the ABV in your homebrew:

1. Take a reading with your hydrometer after you've cooled the wort but before you've pitched the yeast. That is your Original Gravity (OG).
2. Take a reading with your hydrometer after fermentation but before you've primed for bottling. That is your Final Gravity (FG).
3. Plug your numbers into this formula: Alcohol by Volume (ABV) = (OG − FG) ÷ 7.5.

Or, just plug in your OG and FG into an online calculator. We like the one at Brewer's Friend (www.brewersfriend.com/abv-calculator).

Your Homebrew Kit

It's time to put together your homebrew kit. Your local homebrew supply store will have most, if not all of these items. The Internet of course has everything, and you can pick and choose among different sites and compare prices. Many stores and websites will offer a "homebrew kit" that includes all of these items. Here are some sites we recommend:

- Northern Brewer (www.northernbrewer.com)
- Midwest Supplies (www.midwestsupplies.com)
- More Beer! (www.morebeer.com)
- Monster Brew (www.monsterbrew.com)
- Austin Homebrew Supply (www.austinhomebrew.com)

HERE'S ALL YOU REALLY, REALLY NEED TO BREW

- One 5-gallon brew pot
- Two 3- to 5-gallon plastic buckets with lids
- One airlock and rubber stopper
- A strainer
- A long spoon

WHAT WE HAVE IN OUR KIT AND WHAT THESE THINGS DO

- **Brew pot.** A stainless-steel pot, perfect for boiling and creating your wort. Most brew pots are about 5 gallons and that's what we recommend for the recipes in this book. However, the all-grain recipes in the last chapter require a larger pot.
- **Primary fermentation vessel.** A 3- to 5-gallon food-grade plastic bucket or glass carboy. We prefer the carboy because plastic can easily harbor bacteria, but either will do. This is the vessel in which your beer will initially ferment.
- **Secondary vessel.** A 3- to 5-gallon food-grade plastic bucket or glass carboy. This is used if you want to transfer your beer off of the yeast from the primary fermenter, so that it can have a longer fermentation period without risking off-flavors from remaining on the dying yeast. We highly recommend this vessel.
- **Long spoon.** Used for stirring, of course. It's important to use one that will get any syrup or other solids off of the bottom of the pot.
- **Thermometer.** Regular and floating, so you can take an accurate reading of the beer's temperature in its various stages. The floating thermometer comes in handy when you're checking the temperature of the wort while it is cooling down, so you know when to add the yeast and start the fermentation period.
- **Hydrometer.** To measure the gravity in your beer. You'll want to take a measurement before fermentation and compare it with a

The Dipstick Trick

Late one night at the hazy end of our homebrew club's annual holiday party after many samples of homebrew, we were feeling free enough to share what we each hated about homebrewing. *Measuring* was our loud, slightly slurred, complaint. To which a brewing genius replied, "Why don't you just use a dipstick?" After we figured out he wasn't insulting us, we listened intently as he explained. "Get an 18-inch plastic brewing spoon (that you'll use for brewing anyway), then pour known amounts of water into your brew pot to 'calibrate' the spoon as a dipstick. Notch the spoon with a knife or mark it with a permanent marker at ½-gallon intervals as far as you need to." Voilà! No more measuring and pouring (for the most part)! The suggestion was duh simple but so perfect.

sample after fermentation. These measurements will be your Original and Final Gravity readings. They will allow you to determine the beer's Alcohol by Volume.

- **Grain bag.** To hold the grain for steeping or mashing. You can also use smaller bags for hop additions, so there's less to strain before fermentation. You can forgo the grain bag and strain out the grain and hops if you want to, but we love the ease of containing the ingredients in a bag and removing it when needed. Use fine-mesh hop bags for hops (6 by 8 inches for up to 2 ounces of hops; 9 by 12 inches for up to 4 ounces). Use big coarse-mesh bags for whole hops and malted grains. These bags can be washed and sanitized in the dishwasher for reuse.

- **Strainer.** For, um, straining. Your brew can be and can look kinda funky if you don't strain out the hops, barley, spices, and other ingredients when you transfer your wort. The strainer is a fantastic tool in general for your kitchen.

- **Small pot.** To heat up water that you will run through your grains, this is called "sparge water." You'll need a pot that can hold at least 1 gallon of water.
- **Sanitizer.** Not the most fun part of the kit, but perhaps the most important. You must sanitize your equipment, so that all of your hard work is not lost. Infection can ruin a beer. See pages 30–32 for sanitizer recommendations.
- **Auto-siphon.** The best way to transfer your brew from its primary fermenter to the secondary vessel and to the bottling vessel. You don't have to get an auto-siphon, but we think it's just much easier than a traditional siphon.
- **Airlock and stopper.** A fantastic invention that allows a small amount of air out of your brew, while protecting your beer as the bubbling of fermentation begins.
- **Funnel.** You know what a funnel is; it makes pouring the beer into the mouth of a carboy easy and less messy. Some funnels have a strainer built in, so that you don't have to pour through a separate strainer as well.
- **Bottles.** For, well, bottling. These need to be sanitized. You can buy new or recycle used bottles. Use glass bottles.
- **Caps.** They go on the bottles, of course. They also need to be sanitized.
- **Capper.** A supercool tool that seals the caps on top of the bottle, so no air seeps in to spoil the beer.
- **Bottle filler.** Another really nifty device that allows you to fill the bottle without spilling.
- **Bottling bucket.** You need a vessel to transfer your beer into and mix with some priming sugar before you bottle.
- **Digital scale.** For measuring ingredients. Because we make small batches, we're often measuring out amounts of extract, grains, and hops at home. A digital scale can measure even the smallest amounts of hops and yeast in ounces or grams.

You Made My . . . Wish List

 For some people, heading to the homebrew supply store can be like a hikers' trip to REI, where you leave the store with all kinds of gadgets and gear that often end up being *underused*, shall we say. We want brewing to be as easy and as cost-efficient as possible, which is why we've already listed what we think are the essentials in a beginner's brew kit. However, having brewed for a while now, we've picked up some gear that we have found to be very helpful—not essential for brewing—but really helpful for measuring ABVs more quickly, taking temperature readings faster, and getting our wort boiled and cooled faster. If you've found that you're really into the homebrew thing and are willing to invest a little more money into your ~~habit~~ hobby, here's what we'd suggest getting next:

- **Refractometer.** We are not listing this very handy piece of equipment as mandatory to your brewing because it's a bit pricey and a hydrometer can do the job of this instrument as well. *But*, and a big but—We *lerve* our refractometer! Historically used by winemakers to determine the sugar in their grapes with a reading called "brix," the refractometer is a great alternative to a hydrometer to establish your Original Gravity and Final Gravity to determine your ABV. Just a drop of wort viewed in the refractometer at any point during all stages of brewing will give you a clear reading and allow you to make adjustments along the way. Our favorite refractometer has both brix and a calibrated specific gravity scale (otherwise we'd have to convert brix to specific gravity). It's the Brewing Refractometer with Brix Scale, model MT700, from www.morebeer.com, $60.
- **Digital thermometer.** Even though you should never be too far away from your boiling wort, a digital thermometer complete with an alarm set to go off when you've reached your ideal mashing temperature makes us feel downright secure. It's also superfast and gives extremely accurate readings. Just make sure not to submerge the cord

beyond the probe into liquid, or digital thermometer go bye-bye. You can find a decent digital thermometer for $30 to $40.

- **Portable propane burner.** You may have an older gas range that really rocks the casbah. But these days, stoves are calibrated to put out just enough energy to scorch a sole meunière. What we need is power, especially if you're stuck (like one of us is) with an electric range. A propane burner lets you get your boil on in minutes flat and allows great flame control. *Fire warning:* Of course this is for outdoor brewing only and involves flammable gas in the form of a propane tank. You might also consider doing what we did and just buying yourself a nice turkey fryer on sale the day after Thanksgiving from Sears. It has less output than the one we found at the homebrew store, but it came with a 7½-gallon pot (read: brew pot) with an insertable thermometer and a handy little timer with an automatic shutoff! Try the Masterbuilt 30-quart turkey fryer with timer, model 20020209. We've seen it around for $80 to $100. Please use extreme caution.

- **Immersion wort chiller.** An immersion wort chiller is basically a copper coil that is placed directly in the hot wort. As cold water continually passes through the inside of the coil, it absorbs and carries away the heat from the wort. The quicker you can cool down your wort from boiling to the suggested starting temperature range for your yeast, the less time there is for some airborne organism to contaminate your beer. We've mentioned that good sanitation is key, but wort chillers are ideal if you really want to get temperatures down faster than an ice bath allows and want to mitigate the chances that your beer will become infected. You can pick up one of these at the homebrew store for about $75.

Brewing Vocabulary

If you're going to brew the beer, you'd better know how to talk the talk. Here are some basic brewing terms you should familiarize yourself with, so you don't feel lost at the homebrew supply store:

- **Mash.** Process in which the crushed grains are mixed into hot water and enzymes change the starch into fermentable (though some may be unfermentable) sugars for the yeast to eat.
- **Partial mash.** Brewing using a wort made partially from grain and partially from malt extract.
- **All-grain or full mash.** A brew made with all-grains, raw malted barley, instead of malt extracts. This requires space and time and is quite advanced in the brewing world. This is often the practice of professional brewers.
- **Brew in a bag (BIAB).** The process of using a grain bag to mash your grains, instead of a separate lauter tun. This process allows for one-pot brewing and shaves some time off of what can be a very laborious all-grain procedure. This process can also be used in partial mashes and is then called a mini BIAB. (This process is described in more detail in Chapter 14.)
- **Mash tun.** The vessel that contains the mash during all-grain brewing.
- **Base malt.** The malt used as the main source of sugar for fermentation.
- **Malt extract.** A concentrated liquid formed from wort that contains the sugars needed for brewing. This is what most homebrewers use instead of all-grain brewing.
- **Specialty malts.** Smaller amounts of malt used for flavoring and nuance. These can be steeped like tea instead of turned into a mash.
- **Steeping grains.** Used to add flavor, nuance, and/or color for brewers using a malt extract. These do not need to be converted to sugar and can also be steeped like tea.
- **Sparging.** Comes after the mash, when hot water is run through the boiled or steeped grains to extract as many fermentable sugars and flavor properties from those grains as possible. This liquid is added to the wort.

- **Grist.** The mixture of grains that are crushed in a mill and prepared for mashing.
- **Wort.** The gross name chosen for the liquid that is extracted from the mash. It is pronounced *wert*.
- **Adjunct.** A starch used in brewing other than malted barley. It is sometimes used for flavor, sometimes for mouthfeel, and sometimes instead of an amount of malt, making the beer cheaper to make.
- **Hop pellets.** Little things that look like vitamins, these are used by most homebrewers in lieu of a bunch of dried or fresh hops.
- **Bittering hops.** Used early in the boil to bitter the beer, not for aroma.
- **Flavor hops.** Used later in the boil to add some aroma and flavor.
- **Aroma hops.** Added last to the boil, meant to add hop aromas not bitterness or flavor.
- **Attenuation.** Basically the amount of fermentation that happened, meaning how much sugar the yeast ate and how much the Original Gravity decreased. Refers to the final ABV. Lower attenuation creates maltier beers; higher attenuation results in drier beers.
- **Rack.** The process of moving the beer at different stages of homebrewing.
- **Pitch.** The term for adding the yeast to the cooled wort, as in "time to pitch the yeast!"
- **Priming.** The addition of sugar (priming sugar), to beer that has already fermented. This occurs as the beer is being bottled to promote more flavor nuances and/or alcohol and carbonation.
- **Original Gravity.** The measurement of the density of the liquid wort before fermentation, important for later ABV determination.
- **Final Gravity.** The final measurement of the density of the wort after fermentation; using the OG and FG, you can calculate the ABV.

- **Secondary.** Simply removing the beer off of the yeast and protein sediment that has collected in the bottom of the fermenting vessel during primary fermentation and transferring it to another fermentation vessel to continue fermenting. This can greatly improve the flavors of your beer.
- **Flocculation.** Refers to a yeast's ability to clump together at the end of fermentation and drop out of the beer. A yeast strain with low flocculation will take longer to drop out, making cloudier beers. High flocculation can result in a clearer more sparkly beer.

Top 10 Brewing Don'ts

1. DON'T MISHANDLE YOUR GRAINS
Although they don't look it, grains are delicate creatures. If you overmill or overcrush your grains into powder, oversteep your grains, or if you steep or sparge your grains with boiling (too hot) water, you can get a super mouth-puckery, cotton-mouthy astringency. (This is sometimes desired in certain styles, such as an IPA.)

2. DON'T BE DIRTY
OK, we know we mention this to the point of annoyance, but make sure that you sanitize, sanitize, sanitize! A bacterial infection from any number of sources is the number one cause of off-flavors in beers. Contamination can make your beer taste like vegetables and corn. It can also make it sour and downright funky. Bacteria can also be responsible for off-flavors called phenols, which taste like Band-Aids, again, an unwanted flavor in most styles, or anything really.

3. DON'T COVER YOUR BREW POT WHILE BOILING
There's this thing called dimethyl sulfide, or DMS for short, that is released from the wort during the boil. If you cover the wort, the DMS will

not be removed because the DMS condensation rejoins your wort. This can result in notes of seafood and shellfish. Seafood is unacceptable in any style (except maybe Oyster Stout! but not really even then).

4. DON'T UNDERAERATE YOUR COOLED WORT

One thing yeast loves when it begins the fermentation process is oxygen. And while it's not always good to aerate your beer (for instance, you don't want to introduce oxygen to hot wort or when transferring your beer into secondary), just before and after pitching the yeast is prime aeration time, baby. Make sure to stir or shake your cooled wort before and just after adding your yeast. Lack of aeration at this time can result in solvent, off-flavors, and buttery or slick butterscotch notes that brewers call "diacetyl."

5. DON'T UNDERPITCH YOUR YEAST

In our recipes, we've allowed for the correct yeast amount, but as you start to come up with your own recipes, it's important that you pitch enough yeast into your wort to have an active fermentation. Underpitching can also cause the aforementioned off-flavors and aromatics.

6. DON'T LET YOUR BEER FERMENT AT TOO-HIGH TEMPERATURES

Except for a couple of specialty yeast strains, most beer should be fermented below 80°F. High temperatures can kill your yeast and produce harsh hot or solvent characteristics. Brewers call this off-flavor "fusel" or "fusel alcohol."

7. DON'T AERATE YOUR BEER AFTER FERMENTATION

OK, so here it is: Aerate your cooled wort before pitching your yeast. Do not aerate your beer after fermentation, at which point you should be very careful in handling and transferring, using a tube siphon for the latter. Aerating fermented beer can result in oxidation, which creates wet dog and cardboard flavors, and aromatics. Again, this is OK in some styles— like Old Ales and Barley Wines, but not OK in most.

8. DON'T REMOVE YOUR HOMEBREW FROM THE YEAST TOO SOON

Young beer can have flavors and aromatics of green apples (where you don't want them). Brewers call this off-flavor "acetaldehyde." This can also be an indication of a bacterial infection and the cause of buttery diacetyl flavors.

9. DON'T LET YOUR BEER SIT ON THE YEAST TOO LONG

So yeast are unfeeling little buggers, and when they've been sitting around a little too long on top of each other, guess what? They start to eat themselves. That's right, it's yeast cannibalism, otherwise known to brewers as "yeast autolysis." When this happens, the worst of the worst off-flavors occur. Unmistakable characteristics of rotten eggs or sulfur emanate from your homebrew.

10. DON'T BOTTLE YOUR BEER IN CLEAR OR GREEN BOTTLES

The most popular off-flavor that people recognize in beer is skunkiness. A beer gets skunked because of a chemical reaction that takes place in beer when ultraviolet (UV) light hits the invisible hop components in beer. Be sure you bottle your beer in dark brown glass (nope, not even blue) to avoid the dreaded skunked beer!

THREE

June

SUNNY DAYS (FINALLY) ○ **GRILLED CORN** ○ **FRESH FRUIT** ○
CHANGE OF PACE ○ **BLOOMING FLOWERS (ALLERGIES)** ○
PUTTING AWAY THE WINTER CLOTHES

Your June Homebrew

SUMMER ENGLISH PALE: **British-style Pale Ale with slightly sweet,
nutty malt notes and a mellow finish**

WEST COAST HOPPED-UP PALE: **American West Coast–style Pale
Ale with fruity, malty notes and a bitter end**

BLACK SMOKE PALE: **Smoky, toasty malt profile with a clean hop
finish**

To Eat

Black Smoke Pale Split Pea and Ham Soup

June ushers in the summer. This is the perfect time to begin your life
as a homebrewer. You've done your spring-cleaning, and you deserve a reward; a new hobby with a delicious payoff: lovingly crafted
beer. Our recipes for this month go well with summer foods and sunny
days. These recipes are simple starters for the neophyte brewer. All

three are versions of a Pale Ale, a beer that we practically had on an IV drip when we first got into craft beer. The three have very different flavor profiles but share a similar basic brewing process. They all use the four main ingredients in beer and no specialty ingredients.

This is a great time to familiarize yourself with the basic ingredients in beer: water, malt, hops, and yeast (see Chapter 1), the basic workhorses of any brewing recipe. These recipes don't require any unusual ingredients (like sage or anise, which will come later), but they allow you to get inside the beer-making process without overwhelming you. This is like learning the basics of cooking: chopping, sautéing, grilling, and adding salt and pepper. It's a foundation for the experimentation you'll get into later.

Summer English Pale

MAKE THIS BEER IF YOU LIKE: Nutty flavors without too much hop bite. An easy starter recipe that will still impress your friends. British pub–style afternoons.

PAIRS WELL WITH: Mild Cheddar, grilled chicken, fish-and-chips, British biscuits.

STYLE AND BREWING NOTES

The English Pale Ale may be associated with the dark wooded interior of a British pub, but it is also good for drinking throughout warm summer evenings or beachgoing days. It's refreshing and satisfying without being boring. English Pale Ales (similar to the "special bitter" style) are typically low in alcohol; gold to red in color; and have a nutty, caramel malt flavor and touch of fruit, which comes from the yeast. The hops are not overpowering; they are used, instead, to balance the

Ale and keep it from being too sweet. Though the bitterness may be more apparent than in an Amber Ale, it will not hit your taste buds too hard. The final product should be one that will cut through the heat of the afternoon sun without assaulting your palate. It's a perfect beer for a pub-style session talking with friends over a few pints at your first summer barbecue.

This is the first style of beer we ever brewed (ahhh, memories . . .). Most brewers will tell you that this is where their journey began also. It's simple to make and forgiving to newcomers. You can make a few mistakes here and there as you try to get a handle on brewing and still end up with a nice, quaffable brew. Even if you don't hit it out of the park on the first try, you'll have nutty malt flavors and crisp hop notes to enjoy.

Session Ales

The word *session* refers to any style of beer meant to fuel the tongue for hours of chatting and general camaraderie. It's a British term hailing from long sessions at the pub, drinking and talking with friends. Session beers are generally between 3% and 5% ABV, keeping the alcohol from forcing one to quit the evening too early. The British treat their pubs like a second living room, going there to chat the way we Americans meet at the coffee shop. This requires a beer with an interesting, pleasing flavor profile that doesn't kill the palate: not too bitter, not too sweet. The nutty malt and hint of fruit in the English Pale Ale fills the bill for this style of beer. We started out drinking these session beers, then moved on to bigger, bolder, more crazy and complex styles, and have found ourselves coming back to the good old session beer, like a comfortable old slipper. These beers are also perfect for drinking throughout your brewing session.

BREW IT: SUMMER ENGLISH PALE

DIFFICULTY LEVEL: Neophyte

TYPE OF BREWING: Extract with specialty grains

SPECIALTY/EXTRA EQUIPMENT: None

TARGET OG: 1.048

TARGET FG: 1.012

IBUs: 33

TARGET ABV: 4.6

PROPER GLASS: Pint

SHOPPING LIST

1 packet Wyeast London Ale yeast 1028

8 ounces Caramel/Crystal 60 L malt—milled

4 ounces Caramel/Crystal 40 L malt—milled

3.25 pounds liquid Pale malt extract

0.8 ounce East Kent Goldings hop pellets

0.3 ounce Fuggles hop pellets

Makes about 2.5 gallons

PREP

■ *Prepare your yeast (at least 3 hours before you brew):* Crack your packet of London Ale yeast and let it warm up to room temperature. You can do this the day before you brew as well.

STEEP/MASH

■ Heat 3 quarts of water. Attach a thermometer and heat the brew pot until it reaches 160°F. Turn off the heat.

■ Put the specialty grains (Caramel/Crystal 60 L and Caramel/Crystal 40 L malts) in the grain bag (tying the ends) and place it in the brew pot. Cover with a lid, and rest for 30 minutes.

■ Prepare your sparge water by heating 3 quarts of water to 170°F in a separate small pot.

SPARGE

▪ After 30 minutes, remove the grain bag from the brew pot. Put a large fine-mesh strainer over the brew pot. Put the grain bag in the strainer, open the grain bag, and slowly run the hot sparge water through it, making sure to cover all of the grains with water. Do not squeeze the grain bag! Remove the grain bag and discard.

▪ Add an additional 2 gallons of room-temperature water to the brew pot.

▪ Reheat your brew pot water to 155°F; turn off the heat and add the liquid Pale malt extract. Gently stir to make sure the extract doesn't stick to the bottom of the pot.

THE BOIL

▪ Bring the pot to a boil.

▪ As soon as the pot comes to a boil, add your first hop addition, the East Kent Goldings hops, and set your timer for 60 minutes. The hops will dissolve immediately. Stir occasionally, skimming off the big solids with a slotted spoon and looking out for the dreaded boil-over!

▪ At 45 minutes (that is, with 15 minutes left in the boil), add your second hop addition, the Fuggles hops.

PITCH THE YEAST

▪ *Prepare your ice bath:* In your sink or another vessel, prepare an ice bath to cool the beer down in.

▪ *Cool your wort:* Remove the pot from the heat and place it into your ice bath. Place a sanitized thermometer in the wort and let cool until it reaches 70°F or below.

▪ *Clean your stuff:* Sanitize anything that will come into contact with your beer.

▪ *Transfer your wort:* Pour the wort through a sanitized strainer into a 3- or 5-gallon plastic fermenting bucket or through a sanitized strainer and funnel into a 3- or 5-gallon glass carboy.

- *Pitch the yeast:* Shake your packet of prepared yeast, sanitize the outside, tear it open, and throw all of its contents into the cooled wort in the fermenter.

PRIMARY FERMENTATION

- Place an airtight lid equipped with your airlock (filled with vodka) and stopper on the plastic bucket or place the airlock and stopper on a glass carboy. Or use the blow-off tube method (see Chapter 2).
- Keep the container in a dark and relatively cool place (ideal fermentation temperature for this style is between 60° and 72°F) for 7 to 10 days if using secondary or for 12 to 14 days if not.

OPTION: SECONDARY

- Transfer the beer from the primary fermenter to a 3- to 5-gallon bucket or glass carboy with a sanitized tube siphon. (Make sure to leave the sediment behind.)
- Put an airlock on the secondary container and let the beer sit for at least 14 days.
- Bottle for 14 days as described in Chapter 2. Then refrigerate and enjoy!

RULE BREAKERS AND TIPS

- If the specialty grains scare you, relax and cut out that step altogether. Start with the boil and addition of the malt extract and carry on from there. The color and flavor will not be as nice, but you'll have beer!
- No, there's no way around sanitizing your equipment!

PROFESSIONAL BREWS TO ASPIRE TO

Fuller's London Pride: Fuller Smith & Turner, London. A smooth and complex beer with a malty base and a balance of hop flavors from the Target, Challenger, and Northdown varieties; 4.7% ABV.

Firestone Double Barrel Ale: Firestone Walker Brewing Co., Paso Robles, California. A traditional Burton-on-Trent British-style Pale Ale. Aged in oak barrels, this beer has notes of vanilla and toasted oak flavor finished with a hint of English Noble hops; 5% ABV.

8th Street Ale: Four Peaks Brewing Co., Tempe, Arizona. An English-style Best Bitter with a mellow bitterness and a slightly sweet malt flavor. It is brewed with rare imported Kentish hops; 5% ABV.

JUNE HOMEBREW 2

West Coast Hopped-Up Pale

MAKE THIS BEER IF YOU LIKE: India Pale Ales. A crisp, hop bitterness. Pine trees and grapefruit. A touch of caramel malt. West Coast pride.

PAIRS WELL WITH: Burgers with blue cheese, spicy sausage, Cajun-spiced chicken.

STYLE AND BREWING NOTES
The West Coast American–style Pale Ale (APA) is a different beast from its British cousin. We Americans seem to love a bit more bite to our pint in general. Think Sierra Nevada Pale Ale—the classic American Pale that made a new generation of beer drinkers wake up and smell the hops. West Coast Pale Ales have nice fruity, caramel malt notes with bold piney-grapefruit hops. Once you've made the English Pale you may be ready to move up a notch in the world of hops, and this is the perfect recipe.

We, being West Coasters, feel a lot of pride when it comes to the piney, citrusy West Coast American Pale. It is at once the bold sun by the beach in San Diego, the après-ski refresher in the Rockies, and the green pine tree smell of hops grown in Washington and Oregon. The great thing about the hops, besides the fact that they add balance, preservatives, aromatics, dryness, and great flavor to beer, is that they can cover some neophyte mistakes in brewing. They are forgiving, like a black dress, hiding imperfections. This is not to suggest that making a Pale Ale of this style is easy to perfect, but for a homebrew, a nice hoppy Pale can come out well right off the bat, offering citrusy, piney hops as the dominant flavor. Remember, in brewing, hops are your friends.

The other bonus about this recipe for the new brewer, is that you don't need to steep any specialty grains. We want you to focus on the hop character this time, so we've cut out a step. This is definitely a lazy June afternoon endeavor. Relax and smell the hops.

BREW IT: WEST COAST HOPPED-UP PALE

DIFFICULTY LEVEL: Neophyte

TYPE OF BREWING: Extract only

SPECIALTY/EXTRA EQUIPMENT: None

TARGET OG: 1.056

TARGET FG: 1.013

IBUs: 42

TARGET ABV: 5.6

PROPER GLASS: Pint

SHOPPING LIST

1 packet Wyeast American Ale yeast 1056

3 pounds Pale liquid malt extract

12 ounces Amber dry malt extract

0.25 ounce Columbus hop pellets

0.4 ounce Cascade hop pellets

0.25 ounce Centennial hop pellets

0.3 ounce Cascade hop pellets

Makes about 2.5 gallons

PREP

■ *Prepare your yeast (at least 3 hours before you brew):* Crack your packet of American Ale yeast and let it warm up to room temperature. You can do this the day before you brew as well.

STEEP/MASH

■ Heat 3.5 gallons of water. Attach a thermometer and heat the brew pot until it reaches 155°F. Turn off the heat.

■ Add the malt extract (Pale liquid malt extract and Amber dry malt extract). Gently stir to make sure the extract doesn't stick to the bottom of the pot. (Because there are no specialty grains for this brew, you do not need to steep or sparge.)

THE BOIL

■ Bring the pot to a boil. As soon as the pot comes to a boil, add your first hop addition, the Columbus hop pellets, and set the timer for 60 minutes. The hops will dissolve immediately. Stir occasionally, skimming off the big solids with a slotted spoon and looking out for the dreaded boilover!

■ At 30 minutes (that is, with 30 minutes left in the boil), add your second hop addition, the 0.4 ounce of Cascade hop pellets.

■ At 50 minutes (that is, with 10 minutes left in the boil), add your third hop addition, the 0.25 ounce of Centennial hop pellets.

■ At 55 minutes (that is, with 5 minutes left in the boil), add your final hop addition, the 0.3 ounce of Cascade hop pellets.

PITCH THE YEAST

- *Prepare your ice bath:* In your sink or another vessel, prepare an ice bath to cool the beer down in.

- *Cool your wort:* Remove the pot from the heat and place it into your ice bath. Place a sanitized thermometer in the wort and let cool until it reaches 70°F or below.

- *Clean your stuff:* Sanitize anything that will come in contact with your beer.

- *Transfer your wort:* Pour the wort through a sanitized strainer into a 3- or 5-gallon plastic fermenting bucket or through a sanitized strainer and funnel into a 3- or 5-gallon glass carboy.

- *Pitch your yeast:* Shake your packet of prepared yeast, sanitize the outside, tear it open, and throw all of its contents into the cooled wort in the fermenter.

PRIMARY FERMENTATION

- Place an airtight lid equipped with your airlock (filled with vodka) and stopper on the plastic bucket or place the airlock and stopper on a glass carboy. Or use the blow-off tube method (see Chapter 2).

- Keep the container in a dark and relatively cool place (ideal fermentation temperature for this style is between 60° and 72°F) for 7 to 10 days if using secondary or for 12 to 14 days if not.

OPTION: SECONDARY

- Transfer the beer from the primary fermenter to a 3- to 5-gallon bucket or glass carboy with a sanitized tube siphon. (Make sure to leave the sediment behind.)

- Put an airlock on the secondary container and let the beer sit for at least 14 days.

- Bottle for 14 days as described in Chapter 2. Then refrigerate and enjoy!

RULE BREAKERS AND TIPS

- This recipe is pretty easy, so we don't have any shortcuts here, so man up!

PROFESSIONAL BREWS TO ASPIRE TO

Sierra Nevada Pale Ale: Sierra Nevada Brewing Co., Chico, California. The most popular West Coast Pale Ale. Many attempt to copy this style, but few get it so right. Every bottle boasts the same constant quality hop bite; 5.6% ABV.

Dale's Pale Ale: Oskar Blues Brewing Co., Lyons, Colorado. A hugely hopped Pale that delivers a piney nose and flavors of Pale malts and bitter hop bite from start to finish; 6.5% ABV.

Stone Pale Ale: Stone Brewing Co., Escondido, California. A Southern California interpretation of the classic British Pale Ale style. Big, rich malty notes and a fresh hop aroma; 5.4% ABV.

JUNE HOMEBREW 3

Black Smoke Pale

MAKE THIS BEER IF YOU LIKE: Contradictions. A bit of a hoppy bite. Notes of coffee. Barbecue. Smoked meats.

PAIRS WELL WITH: Chipotle peppers, smoked sausage, bacon, smoked Gouda, barbecue.

STYLE AND BREWING NOTES

You may not know it yet, but with this recipe, you've entered into a realm of the beer world that is rife with controversy. There has been a ruckus among craft beer writers, brewers, bloggers, and enthusiasts about the name of this relatively new style of beer. Some of it has to do with people's inability to understand the combination of Dark and Pale in the same name. This controversy has led to different names like Cascadian Dark Ale, coined for the bold Cascade hops from the Pacific Northwest and (the most incendiary) India Black Ale (IBA), which takes care of the Black–Pale confusion. Other suggestions are Dark Bitter Ale, Black Bitter Ale, and Black Hoppy Ale. At the end of the day, we feel like you need to just chill out, pick a name, and drink the beer.

Our Black Smoke Pale Ale (H. G. Wells? *War of the Worlds*? Anyone?) is a beer that has the qualities of a traditional American Pale Ale— fruity, floral, and herbaceous aromatics, a hop bitterness, medium body and alcohol content, a nice caramel malt balance, and a crisp and dry finish—that has been "blackened" with the addition of some very dark and smoky, sumptuous specialty grains. This beer has a good hop presence, but the focus is not on hops, it's on the balance and smoke. You'll see in this brew how adding dark, roasted grains can totally alter a traditional beer style.

BREW IT: BLACK SMOKE PALE

DIFFICULTY LEVEL: Sophomore

TYPE OF BREWING: Extract with specialty grains

SPECIALTY/EXTRA EQUIPMENT: None

TARGET OG: 1.057

TARGET FG: 1.014

IBUs: 39

TARGET ABV: 5.6%

PROPER GLASS: Pint

SHOPPING LIST

1 tube White Labs California Ale yeast WLP001

6 ounces Weyermann's smoked malt—milled

3 ounces Caramel/Crystal 80 L malt—milled

8 ounces Carafa III malt—milled

3.5 pounds Munich liquid malt extract

0.4 ounce (13%) Nugget hop pellets

½ Whirlfloc tablet

Makes about 2.5 gallons

PREP

■ *Prepare your yeast (at least 3 hours before you brew):* Let the White Labs California Ale yeast warm up to room temperature.

STEEP/MASH

■ Heat 3 quarts of water. Attach a thermometer and heat the brew pot until it reaches 160°F. Turn off the heat.

■ Put the specialty grains (Weyermann's smoked, Caramel/Crystal 80 L, and Carafa III malts) in the grain bag (tying the ends) and place it in the brew pot. Cover with a lid and rest for 30 minutes.

■ Prepare your sparge water by heating 3 quarts of water to 170°F in a separate small pot.

SPARGE

■ After 30 minutes, remove the grain bag from the brew pot. Put a large fine-mesh strainer over the brew pot. Put the grain bag in the strainer, open the grain bag, and slowly run the hot sparge water through it, making sure to cover all of the grains with water. Do not squeeze the grain bag! Remove the grain bag and discard.

■ Add an additional 2 gallons of room temperature water to the brew pot.

■ Reheat your brew pot water to 155°F; turn off the heat and add the Munich liquid malt extract. Gently stir to make sure the extract doesn't stick to the bottom of the pot.

THE BOIL

- Bring the pot to a boil.
- As soon as the pot comes to a boil, add your hops, the Nugget hops, and set your timer for 60 minutes. The hops will dissolve immediately. Stir occasionally, skimming off the big solids with a slotted spoon and looking out for the dreaded boilover!
- Add your clarifier: At 55 minutes (that is, when you have 5 minutes left in the boil), add the half tablet of Whirlfloc, stirring to dissolve.

PITCH THE YEAST

- *Prepare your ice bath:* In your sink or another vessel, prepare an ice bath to cool the beer down in.
- *Cool your wort:* Remove the pot from the heat and place it into your ice bath. Place a sanitized thermometer in the wort and let cool until it reaches 70°F or below.
- *Clean your stuff:* Sanitize anything that will come into contact with your beer.
- *Transfer your wort:* Pour the wort through a sanitized strainer into a 3- or 5-gallon plastic fermenting bucket or through a sanitized strainer and funnel into a 3- or 5-gallon glass carboy.
- *Pitch your yeast:* Shake your sanitized tube of yeast, crack it open, and throw all of its contents into the cooled wort in the fermenter.

PRIMARY FERMENTATION

- Place an airtight lid equipped with your airlock (filled with vodka) and stopper on the plastic bucket or place the airlock and stopper on a glass carboy. Or use the blow-off tube method (see Chapter 2).
- Keep the container in a dark and relatively cool place (ideal fermentation temperature for this style is between 68° and 73°F) for 7 to 10 days if using secondary or for 12 to 14 days if not.

■ Transfer the beer from the primary fermenter to a 3- to 5-gallon bucket or glass carboy with a sanitized tube siphon. (Make sure to leave the sediment behind.)

■ Put an airlock on the secondary container and let the beer sit for at least 14 days.

■ Bottle for 14 days as described in Chapter 2, and let the beer carbonate for 7 to 10 days. Then refrigerate and enjoy!

RULE BREAKERS AND TIPS

- OK, dome of silence. So, here's the deal. We used smoked malts in this recipe to avoid using liquid smoke because (1) we've heard so many bad things about it and, OK, (2) we may have had a "bad beer episode" with it ourselves. But if you are an all-extract brewer and you can't score some Rauch malt extract (which is very difficult to find), or you want to add even more smoke to your brew, you might need to use liquid smoke to get a strong flavor. The problem is that many liquid smoke products have more flavorings in them than smoke captured in liquid. Some have spices, vinegar, and other stuff that would suck in a beer. So make sure you find a good one without any of those additions. Try Lazy Kettle all-natural hickory liquid smoke or Wright's concentrated all-natural hickory seasoning liquid smoke. Use liquid smoke *sparingly*! Start with a scant ⅛ teaspoon to 1 teaspoon for a 2.5-gallon batch just before you pitch the yeast, after the wort has cooled down. Pitch it, paddle it, and taste it, as it will change during fermentation—because the sweetness of the wort won't be as strong—so keep that in mind and good luck. Just don't tell anyone.

- Another interesting and kind of cool option is Lapsang Souchong tea (also known as Russian caravan). It's a super-smoky black Chinese tea that is made by drying the tea leaves over pinewood fires. Again, the smoke flavor is very strong, so we suggest starting with 1 ounce at flameout for a 2.5-gallon batch and adjusting with future batches from there.

PROFESSIONAL BREWS TO ASPIRE TO

Hop in the Dark: Deschutes Brewery and Public House, Bend, Oregon. A Black IPA with notes of coffee and chocolate, brewed with oats, Dark, Munich, and Crystal malts. A nice big hop finish; 6.5% ABV.

Aecht Schlenkerla Rauchbier Urbock: Brauerei Heller-Trum, Bamberg, Germany. Big notes of smoke and bacon with sweet notes of caramel and a dry finish; 6.6% ABV.

Alaskan Smoked Porter: Alaskan Brewing Co., Juneau, Alaska. Intense smoky aromas and notes of coffee. Best when aged; 6.5% ABV.

<hr>

TO EAT

Black Smoke Pale Split Pea and Ham Soup

1 pound dried split peas, rinsed and picked through

6 cups chicken stock

2 cups Black Smoke Pale beer

1 large yellow onion, chopped

1 large carrot, chopped

1 large celery stalk, chopped

1 bay leaf

1 ham bone (optional)

½ cup diced ham

Salt and pepper

Serves 8

In a large pot, combine the split peas, stock, beer, onion, carrot, celery, bay leaf, and ham bone. Bring to a boil. Cover; lower the heat to simmer. Cook 1½ to 2 hours, or until the peas are tender and most have fallen apart. Remove the bone and bay leaf. Add the ham; continue to simmer 5 minutes or until the ham is heated through. Add salt and pepper to taste.

Serve with a glass of Black Smoke Pale Ale!

FOUR

July

BARBECUES ☙ FRESH BERRIES ☙ BASTILLE DAY ☙ FIREWORKS ☙
AMBER WAVES OF GRAIN ☙ SWIMMING POOLS ☙ DOG DAYS

Your July Homebrew

TRADITIONAL BAVARIAN HEFEWEIZEN: **Delicate beer with notes of banana and clove**

POOR MAN'S PROVENCE LAVENDER WIT: **Herbaceous Belgian-style beer with lavender notes**

SISTERS OF SUMMER TRIPEL: **Biscuit and citrus with notes of white pepper**

To Eat

Baby Arugula Summer Salad with Sliced Pears and Crumbled Goat Cheese in a Honey-Hefeweizen Vinaigrette

Ah, the fiery month of July. An abundance of fruits like cherries, apricots, and watermelon are at their best now, and summer recipes using these bright seasonal ingredients are in full swing. June has given way to some serious heat, everyone is stripping down, and nothing tastes better in the hot sun than a nice crisp, clean, and cold beer that demands to be consumed out of doors. What does all this mean to us beer geeks and homebrewers? It means that for this time of year we're looking for a beer that is effervescent and nuanced.

We have two Wheat Ales that fit the bill of July. The Hefeweizen is one of the most popular styles of beer in the summer and is a fairly easy beer to brew at home. This is a German Wheat style that is all about the yeast character, while the second beer is a Belgian Wheat style that is all about the spices and addition of lavender. We finish with a Tripel, a bigger Belgian style that still fits the desire for light flavors in the summer. It offers a bit more alcohol but refreshing citrus notes. All three are of the same flavor palate, offering elegance and refreshment at the same time.

JULY HOMEBREW 1

Traditional Bavarian Hefeweizen

MAKE THIS BEER IF YOU LIKE: Bananas Foster. Cloves. No bitter flavors. Fruit. Wheat.

PAIRS WELL WITH: Sushi, summer salads, weisswurst, fruit with whipped cream.

STYLE AND BREWING NOTES

Hefeweizens beg for summer. They are the unfiltered Wheat beers that most neophyte beer drinkers are comfortable with. And though many people couldn't spell or say *Hefeweizen* correctly if their lives depended on it, they seem more familiar with drinking Hefes than with any other Ale.

Hefes were the first craft beer style that blew our minds. While learning about beer working at Father's Office, a craft beer bar in Santa Monica, California, we tasted a true Bavarian-style Hefe for the first time and were floored by the big banana and clove flavors and aromas. Most Hefes we had had before were totally overtaken by the addition of a squeeze of lemon, and so that's what we thought all Hefes tasted like. Oh, how wrong we were! Once we tasted a true Hefe, we couldn't believe that there was no *actual* clove or banana added in the brewing process. Thus began our great respect for that single-celled organism called yeast.

Our recipe here is for a classic Bavarian Hefe similar to the one that started us on the road to craft beer geekdom. This is the true southern German style, meaning the only ingredients are water, malt, hops, and yeast (no spice or fruit additions). This follows the Reinheitsgebot law created by the German brewers of old that requires the brewing of beer with only the four basic ingredients.

There are many different choices when it comes to Hefeweizen yeast, all with different ester qualities. Besides the classic banana and clove, Hefe yeasts can offer citrus, bubble gum, or vanilla notes. Hefes, being a Wheat beer, also call for the addition of wheat to your grain bill. Wheat can add a cloudiness to the brew, a nice body on the tongue, a biscuity, bready wheat flavor, and a hint of sour. The wheat will be mixed with barley, usually the percentage of wheat to barley is at least 60% to 40%. The barley used is generally pale Pilsner malts. Hop flavors are fairly low and are usually relegated to drying qualities rather than bittering. We like to stay authentic when making this style and stick with Noble hops like the spicy, mild and earthy Hallertauer Hersbrucker hops.

Please, respect the hardworking yeast and delicate flavor profile: No f'ing lemon!

BREW IT: TRADITIONAL BAVARIAN HEFEWEIZEN

DIFFICULTY LEVEL: Neophyte

TYPE OF BREWING: Extract with specialty grains

SPECIALTY/EXTRA EQUIPMENT: None

TARGET OG: 1.046

TARGET FG: 1.012

IBUs: 10

TARGET ABV: 4.4

PROPER GLASS: Weizen glass or pint

SHOPPING LIST

1 packet Wyeast Weihenstephaner Weizen yeast
   3068

4 ounces flaked wheat

3 ounces Caravienne malt—milled

3 pounds Wheat liquid malt extract (typically a
   blend of Wheat and Pale malts; check the
   ingredients when you purchase)

0.4 ounce Hallertauer Hersbrucker hop pellets

Makes about 2.5 gallons

PREP

▪ *Prepare your yeast (at least 3 hours before you brew):* Crack your packet of Weizen yeast and let it warm up to room temperature. You can do this the day before you brew as well.

STEEP/MASH

▪ Heat 3 quarts of water. Attach a thermometer and heat the brew pot until it reaches 160°F. Turn off the heat.

▪ Put the specialty grains (flaked wheat and Caravienne malt) in the grain bag (tying the ends) and place it in the brew pot. Cover with a lid and rest for 30 minutes.

- Prepare your sparge water by heating 3 quarts of water to 170°F in a separate small pot.

SPARGE

- After 30 minutes, remove the grain bag from the brew pot. Put a large fine-mesh strainer over the brew pot. Put the grain bag in the strainer, open the grain bag, and slowly run the hot sparge water through it, making sure to cover all of the grains with water. Do not squeeze the grain bag! Remove the grain bag and discard.
- Add an additional 2 gallons of room-temperature water to the brew pot.
- Reheat your brew pot water to 155°F; turn off the heat and add the Wheat liquid malt extract. Gently stir to make sure the extract doesn't stick to the bottom of the pot.

THE BOIL

- Bring the pot to a boil. As soon as the pot comes to a boil, add the Hallertauer Hersbrucker hops and set your timer for 60 minutes. The hops will dissolve immediately. Stir occasionally, skimming off the big solids with a slotted spoon and looking out for the dreaded boil-over!

PITCH THE YEAST

- *Prepare your ice bath:* In your sink or another vessel, prepare an ice bath to cool the beer down in.
- *Cool your wort:* Remove the pot from the heat and place it into your ice bath. Place a sanitized thermometer in the wort and let cool until it reaches 70°F or below.
- *Clean your stuff:* Sanitize anything that will come into contact with your beer.
- *Transfer your wort:* Pour the wort through a sanitized strainer into a 3- or 5-gallon plastic fermenting bucket or through a sanitized strainer and funnel into a 3- or 5-gallon glass carboy.

- *Pitch your yeast:* Shake your packet of prepared yeast, sanitize the outside, tear it open, and throw all of its contents into the cooled wort in the fermenter.

PRIMARY FERMENTATION

- Place an airtight lid equipped with your airlock (filled with vodka) and stopper on the plastic bucket or place the airlock and stopper on a glass carboy. Or use the blow-off tube method (see Chapter 2).
- Keep the container in a dark and relatively cool place (ideal fermentation temperature for this beer is between 64° and 75°F) for 7 to 10 days if using secondary or for 12 to 14 days if not.

OPTION: SECONDARY

- Transfer the beer from the primary fermenter to a 3- to 5-gallon bucket or glass carboy with a sanitized tube siphon. (Make sure to leave the sediment behind.)
- Put an airlock on the secondary container and let the beer sit for at least 14 days.
- Bottle for 14 days as described in Chapter 2. Then refrigerate and enjoy!

RULE BREAKERS AND TIPS

- Hefeweizen is traditionally brewed using the relatively soft water that flows through streams in southern Germany. If your water is funky, consider preboiling it, using a charcoal filter or buying bottled drinking water.
- You can skip the flaked wheat and specialty grains. The body of your beer will be thinner and the color lighter.
- To get more esters out of your yeast, start the fermentation warm and finish it cold (70° to 55°F) for fewer esters, and to make it more like an American-style Hefe, start the fermentation cold and finish it warm (55° to 70°F.)

PROFESSIONAL BEERS TO ASPIRE TO

Paulaner Hefe-Weizen: Paulaner Braurei GmbH & Co., Munich, Germany. Lemon, banana, clove with a nice grain flavor. Though from a large brewery, the quality of this Hefe remains high; 5.5% ABV.

Dancing Man Wheat: New Glarus Brewing Co., New Glarus, Wisconsin. A Bavarian-style Hefe made in the United States, with notes of cinnamon, clove, banana, bubble gum, and grain; 7.2% ABV.

Weihenstephaner Hefeweissbier: Bayerische Staatsbrauerei Weihenstephan, Freising, Germany. Nuanced banana and clove with a dry, earthy, tart finish. A perfectly balanced Hefe from a German brewery established in 1040; 5.4% ABV.

JULY HOMEBREW 2

Poor Man's Provence Lavender Wit

MAKE THIS BEER IF YOU LIKE: Belgium. France. Flowery notes. Complexity. Lack of bitterness. Lavender.

PAIRS WELL WITH: Chicken roasted with herbes de Provence, ricotta cheese, honey gelato.

STYLE AND BREWING NOTES

In July in Provence, French lavender blooms, and the color of the month is a striking purple. We, however, live in Los Angeles. It's nice, but not exactly the French countryside, and the summer colors tend to come from the brownish gray smog that sits lazily above the city. The closest we may get in July (unless a sweet vacation deal comes our way, wink) is a nice homebrew with a touch of lavender in the recipe.

We find that quite a few people are afraid of using this ingredient in food and drink, complaining that it has a soapy perfumey flavor. Others, like us, are drawn to the unique sweet, flowery notes lavender imparts. In fact, lavender is a crucial part of the herbes de Provence (popularized in the 1970s) used in cooking some French fare. This homebrew recipe is our cheap way of visiting Provence in the summer by way of a glass of beer. And since Bastille Day falls in July, adding a French touch to this patriotic month seems appropriate.

Witbiers are Belgian-style Wheat Ales that allow a homebrewer to flex her creativity. Witbiers traditionally have an addition of spice like coriander and a citrus peel like curaçao or lemon. Witbiers are like renegades compared with the refined Hefeweizen. This is not to say that they require any less care from the brewer, need any less balance of flavors, or contain any less nuance. But the Belgians leave the door open on this style to add different combinations of spices, citrus, herbs, and so on. This style will help you become comfortable with adding specialty ingredients into your homebrew.

There are two ways to use lavender in this recipe. You want to make sure to use culinary lavender, not the aromatic kind! The flavors are quite different and aromatic lavender can give off a camphor smell and taste in your beer. *Lavender angustifolia*, or English lavender, is a popular culinary lavender among brewers, or you can take our title for this beer literately and use Provence French lavender, which is a bit more subtle. This is an impressive addition to beer; adding lavender will definitely impress your craft beer–loving friends and force your non-beer-drinking friends to rethink their position. It's kind of a shamelessly glamorous ingredient in homebrew.

BREW IT: POOR MAN'S PROVENCE LAVENDER WIT

DIFFICULTY LEVEL: **Sophomore**

TYPE OF BREWING: **Extract with specialty grains**

SPECIALTY/EXTRA EQUIPMENT: **None**

TARGET OG: **1.050**

TARGET FG: **1.010**

IBUs: **19**

TARGET ABV: **5.3**

PROPER GLASS: **Teardrop or tulip**

SHOPPING LIST

1 tube White Labs Belgian Wit Ale yeast WLP400

4 ounces flaked wheat

2 ounces Caravienne malt—milled

2 pounds Wheat liquid malt extract (typically a
blend of Wheat and Pale malts; check the
ingredients when you purchase)

1 pound Extra-Light dry malt extract

4 ounces honey

0.4 ounce Tettnang hop pellets

0.4 ounce Saaz hop pellets

0.25 ounce coriander seeds, crushed

0.25 ounce bitter orange peel

0.25 ounce lavender

Makes about 2.5 gallons

PREP

■ *Prepare your yeast (at least 3 hours before you brew):* Let the tube of
Wit Ale yeast warm up to room temperature.

STEEP/MASH

■ Heat 3 quarts of water. Attach a thermometer and heat the brew
pot until it reaches 160°F. Turn off the heat.

- Put the specialty grains (flaked wheat and Caravienne malt) in the grain bag (tying the ends) and place it in the brew pot. Cover with a lid and rest for 30 minutes.
- Prepare your sparge water by heating 3 quarts of water to 170°F in a separate small pot.

SPARGE

- After 30 minutes, remove the grain bag from the brew pot. Put a large fine-mesh strainer over the brew pot. Put the grain bag in the strainer, open the grain bag, and slowly run the hot sparge water through it, making sure to cover all of the grains with water. Do not squeeze the grain bag! Remove the grain bag and discard.
- Add an additional 2 gallons of room-temperature water to the brew pot.
- Reheat your brew pot water to 155°F; turn off the heat and add the Wheat liquid extract. Gently stir to make sure the extract doesn't stick to the bottom of the pot. Add the Extra-Light dry malt extract; be careful it doesn't clump. Stir in the honey.

THE BOIL

- Bring the pot to a boil.
- As soon as the pot comes to a boil, add your first hop addition, the Tettnang and 0.2 ounce of the Saaz hop pellets, and set your timer for 60 minutes. The hops will dissolve immediately. Skim off the big solids with a slotted spoon and look out for the dreaded boilover!
- At 55 minutes (that is, when there's 5 minutes left in the boil), add your second hop addition, the remaining 0.2 ounce Saaz hops, along with the coriander, bitter orange peel, and lavender.

PITCH THE YEAST

- *Prepare your ice bath:* In your sink or another vessel, prepare an ice bath to cool the beer down in.

- *Cool your wort*: Remove the pot from the heat and place it into your ice bath. Place a sanitized thermometer in the wort and let cool until it reaches 70°F or below.
- *Clean your stuff*: Sanitize anything that will come into contact with your beer.
- *Transfer your wort*: Pour the wort through a sanitized strainer into a 3- or 5-gallon plastic fermenting bucket or through a sanitized strainer and funnel into a 3- or 5-gallon glass carboy.
- *Pitch your yeast*: Shake your tube of yeast, crack it open, and throw all of its contents into the cooled wort in the fermenter.

PRIMARY FERMENTATION

- Place an airtight lid equipped with your airlock (filled with vodka) and stopper on the plastic bucket or place the airlock and stopper on a glass carboy. Or use the blow-off tube method (see Chapter 2).
- Keep the container in a dark and relatively cool place (ideal fermentation temperature for this style is between 67° and 74°F) for 7 to 10 days if using secondary or for 12 to 14 days if not.

OPTION: SECONDARY

- Transfer the beer from the primary fermenter to a 3- to 5-gallon bucket or glass carboy with a sanitized tube siphon. (Make sure to leave the sediment behind.)
- Put an airlock on the secondary container and let the beer sit for at least 14 days.
- Bottle for 14 days as described in Chapter 2. Then refrigerate and enjoy!

RULE BREAKERS AND TIPS
- Skip the lavender if you want a more traditional Belgian Wit style.
- If you want more lavender flavor, add some to the secondary vessel. Boil the lavender in a small amount of water, let it cool, and throw it all into the secondary vessel.

PROFESSIONAL BEERS TO ASPIRE TO

Blanche De Bruxelles: Brasserie Lefèbvre, Rebecq-Quenast, Belgium. This Witbier is über-traditional and direct from Belgium with a light body and the addition of coriander and orange peel; 4.5% ABV.

Allagash White: Allagash Brewing Co., Portland, Maine. Though a heavily guarded secret, the specific spices have a unique flavor profile (we put money on cloves); note how the spice profile differs from Blanche De Bruxelles and your homebrew; 5.2% ABV.

Eagle Rock Manifesto Wit: Eagle Rock Brewery, Los Angeles. This well-balanced Belgian-style White Ale is brewed with the traditional coriander and citrus peel, but the brewer gets innovative by adding rose petals; 4.7% ABV.

JULY HOMEBREW 3

Sisters of Summer Tripel

MAKE THIS BEER IF YOU LIKE: High alcohol content. Noble hops. Belgian tradition. Making candy.

PAIRS WELL WITH: Sole meunière, scallops, asparagus, artichokes, and lemon curd.

STYLE AND BREWING NOTES

Ah, the Tripel, made popular by the monks and nuns of Belgium who have been brewing and perfecting this style for hundreds of years. Who were we to mess around trying to make it in our kitchens? But we love this style, so we decided to take a stab at it. What the hell, it's just beer, right?

Tripels suffer from many misconceptions. There is a misconception that this beer style must be fermented three times. But actually the name is said to refer to the strength of the beer, not the fermentation. A Tripel is a complex, lighter-colored, full-bodied beer. It's dominated by fruity and citrusy aromatics and herbaceous hops. Tripels have a relatively high alcohol content due to the use of Belgian candi sugar in the boil, which adds flavor and complexity and kicks the ABV up to running somewhere between 7.5% and 9.5%. Tripels usually linger and then finish dry with some spicy characteristics and sparkling effervescence.

Our Sisters of Summer is an homage (not a clone but an homage) to one of our favorite beers of this style, Tripel Karmeliet, whose production is based on a 1679 recipe developed by Carmelite nuns. We pumped up our extract-based recipe with some homemade Belgian candi sugar to elevate the alcohol content. We also used low- to middle-range alpha acid hops with citrus, spicy, and earthy characteristics, so the malt could shine. For added complexity we threw some white pepper in the boil. And, for the star of this style—the yeast—we used our favorite for strong Belgian beers, the Wyeast Trappist High Gravity yeast.

BREW IT: SISTERS OF SUMMER TRIPEL

DIFFICULTY LEVEL: Devout

TYPE OF BREWING: Extract with Specialty Grains

SPECIALTY/EXTRA EQUIPMENT: None

TARGET OG: 1.079

TARGET FG: 1.009

IBUs: 33.6

TARGET ABV: 9.2%

PROPER GLASS: Teardrop or tulip

1 packet Wyeast Trappist High Gravity yeast 3787

1 packet Wyeast Belgian Abbey yeast 1214

4 ounces aromatic Belgian malt—milled

4 ounces Caravienne malt—milled

4 pounds Pilsner liquid malt extract

1 pound 2 ounces cane sugar or homemade Belgian
candi sugar (see page 86)

1 ounce Tettnanger hop pellets

0.5 ounce Saaz hop pellets

0.5 ounce Saaz hop pellets

Makes about 2.5 gallons

PREP

▪ *Prepare your yeast (at least 3 hours before you brew):* Crack your packets of Trappist High Gravity and Belgian Abbey yeasts and let them warm up to room temperature. You can do this the day before you brew as well.

STEEP/MASH

▪ Heat 3 quarts of water. Attach a thermometer and heat the brew pot until it reaches 160°F. Turn off the heat.

▪ Put the specialty grains (aromatic Belgian and Caravienne malts) in the grain bag (tying the ends) and place it in the brew pot. Cover with a lid and rest for 30 minutes.

▪ Prepare your sparge water by heating 3 quarts of water to 170°F in a separate small pot.

SPARGE

▪ After 30 minutes, remove the grain bag from the brew pot. Put a large fine-mesh strainer over the brew pot. Put the grain bag in the strainer, open the grain bag, and slowly run the hot sparge water through it, making sure to cover all of the grains with water. Do not squeeze the grain bag! Remove the grain bag and discard.

- Add an additional 2 gallons of room-temperature water to the brew pot.
- Reheat your brew pot water to 155°F; turn off the heat and add the Pilsner liquid malt extract. Gently stir to make sure the extract doesn't stick to the bottom of the pot.

THE BOIL

- Bring the pot to a boil.
- As soon as the pot comes to a boil, add your first hop addition, the Tettnanger hop pellets, and set your timer for 60 minutes. The hops will dissolve immediately. Stir occasionally, skimming off the big solids with a slotted spoon and looking out for the dreaded boilover!
- At 45 minutes (that is, with 15 minutes left in the boil), add your second hop addition, 0.5 ounce of Saaz hops.
- At 55 minutes (that is, with 5 minutes left in the boil), add your third hop addition, the remaining 0.5 ounce Saaz hops. Skim off the big solids with a slotted spoon. Add the sugar and stir to dissolve.

PITCH THE YEAST

- *Prepare your ice bath:* In your sink or another vessel, prepare an ice bath to cool the beer down in
- *Cool your wort:* Remove the pot from the heat and place it into your ice bath. Place a sanitized thermometer in the wort and let cool until it reaches 70°F or below.
- *Clean your stuff:* Sanitize anything that will come into contact with your beer.
- *Transfer your wort:* Pour the wort through a sanitized strainer into a 3- or 5-gallon plastic fermenting bucket or through a sanitized strainer and funnel into a 3- or 5-gallon glass carboy, aerating as much as possible.
- *Pitch your yeast:* Shake your packets of prepared yeast, sanitize the outside of both, tear them open, and throw all of their contents into the cooled wort in the fermenter.

PRIMARY FERMENTATION

■ Place an airtight lid equipped with your airlock (filled with vodka) and stopper on the plastic bucket or place the airlock and stopper on a glass carboy. Or use the blow-off tube method (see Chapter 2).

■ Keep the container in a dark place and, if you can, try to keep the fermentation temperature around 75°F for 7 to 10 days.

RECOMMENDED: SECONDARY

■ Transfer the beer from the primary fermenter to a 3- to 5-gallon bucket or glass carboy with a sanitized tube siphon. (Make sure to leave the sediment behind.)

■ Put an airlock on the secondary container and let the beer sit for at least 14 days.

■ Bottle for 14 days as described in Chapter 2. Then refrigerate and enjoy!

RULE BREAKERS AND TIPS

- If you don't feel like making or buying Belgian candi sugar, you can use pure white cane or beet sugar.
- You can raise the temperature of your beer by a couple of degrees by snugging the fermentation bucket or glass carboy in some warm blankets. You can also invest in a FermWrap heater ($30), which wraps around your carboy and can increase your beer's temperature by 5° to 20°F. Pretty nifty.

PROFESSIONAL BEERS TO ASPIRE TO

Tripel Karmeliet: Brouwerij Bosteels, Buggenhout, Belgium. A delightful tripel. Smooth, malty character, sweet but not cloying. Nice sharp bitterness that moves quickly to caramel malts and fruity yeasty nose. Alcohol nicely hidden behind the delicious malts. An excellent sipper; 9% ABV.

Westmalle Trappist Tripel: Brouwerij Westmalle, Malle, Belgium. The Tripel that started all Tripels. This is an amazing beer with a great balance; lemon on the lips, sweet and dry with floral and fruity esters, and a lovely lingering finish; 9.5% ABV.

Allagash Tripel Ale: Allgash Brewing Co., Portland, Maine. This strong Golden Ale is marked by passion fruit and herbal notes in the aroma, with suggestions of banana and honey in the complex palate. The Tripel has a remarkably long and smooth finish; 9% ABV.

Make Your Own Belgian Candi Sugar

 Belgian candi sugar is refined from sugar beets and is a fermentable sugar that can help bump up the alcohol content of a beer without making the beer overly sweet. It's a perfect addition to any Belgian Strong Ale and is especially good for using in Tripels. It also happens to be relatively pricey when it comes to beer-brewing ingredients. But the cool thing is that it's pretty easy to make yourself.

Candi sugar is what is called an "invert sugar," meaning that some of its constituents are broken down by inversion (actually splitting its atoms). Whoa. We don't necessarily understand that, but you don't have to be a rocket scientist to make your own invert sugar or candi sugar. Basically it's like making toffee without the butter.

Homemade Belgian Candi Sugar

500 grams of white sugar
Pinch of citric acid
Water

Add the sugar to a small saucepan or pot with a candy thermometer attached. Add enough water to make a thick syrup. Add a pinch of citric acid (available at your local homebrewing store), say ⅛ teaspoon, to the pot. Now slowly bring the mixture to a boil and keep the temperature between what in candy terms are called the hard ball and soft crack stages, which is between 260° and 275°F. Because evaporation will cause the temperature to rise, have a small amount of water on hand and add 1 tablespoon every now and then.

The color will gradually change from clear to light amber to deep red as the boil proceeds. Light candy sugar is a very light beige/yellow color. Dark candy sugar is a very deep red. Once you are at the color you desire (and a lot of that is personal preference; for instance, for the Sisters of Summer Tripel we would stop the browning process at the beige/yellow stage for a light-colored, bright Tripel), raise the temperature to 300°F (hard crack). Once it hits hard crack, turn off the heat and pour the mixture into a rimmed baking sheet lined with some greaseproof paper. As it cools it will go rock hard. Crack it up into pieces and keep it in the freezer until you're ready to use it.

TO EAT

Baby Arugula Summer Salad with Sliced Pears and Crumbled Goat Cheese in a Honey–Hefeweizen Vinaigrette

VINAIGRETTE

1 tablespoon Champagne vinegar

½ tablespoon honey

1 garlic clove, minced

½ shallot, minced

½ tablespoon lemon zest

4 tablespoons extra-virgin olive oil

¾ cup Traditional Bavarian Hefeweizen

Salt (sea or kosher), to taste

SALAD

1 (5-ounce) bag baby arugula

2 seasonal pears, cored and sliced

Plain goat cheese, crumbled, to taste

Freshly ground black pepper, to taste

Serves 4

Make the vinaigrette: In a medium bowl, mix together the vinegar, honey, garlic, shallot, and lemon zest. Drizzle in the olive oil, whisking continuously. Add the Hefeweizen, stirring slowly. Season with salt to taste.

Make the salad by tossing the arugula, pears, and goat cheese. Lightly dress with vinaigrette; toss gently to combine and season with pepper.

Serve with a glass of Traditional Bavarian Hefeweizen!

August

HOT, DAMN HOT ○ OVERRIPE FRUIT ○ LATE SUMMER DINNERS ○
SKIMPY CLOTHES ○ SWIMMING ○ VACATION ○ THIRST QUENCHERS

Your August Homebrew
CRISP SUMMER KÖLSCH: **Biscuit sweet notes with a dry finish**
HONEY CHAMOMILE BLONDE: **Touch of honey and floral notes;**
    mellow drinkin'
LEMON VERBENA BASIL WHEAT: **Hint of citrus and herbaceous**
    basil

To Eat
Lemon Verbena Basil Beer–Marinated Chicken

If there is ever a time for crisp, clean, light-bodied beers, it is during
the dog days of August. Unfortunately, many beer drinkers settle
for the mass-produced, industrialized, fizzy yellow beers. This is chang-
ing as craft brewers answer the call for innovative lighter styles and the
cries for an alternative to "that kind" of beer. We too wanted to brew
beer answering this call.

We start out with a classic Kölsch, a style that had been almost forgotten but is now making a comeback in craft beer culture. Is it a Lager? Is it an Ale? Is it a hybrid? You'll have to decide for yourself. Either way, it's a perfect answer to 98% humidity. The second and third beers for August are light on the palate but use special ingredients that add complexity to the style. Chamomile, honey, basil, and lemon verbena—these are flavors that pair well with hot weather and August dishes. These are not hop-forward beers but rather focus on sweet biscuit notes and delicate specialty ingredients. Clean and complex at the same time.

Crisp Summer Kölsch

MAKE THIS BEER IF YOU LIKE: German austerity. Tradition. The Rhineland. Breaking down myths. Crisp, clean, classic Ales.

PAIRS WELL WITH: Wiener schnitzel, fried pickles, shirred eggs, Emmenthal cheese.

STYLE AND BREWING NOTES

This style of beer, while very old, is just now gaining a foothold in the American craft beer market. Many people are tasting this hybrid style for the first time. Called the German Pale Ale by some, this style hails from Köln (Cologne to us), which is situated in the Rhineland region of Germany. Kölsch is called a hybrid beer because it actually uses both Ale and Lager methods. This beer is fermented with Ale yeast and then goes through a long cold secondary and conditioning, otherwise known as lagering. The result is a superclean and deliciously crisp beer that is crystal clear and sparkling, with a light body. Kölsches have delicate fruity, vinous notes and a clean, dry finish. They also have very slight aromatics of biscuit and bread dough on the nose. Kölsch beers are often overlooked, discounted as run-of-the-mill light beer, because a Kölsch is so soft and so delicate, but we use this beer in our classes and tastings as a great example of the complexity that can be contained in a lighter style of beer. It also dispels the myth that any beer that uses an Ale yeast is big, dark, and strong. This is not an easy beer to perfect in homebrewing because of the lagering step, but you're ready for a new challenge, right?

BREW IT: CRISP SUMMER KÖLSCH

DIFFICULTY LEVEL: Sophomore

TYPE OF BREWING: Extract with specialty grains

SPECIALTY/EXTRA EQUIPMENT: Needs to ferment in
    cooler temperatures (fridge)

TARGET OG: 1.045

TARGET FG: 1.011

IBUs: 25

TARGET ABV: 4.4%

PROPER GLASS: Stange (tall, thin glass) or pint

SHOPPING LIST

1 packet Wyeast Kölsch yeast 2565

4 ounces German Light Munich malt—milled

4 ounces Dextrine (Carapils) malt—milled

2.5 pounds liquid Light malt extract

1 ounce Crystal hop pellets

½ Whirlfloc tablet

0.5 ounce lemon zest (optional)

Makes about 2.5 gallons

PREP

■ *Prepare your yeast (at least 3 hours before you brew):* Crack your packet of Kölsch Ale yeast and let it warm up to room temperature. You can do this the day before you brew as well.

STEEP/MASH

■ Heat 3 quarts of water. Attach a thermometer, and heat the brew pot until it reaches 160°F. Turn off the heat.

■ Put the specialty grains (German Light Munich and Dextrine malts) in the grain bag (tying the ends) and place it in the brew pot. Cover with a lid and rest for 30 minutes.

■ Prepare your sparge water by heating 3 quarts of water to 170°F in a separate small pot.

SPARGE

■ After 30 minutes, remove the grain bag from the brew pot. Put a large fine-mesh strainer over the brew pot. Put the grain bag in the strainer, open the grain bag, and slowly run the hot sparge water through it, making sure to cover all of the grains with water. Do not squeeze the grain bag! Remove the grain bag and discard.

■ Add an additional 2 gallons of room-temperature water to the brew pot.

■ Reheat your brew pot water to 155°F; turn off the heat and add the liquid Light malt extract. Gently stir to make sure the extract doesn't stick to the bottom of the pot.

THE BOIL

■ Bring the pot to a boil.

■ As soon as the brew pot comes to a boil, add your hops, Crystal hop pellets, and set your timer for 60 minutes. The hops will dissolve immediately. Stir occasionally, skimming off the big solids with a slotted spoon and looking out for the dreaded boilover!

- At 55 minutes (that is, with 5 minutes left in the boil), add the half tablet of Whirlfloc and the optional lemon zest, stirring to dissolve the tablet.

PITCH THE YEAST

- *Prepare your ice bath:* In your sink or another vessel, prepare an ice bath to cool the beer down in.
- *Cool your wort:* Remove the pot from the heat and place it into your ice bath. Place a sanitized thermometer in the wort and let cool until it reaches 70°F or below.
- *Clean your stuff:* Sanitize anything that will come into contact with your beer.
- *Transfer your wort:* Pour the wort through a sanitized strainer into a 3- or 5-gallon plastic fermenting bucket or through a sanitized strainer and funnel into a 3- or 5-gallon glass carboy.
- *Pitch your yeast:* Shake your packet of prepared yeast, sanitize the outside, tear it open, and throw all of its contents into the cooled wort in the fermenter.

PRIMARY FERMENTATION

- Place an airtight lid equipped with your airlock (filled with vodka) and stopper on the plastic bucket or place the airlock and stopper on a glass carboy. Or use the blow-off tube method (see Chapter 2).
- Now the trick of this beer is the fermentation temperature. Keep this container in a dark and pretty cool place. We've seen and heard many suggestions, but, if you can, ferment this beer at an average of 58° to 62°F (see Chapter 2 for tips), which is ideal to mitigate fruity esters from taking over your beer. Try fermenting it in a water bath with ice packets. Ferment for 10 to 14 days.

RECOMMENDED: SECONDARY

▪ Transfer the beer from the primary fermenter to a 3- to 5-gallon bucket or glass carboy with a sanitized tube siphon. (Make sure to leave the sediment behind.)

▪ Put an airlock on the secondary container and let the beer sit (ideally still at 58° to 62°F) for at least 14 days.

LAGERING

▪ Kölsch is a hybrid beer that uses Ale yeast strains but is traditionally lagered. Well, this is our lagering process. Ready? Here it is. Make room for your 3- to 5-gallon bucket or glass carboy to rest in your refrigerator. This "cold crashing" will slow down the fermentation to a crawl and will inhibit any esters or phenols that you don't want in this beer style. Lagering also helps your beer clarify and condition even further, so you have a clean, crisp, and refreshing summer beer.

▪ When you have your Kölsch looking and tasting the way that you like, use priming sugar to bottle it as described in Chapter 2.

RULE BREAKERS AND TIPS

• You can do this beer very easily as an extract-only recipe simply by leaving out the German Light Munich and Dextrine malts, which are primarily contributing to mouthfeel and head retention. It won't affect the alcohol content too much.

• Now we say the lemon is optional because a traditional Kölsch does not *ever* have any kind of flavor addition. But we love the brightness that the citrus brings without being overpoweringly lemony. Leave it out and you'll still have a really nice Kölsch here if you're feeling purist.

• Kölsch does well with a soft water source. For extract- and specialty grain–based beer recipes (like we're doing here), your tap water will most likely be fine, but for lighter more nuanced styles, a softer water is best. Don't use softened water, rather boil your water before using it or buy distilled water from the store and use it in this recipe.

PROFESSIONAL BREWS TO ASPIRE TO

Reissdorf Kölsch: Brauerei Heinrich Reissdorf, Cologne, Germany. This Kölsch has a cult following. Smooth, light, yet complex. Hints of jasmine and a cedar-like woody finish; 4.8% ABV.

Karnival Kölsch: Stoudts Brewing Co., Adamstown, Pennsylvania. This German-style Ale is brewed with 2-Row malt, some Red Wheat malt, and German hops for bittering and aroma. Dry and crisp with a hint of fruit; 4.8% ABV.

Yellowtail Pale Ale: Ballast Point Brewing Co., San Diego, California. Uses German hops and German and American malt. Notes of crisp fruit and earthy wheat; 5% ABV.

I'm Spent: What to Do with Your Spent Grain

We hate to waste, and you probably do too, so when you take out your grain bag and dump that used grain into the trash bin, you may feel eco-guilt all over your body. Here are a few suggestions for upcycling that grain and brewing guilt free:

- **Compost:** Spent grain is a perfect addition to your compost.
- **Add to feed:** Many brewers give their spent grain to local cattle, pigs, or chickens.
- **Bake into bread:** Add to bread for a nice rustic, farmhouse touch.
- **Add to cookie dough:** Add a touch to oatmeal cookies to bring an earthy flavor.
- **Mix into pizza dough:** Thicken up that pizza crust by adding a bit of spent grain to the dough.

- **Make your dog happy:** Add to dog biscuit recipes to give a fiber boost to Fido's treats. (*Warning:* Never add hops, or grains that have touched hops or been boiled in hopped wort, to dog food or biscuits. Hops are poison for dogs!)
- **Eat:** Add a touch to hot oatmeal with a little cream and brown sugar. The malty flavor adds complexity and fiber.

AUGUST HOMEBREW 2

Honey Chamomile Blonde

MAKE THIS BEER IF YOU LIKE: Flowery aromas. Low bitterness. A touch of sweetness. Chamomile tea. Blondes that aren't dumb.

PAIRS WELL WITH: Shortbread, sweet corn, mild goat cheese, fresh fruit, lemon bars.

STYLE AND BREWING NOTES

The Blonde style of beer is a bit of an invented category. Its name comes more from the color than any specific flavor profile. An American Blonde Ale tends to be light and biscuity in color and on the palate, sort of like a paler Pale Ale with a touch of sweetness. Some Blondes can be quite boring Ales, others have a nice complexity; the guidelines are pretty lax. Most Blonde Ales, however, do not offer a hoppy bite. Their finish is sweet or clean, but never bitter.

We've added chamomile and honey to our Blonde Ale recipe. Boring Blonde beers offend us (well at least half of us). We're just not crazy about Blonde Ales that have no personality. Some are just too light and sweet and have no character. You'd take them home, but you don't want to have breakfast with them in the morning. The chamomile will add just enough complexity to give it something special on the nose. Like lavender, chamomile is often used in tea, and you may be most familiar with its flowery, apple flavors from brewing some tea to relax at home. (*Chamomile* actually comes from a Greek word that means "ground apple.") Dried chamomile flowers are easy to come by and work much like the lavender does in July's Witbier recipe. If you've planted chamomile in your herb garden, you can harvest it and use the whole plant instead of just the dried flowers, which will provide more of a bitter taste. In fact, chamomile was often used as a bittering agent in beer before hops became a common ingredient. Honey is often added to chamomile tea, so it seemed a perfect accompaniment to this brew. Call it your "sleepy time beer."

We were lucky enough to be invited by New Belgium Brewing Company out of Fort Collins, Colorado, to be a part of their "Trip" series. This is a collaboration series between New Belgium and Elysian Brewing Company out of Seattle, Washington. We traveled up to Elysian and brewed their all-grain version of our Honey Chamomile Blonde beer alongside professional brewer Kevin Watson. We learned so much about brewing techniques from those guys! Trip #13 was released in the summer of 2012 (hopefully you had some!), and we were honored to have collaborated with two of the best breweries in the West!

BREW IT: HONEY CHAMOMILE BLONDE

DIFFICULTY LEVEL: Sophomore

TYPE OF BREWING: Extract with specialty grains

SPECIALTY/EXTRA EQUIPMENT: None

TARGET OG: 1.051

TARGET FG: 1.012

IBUS: 19

TARGET ABV: 5

PROPER GLASS: Pint or teardrop

SHOPPING LIST

1 packet Wyeast Northwest Ale yeast 1332

3 pounds Briess Pilsen Light liquid malt extract

4 ounces Honey malt—milled

0.5 ounce Hallertauer hop pellets

0.25 ounce Czech Saaz hop pellets

0.02 ounce chamomile

½ Whirlfloc tablet

8 ounces honey

Makes about 2.5 gallons

PREP

- *Prepare your yeast (at least 3 hours before you brew):* Crack your packet of Northwest Ale yeast and let it warm up to room temperature. You can do this the day before you brew as well.

STEEP/MASH

- Heat 2 quarts of water. Attach a thermometer and heat the brew pot until it reaches 160°F. Turn off the heat.
- Put the specialty grain (Honey malt) in the grain bag (tying the ends) and place it in the brew pot. Cover with a lid and rest for 30 minutes.
- Prepare your sparge water by heating 4 quarts of water to 170°F in a separate small pot.

SPARGE

- After 30 minutes, remove the grain bag from the brew pot. Put a large fine-mesh strainer over the brew pot. Put the grain bag in the strainer, open the grain bag, and slowly run the hot sparge water through it, making sure to cover all of the grains with water. Do not squeeze the grain bag! Remove the grain bag and discard.
- Add an additional 2 gallons of room temperature water to the brew pot.

- Reheat your brew pot water to 155°F; turn off the heat and add the Briess Pilsen Light liquid malt extract. Gently stir in the malt extract, making sure the extract doesn't stick to the bottom of the pot.

THE BOIL

- Bring the pot to a boil.
- As soon as the pot comes to a boil, add your first hop addition, the Hallertauer hops, and set your timer for 60 minutes. The hops will dissolve immediately. Stir occasionally, skimming off the big solids with a slotted spoon and looking out for the dreaded boilover!
- At 40 minutes (that is, with 20 minutes left in the boil), add your second hop addition, the Czech Saaz hops.
- At 55 minutes (that is, with 5 minutes left in the boil), add the chamomile and the half tablet of Whirlfloc, stirring to dissolve.
- At flameout (that is, when you turn off the heat at the end of the boil), add the honey. Stir gently to make sure it doesn't stick to the bottom of the pot.

PITCH THE YEAST

- *Prepare your ice bath:* In your sink or another vessel, prepare an ice bath to cool the beer down in.
- *Cool your wort:* Remove the pot from the heat and place it into your ice bath. Place a sanitized thermometer in the wort and let cool until it reaches 70°F or below.
- *Clean your stuff:* Sanitize anything that will come into contact with your beer.
- *Transfer your wort:* Pour the wort through a sanitized strainer into a 3- or 5-gallon plastic fermenting bucket or through a sanitized strainer and funnel into a 3- or 5-gallon glass carboy.
- *Pitch your yeast:* Shake your packet of prepared yeast, sanitize the outside, tear it open, and throw all of its contents into the cooled wort in the fermenter.

PRIMARY FERMENTATION

- Place an airtight lid equipped with your airlock (filled with vodka) and stopper on the plastic bucket or place the airlock and stopper on a glass carboy. Or use the blow-off tube method (see Chapter 2).

- Keep the container in a dark and relatively cool place (ideal fermentation temperature for this beer is between 65° and 75°F) for 7 to 10 days if using secondary or for 12 to 14 days if not.

OPTION: SECONDARY

- Transfer the beer from the primary fermenter to a 3- to 5-gallon bucket or glass carboy with a sanitized tube siphon. (Make sure to leave the sediment behind.)

- Put an airlock on the secondary container and let the beer sit for at least 14 days.

- Bottle for 14 days as described in Chapter 2. Then refrigerate and enjoy!

RULE BREAKERS AND TIPS

- Heat up the honey a bit in another pot to make it easier to pour.
- If you don't want to find chamomile at a specialty store, use tea bags. You can even leave the flowers in the bag, throwing in two or three when there's 5 minutes left in the boil.
- You can skip steeping the specialty grains, but the color won't be nearly as nice.

PROFESSIONAL BREWS TO ASPIRE TO

Summer Love American Blonde Ale: Victory Brewing Co., Downington, Pennsylvania. Brewed with earthy European hops, bright American hops and German malts. Hints of lemon; 5.2% ABV.

Lips of Faith Dandelion American Blonde Ale: New Belgium Brewing Co., Fort Collins, Colorado. Dandelion greens, related to chamomile, have a natural bittering effect much like hops. This Blonde is brewed with Pilsner malt, fresh dandelion greens, grains of paradise, and a Belgian yeast strain; 7.8% ABV.

Bikini Blonde: Maui Brewing Co., Lahaina, Hawaii. Notes of bread, citrus rind, and mossy earth. Finishes with hints of lemon and pepper; 5.1% ABV.

AUGUST HOMEBREW 3

Lemon Verbena Basil Wheat

MAKE THIS BEER IF YOU LIKE: Citrus. Wheat beers. Herbaceous notes. Low bitterness. Savory and tart. Thinking outside the box.

PAIRS WELL WITH: Summer pasta with fresh basil, scallops, grilled shrimp, olive oil cake, Thai curry.

STYLE AND BREWING NOTES

The Wheat beers we made in the last chapter were of the Belgian variety. This Wheat Ale recipe has more of an American profile. Unfortunately, most Americans love their Wheat Ale with a slice of lemon on the rim. But brewers will tell you that there's nothing they hate more than seeing a beer they slaved over wind up in a glass with a lemon squeezed into it—this masks all the subtle flavors of the ingredients and kills the head of the beer. (You'll feel the same way once you slave over your beer!) We are strictly NFL (no f'ing lemon) when it comes to this beer controversy. However, because we love lemon as an aroma and flavor in pretty much all things, we wanted to add that refreshing note to this beer without compromising the quality. Lemon verbena became the answer. Like chamomile, lemon verbena is often used in tea. It has a nice hint of citrus without too much sour bite. We realize that basil may seem like a strange addition to beer, but we're big fans of savory ingredients in brews and thought the spice of basil would complement the lemon verbena notes.

We're also using a pretty hip hop in this beer. Sorachi Ace is a Japanese hop that was originally developed for Sapporo. It's known for its high alpha acid content (13% to 16%) and its intense lemony attributes. Its unique citrus flavor has made it popular with homebrewers and professional brewers. We love how it works with the lemon verbena in this brew.

BREW IT: LEMON VERBENA BASIL WHEAT

DIFFICULTY LEVEL: Sophomore
TYPE OF BREWING: Extract with specialty grains
SPECIALTY/EXTRA EQUIPMENT: None
TARGET OG: 1.049
TARGET FG: 1.010
IBUs: 23
TARGET ABV: 5
PROPER GLASS: Teardrop or tulip

SHOPPING LIST

1 packet Wyeast American Wheat Ale yeast 1010
1 ounce Briess Carapils malt—milled
1 ounce Caramel/Crystal 20 L malt—milled
2 pounds liquid Wheat malt extract
1 pound Light dry malt extract
4 ounces honey
0.25 ounce Sorachi Ace hop pellets
0.125 ounce Sorachi Ace hop pellets
0.25 ounce fresh basil leaves, scored
0.25 ounce fresh lemon verbena leaves, scored

Makes about 2.5 gallons

PREP

- *Prepare your yeast (at least 3 hours before you brew):* Crack your packet of American Wheat Ale yeast and let it warm up to room temperature. You can do this the day before you brew as well.

STEEP/MASH

- Heat 2 quarts of water. Attach a thermometer and heat the brew pot until it reaches 160°F. Turn off the heat.
- Put the specialty grains (Briess Carapils and Caramel/Crystal 20 L malts) in the grain bag (tying the ends) and place it in the brew pot. Cover with a lid and rest for 30 minutes.
- Prepare your sparge water by heating 4 quarts of water to 170°F in a separate small pot.

SPARGE

- After 30 minutes, remove the grain bag from the brew pot. Put a large fine-mesh strainer over the brew pot. Put the grain bag in the strainer, open the grain bag, and slowly run the hot sparge water through it, making sure to cover all of the grains with water. Do not squeeze the grain bag! Remove the grain bag and discard.
- Add an additional 2 gallons of room-temperature water to the brew pot.
- Reheat your brew pot water to 155°F; turn off the heat and add the liquid Wheat malt extract. Gently stir to make sure the extract doesn't stick to the bottom of the pot. Add the Light dry malt extract slowly; be careful it doesn't clump. Stir in the honey.

THE BOIL

- Bring the pot to a boil.
- As soon as the pot comes to a boil, add your first hop addition, 0.25 ounce Sorachi Ace hops, and set your timer for 60 minutes. The hops will dissolve immediately. Stir occasionally, skimming off big solids with a slotted spoon and looking out for the dreaded boilover!

- At 55 minutes (that is, when you have 5 minutes left), add your second hop addition, the remaining 0.125 ounce Sorachi Ace hops.
- At flameout (that is, when you turn off the heat at the end of the boil), add the basil and lemon verbena and lightly stir.

PITCH THE YEAST

- *Prepare your ice bath:* In your sink or another vessel, prepare an ice bath to cool the beer down in.
- *Cool your wort:* Remove the pot from the heat and place it into your ice bath. Place a sanitized thermometer in the wort and let cool until it reaches 70°F or below.
- *Clean your stuff:* Sanitize anything that will come into contact with your beer.
- *Transfer your wort:* Pour the wort through a sanitized strainer into a 3- or 5-gallon plastic fermenting bucket or through a sanitized strainer and funnel into a 3- or 5-gallon glass carboy.
- *Pitch your yeast:* Shake your packet of prepared yeast, sanitize the outside, tear it open, and throw all of its contents into the cooled wort in the fermenter.

PRIMARY FERMENTATION

- Place an airtight lid equipped with your airlock (filled with vodka) and stopper on the plastic bucket or place the airlock and stopper on a glass carboy. Or use the blow-off tube method (see Chapter 2).
- Keep the container in a dark and relatively cool place (ideal fermentation temperature for this beer is between 58° and 74°F) for 7 to 10 days if using secondary or for 12 to 14 days if not.

OPTION: SECONDARY

- Transfer the beer from the primary fermenter to a 3- to 5-gallon bucket or glass carboy with a sanitized tube siphon. (Make sure to leave the sediment behind.)

- Put an airlock on the secondary container and let the beer sit for at least 14 days.
- Bottle for 14 days as described in Chapter 2. Then refrigerate and enjoy!

RULE BREAKERS AND TIPS

- Substitute lemon zest for the lemon verbena if you can't get ahold of the verbena. Add 1 teaspoon at flameout.
- You can use lemon verbena tea as a substitute as well, add 1 to 2 tea bags when there are 5 minutes left in the boil.

PROFESSIONAL BREWS TO ASPIRE TO

Trade Winds Tripel: The Bruery, Placentia, California. A Belgian-style Tripel brewed with Thai basil. A peppery, citrusy, super-complex Ale; 7.5% ABV.

Sorachi Ace Saison: Brooklyn Brewery, Brooklyn, New York. A traditional Saison style brewed with a Belgian Ale strain and rare Sorachi Ace hops. Dry-hopped with Sorachi Ace hops and bottle-refermented with Champagne yeast. Crisp notes of lemon zest; 7. 6% ABV.

Organic Honey Basil: Bison Brewing, Berkeley, California. A light-bodied Ale brewed with organic clover honey and fresh, whole leaf organic basil. Herbaceous floral aroma with hints of sweetness and basil in the finish; 5% ABV.

Lemon Verbena Basil Beer–Marinated Chicken

**One 3- to 4-pound broiler/fryer chicken, neck and
giblets removed, cut into 8 pieces (breasts,
drumsticks, thighs, and wings)**

One 12-ounce bottle Lemon Verbena Basil beer

Salt and pepper to taste

½ cup flour

Vegetable shortening

Serves 4

Soak chicken pieces in beer in a sturdy resealable plastic bag or covered container for 1 to 3 hours.

Drain the chicken pieces. Season liberally with salt and pepper.

Place the flour in a shallow dish and dredge the seasoned chicken, shaking off the excess flour. Set aside.

In a cast-iron skillet or other heavy sauté pan, melt enough shortening to come ⅓ inch up the side of the pan. Heat the shortening to 350°F.

Gently lay the chicken into the hot shortening. Do not crowd; you'll need to fry in two batches in a medium pan.

Turn the pieces when medium to deep brown, about 10 minutes, then cook other side until brown, another 10 minutes.

Drain the cooked chicken on a cooling rack set over a cookie sheet.

Serve with a glass of Lemon Verbena Basil Wheat!

September

WEATHER CHANGE ⟳ **HOP HARVEST** ⟳
LABOR DAY WEEKEND ⟳ **AUTUMN BEGINS**

Your September Homebrew

JUST ONE HOP SIMCOE IPA: **Bitter IPA with citrus, stone fruit, and tropical notes**

JUST ONE HOP CASCADE IPA: **Bitter IPA with notes of grass, grapefruit and pine trees**

EAST INDIA PALE ALE (PROAM RECIPE WITH STRAND BREWING COMPANY): **Complex flavors of tamarind, garam masala, curry, citrus and caramel**

To Eat

East India Pale Ale Vegetarian Curry

Get excited because the end of August through the beginning of September is hop harvest season in the beer world. Woo hoo! Many hops are grown in the Northwest region of the United States. Washington and Oregon have prime hop-growing climates and have become the home of many beloved varietals of hops. So, in honor of hops, which do so much for beer, we are brewing IPAs this month that focus on different varietals and allow the new homebrewer to get to know and love hops as much as we and most beer lovers do. If you have found that bitter beers are not your thing, you may want to come back to this chapter after you develop a taste for hops. We can assure you that your palate will change and become accustomed to the bite of hops; it happens to every new craft beer drinker. Some of you are already certified hopheads, so this chapter will be your favorite, no doubt.

The third beer in this chapter is near and dear to our hearts. It's a pro-am (professional brewer with amateur brewers; we'd be the amateurs, of course) recipe that we created with Joel Elliot, owner and brewer at the Strand Brewing Company in Torrance, California. We brewed it together one afternoon at his brewery and served it at an event during Los Angeles Beer Week. All three of us were pleased with the way it turned out, especially because it was kind of a crazy idea and involved a lot of weird ingredients. We were thrilled when Joel emailed us and told us he was going to brew the recipe again to launch a limited line of specialty Strand bottles. Here it is for you to brew and enjoy. Because it was a professional–amateur collaboration, we have included an amateur extract with specialty grains recipe.

Alpha Acid: It Sounds Worse Than It Is

Hops have a measurement called the alpha acid content. This refers to the chemical compounds present in the resin glands of the flowering cones. These alpha acids cause the bitterness that hops impart in beer. The acids are activated when they are added to a hot solution, like the boiling wort in the making of beer. The longer you boil the hops, the more this bitterness is drawn out in your brew. So if you put hops with a high alpha acid content in your boil for 60 minutes, they will impart a bitter bite, but if you put the same hops in for 5 minutes, the effects will be minimal, and you will mostly get only an aromatic essence from those hops. Alpha acid levels in hops can range anywhere from 2% to 13% and higher. This is important when selecting hops for recipes. If you substitute a hop that should have an 11% alpha acid content with one that has a 4% alpha acid content, your beer will lack the balance, dryness, or bitterness you desire. See, alpha acid is actually a *good* thing.

Just One Hop Simcoe IPA

MAKE THIS BEER IF YOU LIKE: Hops. Bitter bite. Stone fruit. Tropical notes. Simplicity.

PAIRS WELL WITH: Spicy mango avocado salad, blackened shrimp, fish tacos, and cheeseburgers.

STYLE AND BREWING NOTES

Simcoe, we love you. As you become a beer lover, you begin to find hop varietals that speak to you, flavors in Pale Ales and IPAs that make you finally fall in love with hops. Simcoe has risen to the top of IPA fame in a very short while, an overnight success. Simcoe hops are a varietal that first showed up on the scene in 2000. It's an American hybrid created by Yakima Chief Ranches in Washington State. Simcoe is now highly sought after in the professional and homebrewing worlds. In fact, it may not be easy for you to get ahold of, so you may have to wait for availability before brewing this IPA. Simcoe has a big following partly because of its bright pine, citrus, grapefruit, and tropical notes but also because it has less of a harsh bite than other popular hops. So it packs a lot of flavor without too much bitter, acidic bite.

Mikkeller is a rebel Danish brewer popular in the craft beer world. He recently came out with a line of single-hop IPAs. Each beer is made with the same ingredients, just a different single type of hop. This is not for the neophyte beer drinker, because the intention is not balance but rather an exploration of a particular hop. Typically a mixture of hops is used in beer, you wouldn't necessarily want a single hop varietal of certain hops. We were inspired by Mikkeller's line and wanted to try a few single-hop Ales at home. We also thought this would be a great learning tool for the new homebrewer, a way to get intimately acquainted with the wide variety of hop flavors out there. Here we have only two, our favorites out of our experimentations, but if you like the challenge, try these recipes with other hop varietals.

BREW IT: JUST ONE HOP SIMCOE IPA

DIFFICULTY LEVEL: Neophyte

TYPE OF BREWING: Extract with specialty grains

SPECIALTY/EXTRA EQUIPMENT: None

TARGET OG: 1.071

TARGET FG: 1.016

IBUs: 74

TARGET ABV: 7.3

PROPER GLASS: Pint

SHOPPING LIST

1 tube of White Labs California Ale yeast WLP001

2 ounces Caramel/Crystal 60 L malt—milled

2 ounces Caramel/Crystal 10 L malt—milled

2 ounces Cara-Amber malt—milled

4 pounds Pale liquid malt extract

0.5 ounce Simcoe hop pellets

0.5 ounce Simcoe hop pellets

1 ounce Simcoe hop pellets

12 ounces Amber dry malt extract

Makes about 2.5 gallons

PREP

- *Prepare your yeast (at least 3 hours before you brew):* Let the tube of California Ale yeast warm up to room temperature.

STEEP/MASH

- Heat 3 quarts of water. Attach a thermometer, and heat the brew pot until it reaches 160°F. Turn off the heat.
- Put the specialty grains (Caramel/Crystal 60 L, Caramel/Crystal 10 L, and Cara-Amber malts) in the grain bag (tying the ends) and place it in the brew pot. Cover with a lid and rest for 30 minutes.
- Prepare your sparge water by heating 3 quarts of water to 170°F in a separate small pot.

SPARGE

- After 30 minutes, remove the grain bag from the brew pot. Put a large fine-mesh strainer over the brew pot. Put the grain bag in the strainer, open the grain bag, and slowly run the hot sparge water through it, making sure to cover all of the grains with water. Do not squeeze the grain bag! Remove the grain bag and discard.
- Add an additional 2 gallons of water to the brew pot.
- Reheat your brew pot to 155°F; turn off the heat and add the Pale liquid malt extract. Gently stir to make sure the extract doesn't stick to the bottom of the pot.

THE BOIL

- Bring the pot to a boil.
- As soon as the pot comes to a boil, add your first hop addition, 0.5 ounce of Simcoe hops, and set your timer for 60 minutes. The hops will dissolve immediately. Skim off the big solids with a slotted spoon and look out for the dreaded boilover!
- At 45 minutes (that is, with 15 minutes left in the boil), add your second hop addition, 0.5 ounce of Simcoe hops.
- At 55 minutes (that is, with 5 minutes left in the boil), add your third hop addition, 1 ounce of Simcoe hops, and stir in the Amber dry malt extract; be careful it doesn't clump.

PITCH THE YEAST

- *Prepare your ice bath:* In your sink or another vessel, prepare an ice bath to cool the beer down in.
- *Cool your wort:* Remove the pot from the heat and place it into your ice bath. Place a sanitized thermometer in the wort and let cool until it reaches 70°F or below.
- *Clean your stuff:* Sanitize anything that will come into contact with your beer.
- *Transfer your wort:* Pour the wort through a sanitized strainer into a 3- or 5-gallon plastic fermenting bucket or through a sanitized strainer and funnel into a 3- or 5-gallon glass carboy.
- *Pitch your yeast:* Shake your tube of prepared yeast, sanitize the outside of the tube, crack it open, and throw all of its contents into the cooled wort in the fermenter.

PRIMARY FERMENTATION

- Place an airtight lid equipped with your airlock (filled with vodka) and stopper on the plastic bucket or place the airlock and stopper on a glass carboy. Or use the blow-off tube method (see Chapter 2).

- Keep the container in a dark and relatively cool place (ideal fermentation temperature for this beer is between 68° and 73°F) for 7 to 10 days if using secondary or for 12 to 14 days if not.

OPTION: SECONDARY
- Transfer the beer from the primary fermenter to a 3- to 5-gallon bucket or glass carboy with a sanitized tube siphon. (Make sure to leave the sediment behind.)
- Put an airlock on the secondary container and let the beer sit for at least 14 days.
- Bottle for 14 days as described in Chapter 2. Then refrigerate and enjoy!

RULE BREAKERS AND TIPS
- If you want to skip the specialty grains, you can add 4 ounces more of the dry malt extract, but be aware that the flavor and the color won't be as nice.
- Substitute Citra, Nelson, or Columbus hops if you can't get ahold of Simcoe. The flavors will be quite different with each hop.

PROFESSIONAL BREWS TO ASPIRE TO
Knuckle Sandwich: Bootlegger's Brewery, Fullerton, California. Big flavors of grass, bitter fruit, and savory herbs. Knuckle Sandwich is definitely a punch in the face, but one that feels good. The alcohol is well hidden; 10% ABV.

Sculpin IPA: Ballast Point Brewing Co., San Diego, California. Showcases bright flavors and aromas of apricot, peach, mango, and lemon. The lighter body also brings out the crispness of the hops; 7% ABV.

Simcoe Single Hop IPA: Mikkeller, Copenhagen, Denmark; brewed at De Proef Brouwerij, Lochristi-Hijfte, Belgium. Brewed with

Simcoe hops and bursting with notes of Fanta orange, passion fruit, and fresh pine; 6.9% ABV.

Just One Hop Cascade IPA

MAKE THIS BEER IF YOU LIKE: The Northwest. Bitter, biting beers. The smell of pine trees. Grapefruit. Hopheads.

PAIRS WELL WITH: Burgers with all the fixin's, fatty meats, grilled steak with crumbled blue cheese.

STYLE AND BREWING NOTES
Do you love hops yet?

Like your last brew, this will be an IPA that teaches you about the characteristics of different hops. We hope by now you are as impressed as we are with how important hops are to the flavor, aroma, and mouthfeel of beer. Cascade hops are favorites in the beer world and are easier to come by than Simcoe. Columbus and Cascade are used in many West Coast Pale Ales and IPAs. Cascade hails from Oregon, and is named after the Cascade Mountains that run through Washington and Oregon. The Northwest is the hop-growing capital in this country. Cascade hops were born out of a breeding program at Oregon State University and made available in 1972. Cascade hops are quite high in alpha acids, which produce the bitterness in hops and are known and loved for their bold piney, grapefruit, and citrus aroma. This recipe is exactly the same as the first one for September but calls for Cascade instead of Simcoe hops. The ABV and IBUs should be pretty much the same as well. The only difference is the hop, but the beer will be a whole new experience on your palate.

BREW IT: JUST ONE HOP CASCADE IPA

DIFFICULTY LEVEL: Neophyte

TYPE OF BREWING: Extract with specialty grains

SPECIALTY/EXTRA EQUIPMENT: None

TARGET OG: 1.071

TARGET FG: 1.016

IBUs: 74

TARGET ABV: 7.3

PROPER GLASS: Pint

SHOPPING LIST

1 tube of White Labs California Ale yeast WLP001

2 ounces Caramel/Crystal 60 L malt—milled

2 ounces Caramel/Crystal 10 L malt—milled

2 ounces Cara-Amber malt—milled

4 pounds Pale liquid malt extract

1 ounce Cascade hop pellets

1.5 ounces Cascade hop pellets

1 ounce Cascade hop pellets

12 ounces dry Amber malt extract

Makes about 2.5 gallons

PREP

■ *Prepare your yeast (at least 3 hours before you brew):* Let the tube of California Ale Yeast warm up to room temperature.

STEEP/MASH

■ Heat 3 quarts of water in brew pot. Attach a thermometer and heat the brew pot until it reaches 160°F. Turn off the heat.

■ Turn off the heat. Put the specialty grains (Caramel/Crystal 60 L, Caramel/Crystal 10 L, and Cara-Amber malts) in the grain bag (tying the ends) and place it in the brew pot. Cover with a lid and rest for 30 minutes.

- Prepare your sparge water by heating 3 quarts of water to 170°F in a separate small pot.

SPARGE

- After 30 minutes, remove the grain bag from the brew pot. Put a large fine-mesh strainer over the brew pot. Put the grain bag in the strainer, open the grain bag, and slowly run the hot sparge water through it, making sure to cover all of the grains with water. Do not squeeze the grain bag! Remove the grain bag and discard.
- Add an additional 2 gallons of water to the brew pot.
- Reheat your brew pot to 155°F; turn off the heat and add the Pale liquid malt extract. Gently stir to make sure the extract doesn't stick to the bottom of the pot.

THE BOIL

- Bring the pot to a boil.
- As soon as the pot comes to a boil, add your first hop addition, 1 ounce of Cascade hops, and set your timer for 60 minutes. The hops will dissolve immediately. Stir occasionally, skimming off the big solids with a slotted spoon and looking out for the dreaded boilover!
- At 45 minutes (that is, with 15 minutes left in the boil), add your second hop addition, 1.5 ounces of Cascade hops.
- At 55 minutes (that is, with 5 minutes left in the boil), add your third hop addition, 1 ounce of Cascade hops, and stir in the Amber dry malt extract.

PITCH THE YEAST

- *Prepare your ice bath:* In your sink or another vessel, prepare an ice bath to cool the beer down in.

- *Cool your wort:* Remove the pot from the heat and place it into your ice bath. Place a sanitized thermometer in the wort and let cool until it reaches 70°F or below.
- *Clean your stuff:* Sanitize anything that will come into contact with your beer.
- *Transfer your wort:* Pour the wort through a sanitized strainer into a 3- or 5-gallon plastic fermenting bucket or through a sanitized strainer and funnel into a 3- or 5-gallon glass carboy.
- *Pitch your yeast:* Shake your tube of yeast, sanitize the outside of the tube, crack it open, and throw all of its contents into the cooled wort in the fermenter.

PRIMARY FERMENTATION

- Place an airtight lid equipped with your airlock (filled with vodka) and stopper on the plastic bucket or place the airlock and stopper on a glass carboy. Or use the blow-off tube method (see Chapter 2).
- Keep the container in a dark and relatively cool place (ideal fermentation temperature for this beer is between 68° and 73°F) for 7 to 10 days if using secondary or for 12 to 14 days if not.

OPTION: SECONDARY

- Transfer the beer from the primary fermenter to a 3- to 5-gallon bucket or glass carboy with a sanitized tube siphon. (Make sure to leave the sediment behind.)
- Put an airlock on the secondary container and let the beer sit for at least 14 days.
- Bottle for 14 days as described in Chapter 2. Then refrigerate and enjoy!

RULE BREAKERS AND TIPS

- If you want to skip the specialty grains, you can add 4 ounces more of the dry malt extract, but be aware that the flavor and the color won't be as nice.
- Substitute Citra, Nelson, or Columbus hops for the Cascade if you want to try a different hop.

PROFESSIONAL BREWS TO ASPIRE TO

Harpoon IPA: Harpoon Brewery, Boston, Massachusetts. Big aromas from dry hopping and a full hop finish. Fresh pine and citrus flavors; 5.9% ABV.

Single Hop Cascade IPA: Mikkeller, Copenhagen, Denmark; brewed at De Proef Brouwerij, Lochristi-Hijfte, Belgium. The third in the series of single-hop IPAs from Mikkeller. Brewed with Cascade hops. Notes of spice and citrus with a hint of elder flower. A touch of sweetness and fruit; 6.9% ABV.

Hop Henge IPA: Deschutes Brewery, Bend, Oregon. Brewed with a large amount of Centennial and Cascade hops and dry-hopped. Brewed with a blend of Crystal, Pale, and Carastan malts, creating biscuit flavors; 8.5% ABV.

SEPTEMBER HOMEBREW 3

East India Pale Ale

MAKE THIS BEER IF YOU LIKE: Indian spices. Complex flavors. Impressing your friends. A brewing challenge.

PAIRS WELL WITH: Bold, spicy Indian dishes; carnitas tacos; carrot cake; and coconut milk curry.

STYLE AND BREWING NOTES

The craft beer world is exploding in Los Angeles; there are tons of great events featuring beer and food pairings, and special and limited beers; there are big celebrations of beer in general. We've been lucky enough to be involved in several of these events but were most excited when asked by the awesome Strand Brewing Company out of Torrence, California, to join them in brewing a pro-am (professional-amateur) beer together for L.A. Beer Week. Not only were we going to be brewing with the very talented master brewer Joel Elliott, but we were going to be serving this beer to the most prolific level-10 beer geeks in Los Angeles. A little intimidating to say the least.

We sat with Joel and drank different beers that we admired and drew inspiration from each one. We tried to think outside the box and get creative with ingredients. Finally, we settled on an East India Pale Ale, meaning East. India. Pale. Ale! We thought tamarind would merge nicely with a touch of a caramel malt note and made that our base flavor. We went a little nuts (that's what happens when you drink while constructing a recipe) and added curry powder, garam masala (that Joel had made at home), chilies, peppercorns, and ginger. The result was a pretty damn crazy delicious beer. It was definitely different; clean, dry, with subtle sweet fruit notes and complex spices. The body was fuller than we anticipated, and the finish was grassy and herbaceous! Nailed it! It was the first pro-am beer keg that blew and we totally won the competition. Well, there was no actual award at the festival, but we felt like winners. We did an all-grain version with Joel, but we've adapted it to an extract with specialty grains recipe for this book.

BREW IT: EAST INDIA PALE ALE

DIFFICULTY LEVEL: Promiscuous

TYPE OF BREWING: Extract with specialty grains

SPECIALTY/EXTRA EQUIPMENT: None

TARGET OG: 1.076

TARGET FG: 1.017

IBUs: 66

TARGET ABV: 7.8

PROPER GLASS: Pint

SHOPPING LIST

1 tube White Labs California Ale yeast WLP001

3 ounces Caramel/Crystal 20 L malt—milled

2 ounces Caramel/Crystal 120 L malt—milled

1 ounce German CaraFoam malt—milled

4 pounds Pale liquid malt extract

1 pound Amber dry malt extract

0.3 ounce Summit hop pellets

0.5 ounce Amarillo hop pellets

8 whole tamarind, shelled and seeded

0.5 ounce Amarillo hop pellets

0.15 ounce freshly grated ginger

1 small dried spicy red pepper

1½ teaspoons black peppercorns

0.5 ounce Amarillo hop pellets

1½ teaspoons garam masala

1½ teaspoons curry powder

1 ounce Amarillo hop pellets—to dry-hop

Makes about 2.5 gallons

Dry Hopping

 Sometimes hop additions during the boil just aren't enough for the hop lover. That's why there's dry hopping. This is the practice of adding more hops to your brew after the initial fermentation. So when you rack to secondary, add the specified amount of hops to your brew for dry hopping. Don't worry about the hops contaminating your beer, hops naturally protect beer, so the addition should be fine for your brew. Hops that you add during dry hopping add a powerful aroma to your brew, which enhances the overall experience of the beer. Because they are added late in the game and not in the boil, they don't contribute to the bitterness of the beer. If you hate the step of racking to a secondary vessel, then add the hops to your primary fermentation container after about 5 days. Dry hopping needs about 14 days in the fermenter.

PREP

- *Prepare your yeast (at least 3 hours before you brew):* Let the White Labs California Ale yeast warm up to room temperature.

STEEP/MASH

- Heat 3 quarts of water. Attach a thermometer and heat the brew pot until it reaches 160°F. Turn off the heat.
- Turn off the heat. Put the specialty grains (Caramel/Crystal 20 L, Caramel/Crystal 120 L, and CaraFoam malts) in the grain bag (tying the ends) and place it in the brew pot. Cover with a lid and rest for 30 minutes.
- Prepare your sparge water by heating 3 quarts of water to 170°F in a separate small pot.

SPARGE

- After 30 minutes, remove the grain bag from the brew pot. Put a large fine-mesh strainer over the brew pot. Put the grain bag in the strainer, open the grain bag, and slowly run the hot sparge water through it, making sure to cover all of the grains with water. Do not squeeze the grain bag! Remove the grain bag and discard.
- Add an additional 2 gallons of water to the brew pot.
- Reheat your brew pot to 155°F; turn off the heat and add the Pale liquid malt extract. Gently stir to make sure the extract doesn't stick to the bottom of the pot. Add the Amber dry malt extract; be careful it doesn't clump.

THE BOIL

- Bring the pot to a boil.
- As soon as the pot comes to a boil, add your first hop addition, Summit hops, and set your timer for 60 minutes. The hops will dissolve immediately. Stir occasionally, skimming off the big solids with a slotted spoon and looking out for the dreaded boilover!
- At 40 minutes (that is, with 20 minutes left in the boil), add your second hop addition, 0.5 ounce of Amarillo hops.
- At 45 minutes (that is, with 15 minutes left in the boil), add the tamarind.
- At 50 minutes (that is, with 10 minutes left in the boil), add your third hop addition, 0.5 ounce of Amarillo hops; also add the ginger, dried pepper, and peppercorns.
- At 55 minutes (that is, with 5 minutes left in the boil), add your fourth hop addition, 0.5 ounce of Amarillo hops; also add the garam masala and curry powder.

PITCH THE YEAST

- *Prepare your ice bath:* In your sink or another vessel, prepare an ice bath to cool the beer down in.

- *Cool your wort:* Remove the pot from the heat and place it into your ice bath. Place a sanitized thermometer in the wort and let cool until it reaches 70°F or below.
- *Clean your stuff:* Sanitize anything that will come into contact with your beer.
- *Transfer your wort:* Pour the wort through a sanitized strainer into a 3- or 5-gallon plastic fermenting bucket or through a sanitized strainer and funnel into a 3- or 5-gallon glass carboy.
- *Pitch your yeast:* Shake your tube of yeast, sanitize the outside of the tube, crack it open, and throw all of its contents into the cooled wort in the fermenter.

PRIMARY FERMENTATION

- Place an airtight lid equipped with your airlock (filled with vodka) and stopper on the plastic bucket or place the airlock and stopper on a glass carboy. Or use the blow-off tube method (see Chapter 2).
- Keep the container in a dark and relatively cool place (ideal fermentation temperature for this beer is between 68° and 73°F) for 7 to 10 days.

SECONDARY AND DRY HOPPING

- Transfer the beer from the primary fermenter to a 3- to 5-gallon bucket or glass carboy with a sanitized tube siphon. (Make sure to leave the sediment behind.)
- Add your dry hops, 1 ounce of Amarillo hops.
- Put an airlock on the secondary container and let the beer sit for 14 days.
- Bottle for 14 days as described in Chapter 2, filtering out the hops through a strainer when you transfer the beer into the bottling bucket. Then refrigerate and enjoy!

RULE BREAKERS AND TIPS

- If you can't get ahold of tamarind, use sweet dried orange peel instead. Add 0.5 ounce to the boil when there are 5 minutes left in the boil.
- If you can't get Amarillo hops, use Summit or Centennial instead.

PROFESSIONAL BREWS TO ASPIRE TO

Rotator IPA Series Spiced IPA: Widmer Brothers Brewing Co., Portland, Oregon. Hoppy IPA brewed with Assam black tea, ginger, cinnamon, clove, star anise, black pepper, and cardamom. The beer and the spices create a super-complex brew; 7% ABV.

Überhoppy: Valley Brewing Co., Stockton, California. Aromas of peach, grapefruit, marmalade, and angel food cake mixed with a tropical fruit chutney, peppercorn, and piney finish. Decadent and strong; 9.5% ABV.

Jai Alai Mango IPA: Cigar City Brewing, Tampa, Florida. Flavors of biscuit and mango. Rich sweet malty notes and a bitter finish; 7.5% ABV.

Aarti Sequeira's Homemade Garam Masala

Living in Los Angeles has some advantages, and one of them is that we've been able to meet a lot of great people in the foodie world. We're very lucky indeed to have befriended Aarti Sequeira, a great Indian food chef and one of the nicest people in the world. Oh, and she also happens to be the star of *Aarti Party* on the Food Network and winner of the sixth season of *The Next Food Network Star*. Anyway, turns out that she and her husband are huge beer fans and we turned her husband on to his favorite beer!

She's given us a great homemade garam masala recipe that we use in our East India Pale Ale. It leaves out the cumin and the peppercorns.

Aarti says that just like curry, there's no *one* blend of garam masala. She grew up with a version that was solely cinnamon and cloves. Most garam masalas contain cardamom, cinnamon, cloves, and black peppercorns, and sometimes add cumin and coriander. Those bought at the grocery store usually contain some other stuff too and probably won't contain very much cardamom, cloves, or cinnamon because they're more expensive spices. We wanted a blend that was more sweet and spicy than savory and earthy, specific to the tamarind and ginger in our beer. So, after some discussion, here's what Aarti came up with for us. She says that you should be able to find all of these ingredients at your friendly neighborhood Indian market, gourmet market, or online source such as Penzeys Spices or Kalustyan's Spices and Sweets.

AARTI SEQUEIRA'S HOMEMADE GARAM MASALA

3 large cinnamon sticks (the kind you get at Indian stores; it's about 3 tablespoons of cinnamon bark bits)

3 tablespoons whole cloves

¼ cup green cardamom pods, shelled, husks discarded (about 2 tablespoons of seeds)

4 large black cardamom pods, shelled, husks discarded (about 1 tablespoon of seeds), optional

Pour all the ingredients into a spice or coffee grinder and grind until fine. Store in an airtight container away from direct sunlight.

Use 1½ teaspoons (or more if you like) of this garam masala in your East India Pale Ale by adding it to your brew pot when there are 5 minutes left in the boil. Also use it in the recipe on page 126 and in any recipe that calls for this delicious spice mix! Thanks, Aarti! You rock.

East India Pale Ale Vegetable Curry

1 small yellow onion, finely chopped

4 garlic cloves, minced

1 tablespoon minced or grated gingerroot

3 tablespoons vegetable oil

3 tablespoons curry powder

1 teaspoon Aarti Sequeira's Homemade Garam
   Masala (see page 124)

1 tablespoon salt

1 teaspoon turmeric

1 teaspoon paprika

½ teaspoon freshly ground black pepper

3 medium potatoes, peeled and cut into ½-inch
   pieces

1 large carrot, cut into ½-inch pieces

1 cup cauliflower florets

1 small red bell pepper, cut into ½-inch pieces

1 tomato, coarsely chopped

1 zucchini, cut into ½-inch pieces

½ cup green peas (frozen or fresh)

1 cup East India Pale Ale

½ cup coconut milk

½ cup plain yogurt

1 whole sanam chili

1 bay leaf

2 sprigs cilantro, chopped

6 cups cooked basmati rice

Serves 6

In a large pot over medium-low heat, sweat the onion, garlic, and ginger in the vegetable oil until the onion is translucent. Add the curry powder, garam masala, salt, tumeric, paprika, and black pepper, and cook 2 minutes, stirring constantly. Add the potatoes, carrot, cauliflower, bell pepper, tomato, zucchini, and peas, tossing to coat with the spices.

Add the beer, coconut milk, yogurt, chili, and bay leaf. Bring to a boil. Reduce the heat to medium low and simmer, covered, for 45 minutes, stirring frequently. Remove the chili and bay leaf. Garnish with the cilantro. Serve over basmati rice.

Serve with a glass of East India Pale Ale!

SEVEN

October

FALLEN LEAVES ○ HORROR MOVIE MARATHON ○
ROASTED SQUASH ○ TRICK-OR-TREATING ○
BRATS AND SAUERKRAUT ○ CANDY CORN

Your October Homebrew

DER NACKTE BRAUER FESTBIER (THE NAKED BREWER FESTBIER):
Toasty, biscuit, nutty notes; light bodied and dry

IMPERIAL BLOOD RED: Chewy caramel malt with a big hop bite

CONTROVERSIAL PUMPKIN ALE: Pumpkin notes with vanilla and
holiday spice

To Eat

Controversial Pumpkin Cheesecake with Spent Grain Crust

October is one our favorite months and not just because we have free rein to dress up like sluts on the last day of it. We love the cool evening walks. The decorated Halloween houses, the silly costumes, and multiple excuses to eat loads of candy. October is festive and kind of evil and a bit sexy. We start out this month brewing a beer in the style of an Oktoberfest. Frankly, we couldn't decide where in the book to put this beer. Because back in the day in Bavaria, Oktoberfest-style beer (also known as Märzen) was traditionally brewed in March (März) for the Oktoberfest celebration (which actually starts in September). Brewing was a seasonal venture, and the brewing season ended in the spring and resumed in the fall. This style could really be placed in March, September, or October. We finally settled on October because that's when most people in America think to drink Oktoberfest-style beers. The air is crisp, the pumpkins are harvested, and you see images of revelers in lederhosen drinking from steins on the Wies'n in Munich.

We're also making an Imperial Blood Red this month. It's a delicious American Red Ale with a scary name just in time for Halloween, although the name's the only thing that will scare you. And finally, we're making Controversial Pumpkin Ale, a style of beer that one of us hates and one of us loves. It stirs up trouble between us every year.

OCTOBER HOMEBREW 1

Der Nackte Brauer Festbier (The Naked Brewer Festbier)

MAKE THIS BEER IF YOU LIKE: German weddings. Lederhosen. Nutty malt. Low bitterness. Women carrying many, many heavy beers at once.

PAIRS WELL WITH: Sauerkraut and sausages, pretzels and mustard, speck, Wiener schnitzel.

STYLE AND BREWING NOTES

Oktoberfest. You've heard of it, you've seen pictures, you're curious about the funny costumes. This is beer mecca for many of us and also happens to be the world's largest fair. This ultimate beer party consists of 16 or so days of drinking in Munich to celebrate the anniversary of the wedding of Crown Prince Ludwig and Princess Therese of Bavaria in 1810. Also known generally as Märzen, this style is a German Lager that was meant to be kept in cold storage from spring through the hot summer, for at least 5 months, to be consumed at the end of September. It typically has low to medium hops, malty and caramel characteristics, and a toasty finish.

Our Festbier (to be enjoyed any time of the year) is an homage to Germany's vast and prestigious brewing history. We pretty much stick to the traditional ingredients and rules, save one thing. We use a German Ale yeast instead of a Lager yeast, and we ferment at temperatures that more closely resemble Ale temperatures. Why, you may ask? Because when we first started brewing this beer, we had no equipment or way to ferment a beer at 50°F for any period of time. So instead we used a German-style Kölsch yeast that finishes very dry. In homebrewing, as in life, you gotta work with what you have.

BREW IT: DER NACKTE BRAUER FESTBIER (THE NAKED BREWER FESTBIER)

DIFFICULTY LEVEL: Sophomore

TYPE OF BREWING: Extract with specialty grains

SPECIALTY/EXTRA EQUIPMENT: Refrigerator space

TARGET OG: 1.054

TARGET FG: 1.015

IBUs: 26

TARGET ABV: 5.2%

PROPER GLASS: Pint

SHOPPING LIST

1 packet Wyeast Kölsch yeast 2565

8 ounces CaraMunich III malt—milled

4 ounces Vienna malt—milled

4.25 pounds liquid Munich malt extract

0.75 ounce Hallertauer hop pellets

0.25 ounce Tettnanger hop pellets

½ Whirlfloc tablet

Makes about 2.5 gallons

PREP

▪ *Prepare your yeast (at least 3 hours before you brew):* Crack your packet of Kölsch yeast and let it warm up to room temperature. You can do this a day before you brew as well.

STEEP/MASH

▪ Heat 3 quarts of water. Attach a thermometer and heat the brew pot until it reaches 160°F. Turn off the heat.

▪ Prepare your sparge water by heating 3 quarts of water to 170°F in a separate small pot.

SPARGE

▪ Put the specialty grains (CaraMunich III and Vienna malts) in the grain bag (tying the ends) and place it in the brew pot. Cover with a lid and rest for 30 minutes.

▪ After 30 minutes, remove the grain bag from the brew pot. Put a large fine-mesh strainer over the brew pot. Put the grain bag in the strainer, open the grain bag, and slowly run the hot sparge water through it, making sure to cover all of the grains with water. Do not squeeze the grain bag! Remove the grain bag and discard.

▪ Add an additional 2 gallons of water to the brew pot.

▪ Reheat your brew pot to 155°F; turn off the heat and add the liquid Munich malt extract. Gently stir to make sure the extract doesn't stick to the bottom of the pot.

THE BOIL

- Bring the pot to a boil.

- As soon as the pot comes to a boil, add your first hop addition, Hallertauer hops, and set your timer for 60 minutes. The hops will dissolve immediately. Stir occasionally, skimming off the big solids with a slotted spoon and looking out for the dreaded boilover!

- At 40 minutes (that is, with 20 minutes left in the boil), add your second hop addition, Tettnanger hops.

- At 55 minutes (that is, with 5 minutes left in the boil), add the half tablet of Whirlfloc, stirring to dissolve.

PITCH THE YEAST

- *Prepare your ice bath:* In your sink or another vessel, prepare an ice bath to cool the beer down in.

- *Cool your wort:* Remove the pot from the heat and place it into your ice bath. Place a sanitized thermometer in the wort and let cool until it reaches 70°F or below.

- *Clean your stuff:* Sanitize anything that will come into contact with your beer.

- *Transfer your wort:* Pour the wort through a sanitized strainer into a 3- or 5-gallon plastic fermenting bucket or through a sanitized strainer and funnel into a 3- or 5-gallon glass carboy.

- *Pitch your yeast:* Shake your packet of prepared yeast, sanitize the outside, tear it open, and throw all of its contents into the cooled wort in the fermenter.

PRIMARY FERMENTATION

- Place an airtight lid equipped with your airlock (filled with vodka) and stopper on the plastic bucket or place the airlock and stopper on a glass carboy. Or use the blow-off tube method (see Chapter 2).

- Keep the container in a dark and relatively cool place (ideal fermentation temperature for this style is between 56° and 70°F) for 7 to 10 days.

SECONDARY AND LAGERING
- Transfer the beer from the primary fermenter to a 3- to 5-gallon bucket or glass carboy with a sanitized tube siphon. (Make sure to leave the sediment behind.)
- Put an airlock on the secondary container, make room in the fridge, and store the beer there for 3 to 4 weeks.
- Bottle for 14 days as described in Chapter 2. Then refrigerate and enjoy!

RULE BREAKERS AND TIPS
- One great tip we got from Mark Jilg, owner of Craftsman Brewing Co., is "If you don't have temperature, use time." Meaning, if you can't ferment at Lager temperatures, give the beer some additional time for the undesirable esters (which a warmer fermentation may have created) to blow off.

PROFESSIONAL BREWS TO ASPIRE TO
Trocken Hopfen Marzen: St. Louis Brewing Co., St. Louis, Missouri. This dry-hopped Märzen is an American interpretation of a classic German beer style. Dry-hopped with Hallertauer Mittelfrüh; 5.5% ABV.

Munsterfest: Three Floyds Brewing Co., Munster, Indiana. A Bavarian-style Oktoberfest beer brewed with malted barley, aromatic German Noble hops, and traditional yeast and brewed in strict accordance with the German beer purity law of 1516; a traditional 6% ABV.

Late Harvest: Bear Republic Brewing Co., Healdsburg, California. An Oktoberfest beer with big malt characteristics, Noble hops, and a nice dry finish. Traditional and balanced; 6.3% ABV.

OCTOBER HOMEBREW 2

Imperial Blood Red

MAKE THIS BEER IF YOU LIKE: Vampire movies. Bitter beers. Chewy caramel malt. Regal beers.

PAIRS WELL WITH: Spicy pulled pork, toffee cookies, blue cheese, and flan.

STYLE AND BREWING NOTES

No blood necessary for this brew (although one of our Facebook fans admitted to adding blood to a homebrew recipe—whoa). The blood-red image, besides being appropriate for Halloween, refers to the lovely ruby red color of this brew, which comes from the malt. A Red Ale can refer to either the mellow Irish Red or the bolder American-style Red. The Irish Red is a low-hop, low-alcohol malty, nutty brew. The American Red, in true American style, is a louder brew. American Reds tend to have nice rich malt with notes of caramel balanced by a bold bitter hop. This can be similar to the American West Coast–style Pale Ale. Reds can swing more malty or bitter, depending on the brewer's taste. This brew is an Imperial Red, which basically means higher in alcohol and richer in malt and hop flavor profiles. Imperial (which means it's almost a double) Red just seems a bit scarier, so we think it's perfect for Halloween. Luckily it's not very scary to brew.

When we were slinging craft beers from behind the bar together, we waited patiently for the seasonal brews to roll in. One such was Evil

Dead Red from AleSmith Brewing Co. in San Diego, California. This was our intro to the big Red beer style. We loved the candied, caramel effect from the rich malt flavor mixed with the unforeseen bite of hops on the finish—perfectly vampiric actually. Our homebrew recipe is an attempt to capture that taste, which pairs perfectly with Halloween night.

BREW IT: IMPERIAL BLOOD RED

DIFFICULTY LEVEL: Sophomore

TYPE OF BREWING: Extract with specialty grains

SPECIALTY/EXTRA EQUIPMENT: None

TARGET OG: 1.080

TARGET FG: 1.014

IBUs: 78

TARGET ABV: 8.7

PROPER GLASS: Pint

SHOPPING LIST

1 tube White Labs California Ale yeast WLP001

1 ounce Caramel/Crystal 80 L malt—milled

2 ounces CaraMunich malt—milled

1 ounce Chocolate malt—milled

3 pounds Extra-Light dry malt extract

1 pound Amber dry malt extract

0.6 ounce Centennial hop pellets

0.6 ounce Centennial hop pellets

0.5 ounce Centennial hop pellets

0.6 ounce Cascade hop pellets

1 ounce Cascade hop pellets—dry-hopped

Makes about 2.5 gallons

PREP

■ *Prepare your yeast (at least 3 hours before you brew):* Let the tube of California Ale yeast warm up to room temperature.

STEEP/MASH

■ Heat 3 quarts of water. Attach a thermometer and heat the brew pot until it reaches 160°F. Turn off the heat.

■ Put the specialty grains (Caramel/Crystal 80 L, CaraMunich, and Chocolate malts) in the grain bag (tying the ends) and place it in the brew pot. Cover with a lid and rest for 30 minutes.

■ Prepare your sparge water by heating 3 quarts of water to 170°F in a separate small pot.

SPARGE

■ After 30 minutes, remove the grain bag from the brew pot. Put a large fine-mesh strainer over the brew pot. Put the grain bag in the strainer, open the grain bag, and slowly run the hot sparge water through it, making sure to cover all of the grains with water. Do not squeeze the grain bag! Remove the grain bag and discard.

■ Add an additional 2 gallons of water to the brew pot.

■ Reheat your brew pot to 155°F; turn off the heat and add the Extra-Light dry malt and Amber dry malt extracts. Gently stir to make sure the extracts don't stick to the bottom of the pot; be careful they don't clump.

THE BOIL

■ Bring the pot to a boil.

■ As soon as the pot comes to a boil, add your first hop addition, 0.6 ounce of Centennial hops, and set your timer for 60 minutes. The hops will dissolve immediately. Stir occasionally, skimming off the big solids with a slotted spoon and looking out for the dreaded boilover!

■ At 30 minutes (that is, with 30 minutes left in the boil), add your second hop addition, 0.6 ounce of Centennial hops.

- At 45 minutes (that is, with 15 minutes left in the boil), add your third hop addition, 0.5 ounce of Centennial hops.
- At 55 minutes (that is, with 5 minutes left in the boil), add your fourth hop addition, 0.6 ounce of Cascade hops.

PITCH THE YEAST

- *Prepare your ice bath:* In your sink or another vessel, prepare an ice bath to cool the beer down in.
- *Cool your wort:* Remove the pot from the heat and place it into your ice bath. Place a sanitized thermometer in the wort and let cool until it reaches 70°F or below.
- *Clean your stuff:* Sanitize anything that will come into contact with your beer.
- *Transfer your wort:* Pour the wort through a sanitized strainer into a 3- or 5-gallon plastic fermenting bucket or through a sanitized strainer and funnel into a 3- or 5-gallon glass carboy.
- *Pitch your yeast:* Shake your tube of yeast, sanitize the outside of the tube, crack it open, and throw all of its contents into the cooled wort in the fermenter.

PRIMARY FERMENTATION

- Place an airtight lid equipped with your airlock (filled with vodka) and stopper on the plastic bucket or place the airlock and stopper on a glass carboy. Or use the blow-off tube method (see Chapter 2).
- Keep this container in a dark and relatively cool place (ideal fermentation temperature for this style is between 68° and 73°F) for 7 to 10 days.

SECONDARY AND DRY HOPPING

- Transfer the beer from the primary fermenter to a 3- to 5-gallon bucket or glass carboy with a sanitized tube siphon. (Make sure to leave the sediment behind.)

- Add your dry hops, 1 ounce of Cascade hops.
- Put an airlock on the secondary container and let the beer sit for 14 more days.
- Bottle for 14 days as described in Chapter 2, filtering out the hops through a strainer when you transfer the beer into the bottling bucket. Then refrigerate and enjoy!

RULE BREAKERS AND TIPS
- You can skip the dry hopping on this Ale and still have a nice, bold bitter brew. However, there will be more aroma if you dry-hop.

PROFESSIONAL BEERS TO ASPIRE TO

Evil Dead Red: AleSmith Brewing Co., San Diego, California. Piney hop aroma with a rich, chewy, toffee malt sweetness; 6.66% ABV.

Red Rocket Ale: Bear Republic Brewing Co., Healdsburg, California. A sort of Scottish-style Red Ale that hits the palate with sweet, caramel malt flavors; 6.8% ABV.

Lagunitas Lucky 13: Lagunitas Brewing Co., Petaluma, California. *Big* aromas of Amarillo hops and rich, smoky sweet malt; 8.3% ABV.

OCTOBER HOMEBREW 3

Controversial Pumpkin Ale

MAKE THIS BEER IF YOU LIKE: Controversy. Debates. Pumpkin Pie. Brown Ales. On-the-nose holiday drinks.

PAIRS WELL WITH: Pumpkin pie (duh), pecan cookies, candied bacon, and butternut squash.

STYLE AND BREWING NOTES

Why would controversy surround such a beloved squash? Because there are many beer drinkers in the craft beer world who would prefer to have their pumpkin served only in a pie crust, not in their beer glass. Within our own Beer Chicks duo we have a debate: brunette being against it; blonde being for it. The rift is palpable during the holiday season. This controversy mostly comes from the fact that many pumpkin Ales seem to simply have hints of spice without the full flavor and richness of pumpkin pie. In fact, some pumpkin Ales don't actually use any pumpkin at all and just depend on the spices to create that illusion. And if those strong spices seem a bit cloying to you, then pumpkin Ales may not be your thing. But let's face it, around Halloween and throughout the holiday season, serving a pumpkin homebrew to your guests is a welcome hospitality.

The key with pumpkin Ale, as with pumpkin pie, is to go easy on the spices. If you're left with only allspice or clove on your tongue, you probably went overboard. That doesn't mean that the complexity of spices in this beer isn't beautiful; the layers should provide a great drinking experience from your first sip in the glass to a rich layer of flavors by the last lap.

Pumpkin is a great ingredient to use because of the dual life it offers in your kitchen. You will roast it and boil it for your brew, but then can use it for pumpkin cheesecake, if you are so inclined (see page 144 for the recipe). We like making the most use out of our brewing ingredients, and a homebrew pumpkin cheesecake fits perfectly into those parameters.

BREW IT: CONTROVERSIAL PUMPKIN ALE

DIFFICULTY LEVEL: Promiscuous

TYPE OF BREWING: Extract with specialty grains

SPECIALTY/EXTRA EQUIPMENT: Baking sheet

TARGET OG: 1.045

TARGET FG: 1.013

IBUs: 23

TARGET ABV: 4.3

PROPER GLASS: Pint

SHOPPING LIST

1 packet Wyeast Whitbread Ale yeast 1099

1 medium pie pumpkin

5 ounces Biscuit malt—milled

2 ounces Caramel/Crystal 60 L malt—milled

2 ounces Chocolate malt—milled

3 pounds Amber liquid malt extract

0.7 ounce Fuggles hop pellets

1 ounce molasses

1½ teaspoons pumpkin pie spice

Makes about 2.5 gallons

PREP

■ *Prepare your yeast (at least 3 hours before you brew):* Crack your packet of Whitbread Ale yeast and let it warm up to room temperature. You can do this a day before you brew as well.

■ *Roast your pumpkin:* Wash the pie pumpkin, cut it into quarters and scrape out the seeds. Place it on a baking sheet and roast in a preheated 350°F oven for about 1 hour, or until the flesh is soft and is starting to brown. Scrape out the flesh and set aside 2 pounds in a bowl.

STEEP/MASH

▪ Heat 4 quarts of water. Place the 2 pounds of roasted pumpkin in a grain bag (tying the ends) and add it to the water. Attach a thermometer, and heat the brew pot until it reaches 160°F. Turn off the heat.

▪ Remove the pot from the heat. Put the specialty grains (Biscuit, Caramel/Crystal 60 L, and Chocolate malts) in a second grain bag (tying the ends) and place it in the brew pot. Cover with a lid and rest for 30 minutes.

▪ Prepare your sparge water by heating 3 quarts of water to 170°F in a separate small pot.

SPARGE

▪ After 30 minutes, remove the grain bags from the brew pot. Put a large fine-mesh strainer over the brew pot. Put the bag with grains in the strainer, open the grain bag, and slowly run the hot sparge water through it, making sure to cover all of the grains with water. Do not squeeze the grain bag! Run some of the water through the bag with the pumpkin as well. Set both the grain bag and pumpkin aside and save them to use in the pumpkin cheesecake recipe (see page 144).

▪ Add an additional 2 gallons of water to the brew pot.

▪ Reheat your brew pot to 155°F; turn off the heat and add the Amber liquid malt extract. Gently stir to make sure the extract doesn't stick to the bottom of the pot.

THE BOIL

▪ Bring the pot to a boil.

▪ As soon as the pot comes to a boil, add the Fuggles hops and set your timer for 60 minutes. The hops will dissolve immediately. Stir occasionally, skimming off the big solids with a slotted spoon and looking out for the dreaded boilover!

▪ At flameout (that is, at the end of boil, when you turn the heat off), stir in the molasses and add the pumpkin pie spice.

PITCH THE YEAST

- *Prepare your ice bath:* In your sink or another vessel, prepare an ice bath to cool the beer down in.
- *Cool your wort:* Remove the pot from the heat and place it into your ice bath. Place a sanitized thermometer in the wort and let cool until it reaches 70°F or below.
- *Clean your stuff:* Sanitize anything that will come into contact with your beer.
- *Transfer your wort:* Pour the wort through a sanitized strainer into a 3- or 5-gallon plastic fermenting bucket or through a sanitized strainer and funnel into a 3- or 5-gallon glass carboy.
- *Pitch your yeast:* Shake your packet of prepared yeast, sanitize the outside, tear it open, and throw all of its contents into the cooled wort in the fermenter.

PRIMARY FERMENTATION

- Place an airtight lid equipped with your airlock (filled with vodka) and stopper on the plastic bucket or place the airlock and stopper on a glass carboy. Or use the blow-off tube method (see Chapter 2).
- Keep the container in a dark and relatively cool place (ideal fermentation temperature for this style is between 64° and 75°F) for 7 to 10 days if using secondary or for 12 to 14 days if not.

RECOMMENDED: SECONDARY

- Check your spice! We recommend using a secondary vessel for this style. You can taste the beer at this point and add more pumpkin pie spice if you feel it needs it. Boil ½ teaspoon of pumpkin pie spice in a bit of water, let it cool to room temperature, and add the mixture to your secondary vessel.
- Transfer the beer from the primary fermenter to a 3- to 5-gallon bucket or glass carboy with a sanitized tube siphon. (Make sure to leave the sediment behind.)

■ Put an airlock on the secondary container and let the beer sit for at least 14 days.

■ Bottle for 14 days as described in Chapter 2. Then refrigerate and enjoy!

RULE BREAKERS AND TIPS

- Yes, you can use canned pumpkin, *but we strongly discourage it*! Though it may seem easier, cleanup is far worse because the canned pumpkin is so soft and mushy.

- You can skip the pumpkin altogether and still have a lovely "pumpkin" Ale. The spices are really what make this beer reminiscent of pumpkin pie. You can still tell people you added fresh pumpkin, we won't tell.

- You can skip steeping the grains here; if you do, you may want to just skip the pumpkin addition altogether. Add 4 ounces of dry extract or honey instead.

- If you don't have pumpkin pie spice, mix together some allspice, nutmeg, cinnamon, and ginger to taste.

PROFESSIONAL BEERS TO ASPIRE TO

Punkin Ale: Dogfish Head Craft Brewery, Milton, Delaware. A big brown Ale with notes of pumpkin, brown sugar, and pumpkin pie spices; 7% ABV.

Pumpkin Ale: Kern River Brewing Co., Kern River, California. A seasonal Ale brewed with real pumpkin and a touch of allspice. Finishes dry with a hint of spice; 6% ABV.

The Great Pumpkin: Elysian Brewing Co., Seattle, Washington. Intense pumpkin, sugar, and spice on the nose with a warming, bready, toasty malt character; 8.1% ABV.

Controversial Pumpkin Cheesecake with Spent Grain Crust

CRUST

½ cup ground ginger snaps

½ cup spent grain

½ tablespoon granulated sugar

1 tablespoon salted butter, softened

FILLING

Four 8-ounce packages cream cheese, softened

1 cup packed light brown sugar

1 cup pureed well-drained spent pumpkin

1 teaspoon vanilla extract

½ teaspoon ground cinnamon

¼ teaspoon ground ginger

¼ teaspoon ground allspice

⅛ teaspoon ground nutmeg

¼ teaspoon salt

4 large eggs, room temperature

¼ cup sour cream

Serves 8

Set the oven rack to the middle position and preheat the oven to 350°F. Wrap foil around the outside of a 9-inch springform pan to prevent leaking from water bath later. Lightly grease the bottom and sides of the pan.

Make the crust: In a food processor, pulse the ginger snaps, spent grain, and granulated sugar until coarsely ground. Add the butter, and pulse until incorporated. Press the mixture into the bottom of the prepared pan. Bake for 10 minutes. Set aside to cool.

Turn the oven down to 325°F and heat 2 cups of water in a pot until it is hot but not boiling.

Make the filling: In a large bowl or stand mixer, beat the cream cheese until smooth. Add the brown sugar and continue beating until fluffy. Add the pumpkin, vanilla, cinnamon, ginger, allspice, nutmeg, and salt and mix until combined. Add the eggs, one at a time, beating until thoroughly incorporated. Add the sour cream and mix until combined.

Pour the mixture over the cooled crust. Place the pan in large baking dish on the oven rack and pour hot water into the baking dish, being careful not to overfill (you don't want hot water sloshing around as you pull the oven rack in and out!). Bake 1 hour. Turn off the heat but leave the cheesecake in oven for 1 hour more. Use the toothpick test to determine if the cheesecake is done.

Serve with a pint of Controversial Pumpkin Ale!

November

THANKSGIVING ○ ROASTED MEATS ○ FAMILY DINNERS ○
ENDLESS PIE ○ FIRESIDE DRINKING ○ HOLIDAY OVERLOAD

Your November Homebrew

PECAN PIE BROWN ALE: **Sweet and nutty with a touch of caramel and biscuit**

CRANBERRY BELGIAN PALE: **Earthy and dry, with a hint of tart cranberries**

SAGE CHESTNUT ESB: **Malty, nutty Ale with a nice hop balance and herbaceous sage notes**

To Eat

Sage Chestnut ESB Stuffing

November is the beginning of the onslaught of heavy food, cold weather, and holiday fervor. You'll need a beer to deal with all of those things, and especially your weird uncle Steven. The beers for this month focus on ingredients that you will probably also be using in your holiday food recipes. These brews are meant to parallel some of the traditional holiday dishes. We get all sentimental in November and December, and we like to marinate in that feeling. Call us old-fashioned. This is the time for comforting beers that echo the flavors of the season. These are not hop-forward Ales, but they mostly showcase malty, nutty notes, herbaceous aromas, and rich fruit. Indulge in these flavors and set aside the hop bite for a month.

These will also be welcome refreshments for your family and friends. Bring the brew to Thanksgiving dinner and you may be able to bypass the "So what are you doing with your life?" and "When are you getting married?" conversations. Or at least you can have delicious homebrew to drink throughout the arguing.

NOVEMBER HOMEBREW 1

Pecan Pie Brown Ale

MAKE THIS BEER IF YOU LIKE: Nutty Ales. Low IBU beers. Subtle flavors. Pecan pie (of course). Easy drinking beers.

PAIRS WELL WITH: Do we need to say it? Pecan pie, vanilla cake, glazed salmon, and pad Thai.

STYLE AND BREWING NOTES

The Brown Ale is an English style that differs slightly from an ESB or Pale Ale; it focuses more on the sweet, nutty, caramel malty notes of the beer. The hops are less present and should be a backdrop to the notes in the malt. The hops keep the beer from being too sweet, but Brown Ales do often have a deep, rich toffee flavor. Brown Ales are typically low in alcohol as well, so you can have a few.

Nuts in general are a perfect accompaniment to Brown Ales. You'll find that many Brown Ales reference nuts in the name, as in Rogue's

Hazelnut Brown. We're not actually adding pecan pie to the boil (though, if you ever get the chance, why the hell not, see what happens!) but instead are adding roasted pecans and using a Biscuit malt and molasses that will create a subtle, nutty, sweet Ale with a hint of the flavor of pie crust.

When adding nuts to a brew, it's important to remember that they tend to impart a very subtle flavor, so don't expect pecan to be the strongest flavor in the finished product. Beware of the oils in the nuts, as they can ruin the head retention in your brew. This is why the roasting step is important.

Our first experience adding nuts to a brew came during our visit to Sierra Nevada Brewing Co. in Chico, California, where we were invited up for a tour with a bunch of beer enthusiasts during its Beer Camp program. We brewed a beer with locally roasted almonds called the Almond Märzen Project (endless punnery is a pastime in the beer world . . .); the end result was a lovely, drinkable Märzen with rich malty notes. The almonds were subtle, but present. Being a part of this brewing process encouraged us to try a nutty Ale of our own. We had also tasted Abita Brewing Co.'s seasonal Brown Ale made with pecans

Beer Nutz

Nuts and beer are a classic snack combination. We decided to unite them by using the beer as a glaze for roasted, spiced pecans. These make a lovely gift for the holidays.

1 egg white, lightly beaten
½ cup Pecan Pie Brown Ale
1½ teaspoons salt
2 cups pecans (try almonds or walnuts, too!)

SPICE MIX

⅓ cup granulated sugar

2 teaspoons ground cinnamon

1 teaspoon ground ginger

1 teaspoon salt

Preheat the oven to 300°F. Mix the egg white, beer, and 1½ teaspoons salt in a medium bowl and soak the nuts in the mixture for 5 minutes. Meanwhile make the spice mix by combining the sugar, cinnamon, ginger, and 1 teaspoon salt in a large bowl. Drain the nuts and toss them in the spice mix, coating well. Spread the nuts in a single layer on a baking sheet lined with parchment paper or a silicone mat. Bake in the center of the oven for 30 minutes, or until the coating is no longer sticky. Check often, shaking the pan once or twice during cooking to avoid burning. Cool for about 10 minutes and serve.

while doing a book signing at New Orleans on Tap, a beer festival that showcases local brews and benefits the SPCA. Pecans are a traditional Southern ingredient, and their beer pairs well with big Southern dishes, adding a toasty, sweet note.

BREW IT: PECAN PIE BROWN ALE

DIFFICULTY LEVEL: Sophomore

TYPE OF BREWING: Extract with specialty grains

SPECIALTY/EXTRA EQUIPMENT: Baking sheet

TARGET OG: 1.045

TARGET FG: 1.011

IBUs: 23

TARGET ABV: 4.5

PROPER GLASS: Pint

SHOPPING LIST

12 ounces shelled pecans

1 packet Wyeast British Ale yeast 1098

6 ounces Caramel/Crystal 60 L malt—milled

4 ounces Biscuit malt—milled

2 ounces Chocolate malt—milled

3 pounds Pale liquid malt extract

1 ounce molasses

0.7 ounce Fuggles hop pellets

Makes about 2.5 gallons

PREP

■ Prepare your pecans (2 to 3 days before you brew): The goal here is to remove most of the oil in the pecans. The oil is not good for your brew and will ruin the head retention of the beer. Spread the pecans out on a baking sheet and roast in a 350°F oven for 15 to 20 minutes. Remove the nuts from the pan and spread them on paper towels to cool; the towels will absorb the oils. Chop the nuts into course pieces and bake again for 15 to 20 minutes. Again spread them on paper towels to absorb the oil. Repeat the roasting 4 more times, being careful not to burn them. Don't be alarmed if the nuts smoke a little bit. Leave them on paper towels or in a paper bag for 2 to 3 days before you use them in brewing.

■ *Prepare your yeast (at least 3 hours before you brew):* Crack your packet of British Ale yeast and let it warm up to room temperature. You can do this the day before you brew as well.

STEEP/MASH

■ Heat 4 quarts of water. Attach a thermometer and heat the brew pot until it reaches 160°F. Turn off the heat.

■ Put the specialty grains (Caramel/Crystal 60 L, Biscuit, and Chocolate malts) and the roasted pecans in the grain bag (tying the ends) and place it in the brew pot. Cover with a lid and rest for 30 minutes.

■ Prepare your sparge water by heating 2 quarts of water to 170°F in a separate small pot.

SPARGE

■ After 30 minutes, remove the grain bag from the brew pot. Put a large fine-mesh strainer over the brew pot. Put the grain bag in the strainer, open the grain bag, and slowly run the hot sparge water through it, making sure to cover all of the grains with water. Do not squeeze the grain bag! Remove the grain bag and discard.

■ Add an additional 2 gallons of water to the brew pot.

■ Reheat your brew pot to 155°F; turn off the heat and add the Pale liquid malt extract. Gently stir to make sure the extract doesn't stick to the bottom of the pot.

THE BOIL

■ Bring the pot to a boil.

■ As soon as the pot comes to a boil, add the Fuggles hops and set your timer for 60 minutes. The hops will dissolve immediately. Stir occasionally, skimming off the big solids with a slotted spoon and looking out for the dreaded boilover!

■ At flameout (that is, when the boil is over and you turn off the heat), stir in the molasses.

PITCH THE YEAST

■ *Prepare your ice bath:* In your sink or another vessel, prepare an ice bath to cool the beer down in.

■ *Cool your wort:* Remove the pot from the heat and place it into your ice bath. Place a sanitized thermometer in the wort and let cool until it reaches 70°F or below.

■ *Clean your stuff:* Sanitize anything that will come into contact with your beer.

- *Transfer your wort:* Pour the wort through a sanitized strainer into a 3- or 5-gallon plastic fermenting bucket or through a sanitized strainer and funnel into a 3- or 5-gallon glass carboy.
- *Pitch your yeast:* Shake your packet of prepared yeast, sanitize the outside, tear it open, and throw all of its contents into the cooled wort in the fermenter.

PRIMARY FERMENTATION

- Place an airtight lid equipped with your airlock (filled with vodka) and stopper on the plastic bucket or place the airlock and stopper on a glass carboy. Or use the blow-off tube method (see Chapter 2).
- Keep the container in a dark and relatively cool place (ideal fermentation temperature for this style is between 64° and 75°F) for 7 to 10 days if using secondary or 12 to 14 days if not.

OPTION: SECONDARY

- Transfer the beer from the primary fermenter to a 3- to 5-gallon bucket or glass carboy with a sanitized tube siphon. (Make sure to leave the sediment behind.)
- Put an airlock on the secondary container and let the beer sit for 14 days.
- Bottle for 14 days as described in Chapter 2. Then refrigerate and enjoy!

RULE BREAKERS AND TIPS

- Skip the pecans and you'll still have a nice nutty English-style Brown Ale that will pair well with pecan pie.

PROFESSIONAL BREWS TO ASPIRE TO

Southern Pecan Nut Brown Ale: Lazy Magnolia Brewing Co., Kiln, Mississippi. Brewed with whole, roasted pecans. The pecans are used just like grain and add a nutty flavor and depth to the beer. Notes of caramel, and nutty flavors with a low hop profile; 4.39% ABV.

Pecan Harvest Ale: Abita Brewing Co., Abita Springs, Louisiana. Made with real, toasted Louisiana pecans. The natural oils from the pecans add a light pecan finish and aroma; 5% ABV.

Hazelnut Brown Nectar: Rogue Ales, Newport, Oregon. A traditional European Brown Ale with a hazelnut aroma, sweet nutty flavor, and a smooth finish; 6.2% ABV.

NOVEMBER HOMEBREW 2

Cranberry Belgian Pale

MAKE THIS BEER IF YOU LIKE: Earthy Belgian Ales. A bit of spice and fruit. Cranberry sauce with your turkey. A touch of tart.

PAIRS WELL WITH: Turkey, stuffing, pheasant, cranberry sauce, noodle kugel.

STYLE AND BREWING NOTES

The Belgian version of the Pale Ale is quite different from the American. The Belgians place less emphasis on the bitter, piney hops and more on complex notes of spice, fruit, citrus, pepper, and earth. We think this difference works well for November's dishes. The earthiness of a Belgian Pale Ale is big and balanced enough to drink with roasted game hen or turkey, without overpowering the food. We've added an odd ingredient to this brew: cranberries. Something about the tart fruit and spice of the beer blend well to create a beer perfect for Thanksgiving. It's more common to add tart fruit to sour beers like Lambics or a

Berliner Weisse, but we decided to venture outside the box on this one, and it paid off. Those in your family who don't love beer but who would drink a tart cocktail will warm up to this homebrew.

Sometimes we double this recipe to 5 gallons and ferment half with the cranberries and half without any fruit. This way you end up with a nice selection of beers for the Thanksgiving table; one earthy, spicy, and dry, the other earthy with a touch of tart berries.

BREW IT: CRANBERRY BELGIAN ALE

DIFFICULTY LEVEL: **Promiscuous**
TYPE OF BREWING: **Extract with specialty grains**
SPECIALTY/EXTRA EQUIPMENT: **Pot for steaming, immersion blender**
TARGET OG: **1.052**
TARGET FG: **1.013**

IBUs: **24**
TARGET ABV: **5.1**
PROPER GLASS: **Tulip or teardrop**

SHOPPING LIST

1 packet Wyeast Belgian Ardennes yeast 3522

3 ounces Belgian Aromatic malt—milled

4 ounces Belgian Biscuit malt—milled

6 ounces Belgian CaraMunich malt—milled

2.5 pounds Briess Pilsen Light liquid malt extract

1 pound Amber liquid malt extract

0.5 ounce Saaz hop pellets

0.3 ounce Styrian Goldings hop pellets

0.25 ounce Fuggles hop pellets

2.5 pounds fresh cranberries

Makes about 2.5 gallons

PREP

- *Prepare your yeast (at least 3 hours before you brew):* Crack your packet of Belgian Ardennes yeast and let it warm up to room temperature. You can do this the day before you brew as well.

STEEP/MASH

- Heat 3 quarts of water. Attach a thermometer and heat the brew pot until it reaches 160°F. Turn off the heat.
- Put the specialty grains (Belgian Aromatic, Belgian Biscuit, and Belgian CaraMunich malts) in the grain bag (tying the ends) and place it in the brew pot. Cover with a lid and rest for 30 minutes.
- Prepare your sparge water by heating 3 quarts of water to 170°F in a separate small pot.

SPARGE

- After 30 minutes, remove the grain bag from the brew pot. Put a large fine-mesh strainer over the brew pot. Put the grain bag in the strainer, open the grain bag, and slowly run the hot sparge water through it, making sure to cover all of the grains with water. Do not squeeze the grain bag! Remove the grain bag and discard.
- Add an additional 2 gallons of water to the brew pot.
- Reheat your brew pot to 155°F; turn off the heat and add the Briess Pilsen Light and Amber liquid malt extracts. Gently stir to make sure the extracts don't stick to the bottom of the pot.

THE BOIL

- Bring the pot to a boil.
- As soon as the pot comes to a boil, add your first hop addition, the Saaz hops and set your timer for 60 minutes. The hops will dissolve immediately. Stir occasionally, skimming off the big solids with a slotted spoon and looking out for the dreaded boilover!
- At 30 minutes (that is, with 30 minutes left to the boil), add your second hop addition, the Styrian Goldings hops.

- At 55 minutes (that is, with 5 minutes left to the boil), add your third hop addition, the Fuggles hops.

PITCH THE YEAST

- *Prepare your ice bath:* In your sink or another vessel, prepare an ice bath to cool the beer down in.
- *Cool your wort:* Remove the pot from the heat and place it into your ice bath. Place a sanitized thermometer in the wort and let cool until it reaches 70°F or below.
- *Clean your stuff:* Sanitize anything that will come into contact with your beer.
- *Transfer your wort:* Pour the wort through a sanitized strainer into a 3- or 5-gallon plastic fermenting bucket or through a sanitized strainer and funnel into a 3- or 5-gallon glass carboy.
- *Pitch your yeast:* Shake your packet of prepared yeast, sanitize the outside, tear it open, and throw all of its contents into the cooled wort in the fermenter.

PRIMARY FERMENTATION

- Place an airtight lid equipped with your airlock (filled with vodka) and stopper on the plastic bucket or place the airlock and stopper on a glass carboy. Or use the blow-off tube method (see Chapter 2).
- Keep the container in a dark and relatively cool place (ideal fermentation temperature for this style is between 65° and 76°F) for 7 to 10 days.

SECONDARY AND CRANBERRY ADDITION

- Freeze the cranberries at least 24 hours before you transfer your beer to secondary to make sure they get thoroughly frozen hard. On transfer day, take them out and steam them in a double-pot steamer. Use enough water in the bottom of the pot for the cranberries to be dumped into after steaming for boiling. Steam the cranberries for 5 minutes, and then dump the berries into the boiling water. Turn off the heat and carefully roughly blend using an immersion blender. Do not completely puree the berries, leave some solids. Simmer for 10 to 15 minutes. Cool to room temperature.

■ Add the cooled and blended cranberry mixture to a second 3- to 5-gallon bucket or glass carboy. Transfer the beer from the primary fermenter to this secondary container with a sanitized tube siphon. (Make sure to leave the sediment behind.)

■ Put an airlock on the secondary container and let the beer sit for 14 days.

NECESSARY: TERTIARY FERMENTATION

■ Transfer the beer from the secondary vessel to a 3- to 5-gallon bucket or glass carboy with a sanitized tube siphon. (Make sure to leave the sediment and as much of the cranberry pulp as possible behind.)

■ Put an airlock on the secondary container and let the beer sit for 2 to 3 more weeks.

■ Bottle for 14 days as described in Chapter 2. Then refrigerate and enjoy!

RULE BREAKERS AND TIPS

• If you prefer the easy way out, you can substitute juice instead of real cranberries. After the primary fermentation, add 8 ounces of room-temperature organic cranberry juice (unsweetened, 100% juice). Two days later you are ready to bottle.

Sage Chestnut ESB

MAKE THIS BEER IF YOU LIKE: Malty Ales. Thanksgiving in the desert. Stuffing with your turkey. Herbaceous aromatics. Unusual beers.

PAIRS WELL WITH: Roasted turkey, roasted chicken, beer-braised short ribs, sage pumpkin ravioli, chestnut soup.

STYLE AND BREWING NOTES

ESB stands for Extra Special Bitter—though it's not particularly extra, special, or bitter. It is a British style of Ale that was named such to differentiate it from the Best Bitter, which is a lower-alcohol brew, much like a Pale Ale. The *Best* referred to the use of the best ingredients on hand. ESBs tend to be drier than Brown Ales but not quite as bitter as IPAs. We love them because of their balance and manageable alcohol content. They make for a perfect fall afternoon brew.

Sage is often associated with winter foods, particularly as a key ingredient in stuffing for turkey. We like to brew this in time for Thanksgiving to serve with dinner and to add to our stuffing recipe (page 163). The herbaceous flavor of sage is an unusual one in beverages, but we love it. Against a nutty, malt background and with herbaceous hops, the sage creates a complex brew that works well in cold weather. As fans of hiking in the desert, we find that waft of sage a welcome reminder of beautiful desert landscapes. The first time we had sage in beer was in Craftsman Brewing Co.'s Triple White Sage, a beer that Mark Jilg, owner and brewmaster, makes with local handpicked sage from the Pasadena foothills. It's a cult favorite here in California and an homage to indigenous plant life. Against a nutty, malt background and with herbaceous hops, the sage creates a complex brew that works well in cold weather. Sage has long been used for its medicinal properties as a tonic and for warding off evil spirits, so we like to burn a little sage while brewing this one, just to cleanse the air and get in the mood. Sage was one of several herbs, flowers, and plants used in the homebrewing days of old to balance the sweetness in beer before hops were widely used.

Chestnuts (which are actually a fruit) are a perfect complement to the nutty character of the malt used in an ESB recipe. They are one of the oldest foods on the planet and are more akin to the sweet potato in texture than to any nut. The sweet nature of roasted or boiled chestnuts mirrors the sweetness you will smell in your wort. You don't have to roast them over an open fire (though it would be damn authentic) but it's important to use roasted chestnuts in your brew because raw chestnuts have an undesirable tannic quality and, like the pecans in the Pecan Pie Brown Ale, add too much oil to the brew.

BREW IT: SAGE CHESTNUT ESB

DIFFICULTY LEVEL: Promiscuous
TYPE OF BREWING: Partial mash
SPECIALTY/EXTRA EQUIPMENT: Baking sheet
TARGET OG: 1.055
TARGET FG: 1.016
IBUs: 35
TARGET ABV: 5.1
PROPER GLASS: Pint

SHOPPING LIST

1 packet Wyeast London ESB Ale yeast 1968
1 pound dry-roasted chestnuts
1.5 pounds Pale 2-row malt—milled
8 ounces Biscuit malt—milled
6 ounces Caramel/Crystal 40 L malt—milled
6 ounces Caramel/Crystal 20 L malt—milled

2 ounces Briess 2-row Chocolate malt—milled

2 pounds Golden liquid malt extract

1 ounce Fuggles hop pellets

0.25 ounce East Kent Goldings hop pellets

0.25 ounce Fuggles hop pellets

⅛ ounce fresh Great Basin sagebrush leaves (*Artemisia tridentate*), aka desert sage

Makes about 2.5 gallons

PREP

■ *Prepare your yeast (at least 3 hours before you brew):* Crack your packet of London ESB Ale yeast and let it warm up to room temperature. You can do this the day before you brew as well.

■ Prepare your chestnuts: This is almost the same process as described on page 150 for pecans, but doesn't take as much roasting because chestnuts don't have as much oil. Preheat the oven to 350°F. Using a sharp knife, carefully cut an X into the shell of each chestnut to help lift the shell from the nut during roasting. Spread the chestnuts out on a baking sheet and bake for 15 minutes. Cool on paper towels to soak up the oil. Remove the meat from the shells and chop the chestnuts into coarse pieces and roast again for 15 minutes more. Cool on paper towels or in a paper bag to absorb the oil.

STEEP/MASH

■ Heat 4 quarts of water. Attach a thermometer and heat the brew pot until it reaches 160°F. Turn off the heat.

■ Put the grains (Pale 2-row, Biscuit, Caramel/Crystal 40 L, Caramel/Crystal 20 L, and Briess 2-row malts) in a grain bag (tying the ends) and put the chestnuts in another grain bag (tying the ends) and place them in the brew pot. Cover with a lid and rest for 60 minutes, maintaining a temperature of 155°F by turning the heat on for a few minutes if necessary.

- Prepare your sparge water by heating 4 quarts of water to 170°F in a separate small pot.

SPARGE

- After 60 minutes, remove both grain bags from the brew pot. Put a large fine-mesh strainer over the brew pot. Put the bag with the grains in the strainer, open the grain bag, and slowly run the hot sparge water through it, making sure to cover all of the grains with water. Do not squeeze the grain bag! Run some water through the chestnut bag as well. Remove the bags.
- Add an additional 2 gallons of water to the brew pot.
- Reheat your brew pot to 155°F; turn off the heat and add the Golden liquid malt extract. Gently stir to make sure the extract doesn't stick to the bottom of the pot.

THE BOIL

- Bring the pot to a boil.
- As soon as the pot comes to a boil, add your first hop addition, 0. 5 ounce of the Fuggles hops and set your timer for 60 minutes. The hops will dissolve immediately. Stir occasionally, skimming off the big solids with a slotted spoon and looking out for the dreaded boil-over!
- At 45 minutes (that is, with 15 minutes left in the boil), add your second hop addition, the East Kent Goldings hops.
- At 58 minutes (that is, with 2 minutes left in the boil), add your third hop addition, 0.5 ounce of Fuggles hops.
- At flameout (that is, when the boil is over and you turn off the heat), add the sage.

PITCH THE YEAST

- *Prepare your ice bath:* In your sink or another vessel, prepare an ice bath to cool the beer down in.

- *Cool your wort:* Remove the pot from the heat and place it into your ice bath. Place a sanitized thermometer in the wort and let cool until it reaches 70°F or below.
- *Clean your stuff:* Sanitize anything that will come into contact with your beer.
- *Transfer your wort:* Pour the wort through a sanitized strainer into a 3- or 5-gallon plastic fermenting bucket or through a sanitized strainer and funnel into a 3- or 5-gallon glass carboy.
- *Pitch your yeast:* Shake your packet of prepared yeast, sanitize the outside, tear it open, and throw all of its contents into the cooled wort in the fermenter.

PRIMARY FERMENTATION

- Place an airtight lid equipped with your airlock (filled with vodka) and stopper on the plastic bucket or place the airlock and stopper on a glass carboy. Or use the blow-off tube method (see Chapter 2).
- Keep the container in a dark and relatively cool place (ideal fermentation temperature for this style is between 64° and 72°F) for 7 to 10 days if using secondary or for 12 to 14 days if not.

OPTION: SECONDARY

- This is a good time to taste your beer and see how the flavors are coming. If you desire more sage flavor, boil some sage in a small amount of water in a small grain bag, let it cool, and add that to your secondary vessel.
- Transfer the beer from the primary fermenter to a 3- to 5-gallon bucket or glass carboy with a sanitized tube siphon. (Make sure to leave the sediment behind.)
- Put an airlock on the secondary container and let the beer sit for at least 14 days.
- Bottle for 14 days as described in Chapter 2. Then refrigerate and enjoy!

RULE BREAKERS AND TIPS

- You can purchase dried chestnut chips and forgo the roasting. Just add them to the steeping grains.
- You can use dried culinary sage instead of desert sage; the flavor may be a bit more subdued.
- You can use chestnut liqueur in your beer instead of actual chestnuts (yeah, it's kind of cheating). Add during bottling. Taste a drop in a sample glass of your brew to determine how much to add.

PROFESSIONAL BREWS TO ASPIRE TO

Anvil ESB: AleSmith Brewing Co., San Diego, California. An American-style ESB with rich, toasty malt notes and balancing hops; 5.5% ABV.

Mammoth IPA 395: Mammoth Brewing Co., Mammoth Lakes, California. Named after Route 395, this big IPA celebrates the aromas of hops, desert sage, and mountain juniper of the region; 8% ABV.

Triple White Sage: Craftsman Brewing Co., Pasadena, California. Complex and earthy Belgian-style triple with big sage flavors and aroma. A cult favorite; 9% ABV.

TO EAT

Sage Chestnut ESB Stuffing

1 (1-pound) loaf white bread, stale or dried in a
    200°F oven, cut into 1-inch cubes
1 large yellow onion, chopped
3 large celery stalks, chopped

¼ cup (½ stick) salted butter

1 cup Sage Chestnut ESB

1 teaspoon dried sage

1 teaspoon dried thyme

½ teaspoon freshly ground black pepper

½ cup chopped chestnuts, cooked

2 large eggs

½ cup chicken stock

1 teaspoon salt

Serves 8

Preheat the oven to 375°F. Butter a 9-by-13-inch baking dish. Place bread cubes in a very large bowl.

In a large sauté pan, cook the onion and celery over medium-low heat in the butter until barely translucent. Add ½ cup of the beer and simmer until half of the liquid has cooked off. Add the sage, thyme, pepper, and chestnuts, and cook until heated through. Pour the mixture over the bread cubes, tossing to combine.

In a medium bowl, beat the eggs with remaining ½ cup of beer, the chicken stock, and salt. Pour the egg mixture over the bread mixture, combining well.

Pour mixture into the prepared baking dish. If the stuffing looks dry, add another ½ cup of stock or beer to moisten. Cover the dish with foil, and bake for 30 minutes. Remove the foil, and bake an additional 10 minutes or until top begins to brown.

Pair with a glass of Sage Chestnut ESB or Cranberry Belgian Pale or both!

NINE

December

SNOW ◯ LOTS OF GIFTS ◯ BIG JARS OF HOLIDAY COOKIES ◯ SPICED
BEVERAGES BY THE FIRE ◯ SOMETHING THAT KEEPS YOU NICE AND WARM

Your December Homebrew

CHRISTMAS SPICED PORTER: **Chocolate and coffee notes with bold
flavors of allspice, licorice, ginger, and orange peel**

FIG AND CLOVE DUBBEL: **Dark fruit and spicy clove notes with an
earthy finish**

ALPINE JUNIPER BRAGGOT: **A Scandinavian holiday mead Ale
fermented with juniper berries**

To Eat

Fig and Clove Dubbel Chutney

Our favorite beer season has arrived! December gives us all the
excuse to overeat, overdrink, overpurchase, and generally em-
body excess. These are the cold winter nights at the gastropub where
the inevitable answer to "Should we have another round?" is a resound-
ing "Hell yes!" We created these recipes with the rich and decadent

holiday foods of December in mind. As in November, we love bringing these homebrews to our family gatherings to pair with holiday dinner courses. We even dare to open an effervescent Belgian-style Dubbel instead of Champagne on New Years Eve (OK, we drink the Champagne too). This is also your month to gift some homebrew, so show off your new talent, and give a gift made with love.

The first December beer is Christmas Spiced Porter, a dark winter beer full of notes of chocolate, dark fruit, coffee, vanilla, anise, and orange peel. The second beer is a Belgian-style Dubbel that is rounded out with notes of dark figs and spice. And finally, we have a recipe for an easy Ale mead called Braggot. This treat is made with equal parts honey and grains and harks back to ancient pagan winter solstice celebrations. Perfect for cold winter December nights, and all you heathen pagans out there.

DECEMBER HOMEBREW 1

Christmas Spiced Porter

MAKE THIS BEER IF YOU LIKE: Christmas spices. Fruitcake. Lattes with cinnamon. Mulled wine. Star anise.

PAIRS WELL WITH: Chocolate chocolate chip cookies, fig pudding, stolen, fruitcake, and roast goose.

STYLE AND BREWING NOTES
The Porter is an Ale named after the river porters of London, with whom the style was very popular. Porters typically have very similar characteristics to Stouts. In fact, the word *stout* used to refer to a stronger Porter, as in "Guinness Stout Porter," the beer's original name. Now the two styles are pretty much the same. You could brew a Porter and call it a Stout and most people wouldn't be the wiser.

Porters use malt that imparts a chocolate and roasted coffee flavor that typically finishes dry. Our Porter here has ingredients that give the brew an appropriate holiday personality. As with the Controversial Pumpkin Ale (page 138), you have to watch that the spices in your Porter or Stout don't overwhelm the beer; however, the darker malt profile in these brews stands up better to stronger spices than does the Brown Ale base of the typical pumpkin ale. The coffee and chocolate notes are big and bold, so a heavier hand with spices is welcome. The dominant flavors will come from the roasted grains, anise, and allspice, but we've added vanilla, orange peel, and ginger to emphasize sweeter notes.

There's nothing more comforting to us than sticking our noses over the pot during the boil of this recipe. Not sure what that says about us, but . . . it's warm and the notes of orange peel and spice make us feel smack dab in the middle of the holidays. And the hops add that green note that makes us think of decorating trees and cool winter evenings, like brewing up a Christmas stew.

BREW IT: CHRISTMAS SPICED PORTER

DIFFICULTY LEVEL: Sophomore
TYPE OF BREWING: Extract with specialty grains
SPECIALTY/EXTRA EQUIPMENT: None
TARGET OG: 1.045
TARGET FG: 1.013
IBUs: 25
TARGET ABV: 4.5
PROPER GLASS: Pint

SHOPPING LIST

1 packet Wyeast Ringwood Ale yeast 1187
4 ounces roasted Barley malt—milled
3 ounces Chocolate malt—milled

4 ounces Caramel/Crystal 60 L malt—milled

1 ounce British Black Patent malt—milled

3 pounds liquid Munich malt extract

0.3 ounce Northdown hop pellets

0.5 ounce peeled and coarsely chopped gingerroot

0.12 ounce whole pieces star anise (not ground)

1 vanilla bean, split in half

0.4 ounce Willamette hop pellets

0.3 ounce dried sweet orange peel

½ teaspoon ground allspice

Makes about 2.5 gallons

PREP

■ *Prepare your yeast (at least 3 hours before you brew):* Crack your packet of Ringwood Ale yeast and let it warm up to room temperature. You can do this the day before you brew as well.

STEEP/MASH

■ Heat 3 quarts of water. Attach a thermometer, and heat the brew pot until it reaches 160°F. Turn off the heat.

■ Put the specialty grains (roasted Barley, Chocolate, Caramel/Crystal 60 L, and British Black Patent malts) in the grain bag (tying the ends) and place it in the brew pot. Cover with a lid and rest for 30 minutes.

■ Prepare your sparge water by heating 3 quarts of water to 170°F in a separate small pot.

SPARGE

■ After 30 minutes, remove the grain bag from the brew pot. Put a large fine-mesh strainer over the brew pot. Put the grain bag in the strainer, open the grain bag, and slowly run the hot sparge water through it, making sure to cover all of the grains with water. Do not squeeze the grain bag! Remove the grain bag and discard.

- Add an additional 2 gallons of water to the brew pot.
- Reheat your brew pot to 155°F; turn off the heat and add the liquid Munich malt extract. Gently stir to make sure the extract doesn't stick to the bottom of the pot.

THE BOIL

- Bring the pot to a boil.
- As soon as the pot comes to a boil, add your first hop addition, the Northdown hops, and set your timer for 60 minutes. The hops will dissolve immediately. Stir occasionally, skimming off the big solids with a slotted spoon and looking out for the dreaded boilover!
- At 45 minutes (that is, with 15 minutes left in the boil), add the ginger, star anise, and half of the vanilla bean.
- At 50 minutes (that is, with 10 minutes left in the boil), add your second hop addition, the Willamette hops.
- At 55 minutes (that is, with 5 minutes left in the boil), add the orange peel, remaining half of the vanilla bean, and allspice.

PITCH THE YEAST

- *Prepare your ice bath:* In your sink or another vessel, prepare an ice bath to cool the beer down in.
- *Cool your wort:* Remove the pot from the heat and place it into your ice bath. Place a sanitized thermometer in the wort and let cool until it reaches 70°F or below.
- *Clean your stuff:* Sanitize anything that will come into contact with your beer.
- *Transfer your wort:* Pour the wort through a sanitized strainer into a 3- or 5-gallon plastic fermenting bucket or through a sanitized strainer and funnel into a 3- or 5-gallon glass carboy.
- *Pitch your yeast:* Shake your packet of prepared yeast, sanitize the outside, tear it open, and throw all of its contents into the cooled wort in the fermenter.

PRIMARY FERMENTATION

- Place an airtight lid equipped with your airlock (filled with vodka) and stopper on the plastic bucket or place the airlock and stopper on a glass carboy. Or use the blow-off tube method (see Chapter 2).

- Keep the container in a dark and relatively cool place (ideal fermentation temperature for this style is between 64° and 74°F) for 7 to 10 days if using secondary or for 12 to 14 days if not.

RECOMMENDED: SECONDARY

- Transfer the beer from the primary fermenter to a 3- to 5-gallon bucket or glass carboy with a sanitized tube siphon. (Make sure to leave the sediment behind.)

- Put an airlock on the secondary container and let the beer sit for at least 14 days.

- Bottle for 14 days as described in Chapter 2. Then refrigerate and enjoy!

RULE BREAKERS AND TIPS

- If you want to forgo the vanilla bean, you can add 0.25 ounce vanilla extract or syrup to the fermenter at bottling time. The flavor may be less authentic, but the extract is easier.

- Note that a little star anise goes a long, long way! You may want to soak some in hot water like tea and then smell and taste to see if you like the aroma and flavor as much as we do. If you're not that into it, cut it out of the recipe, or halve the amount called for.

- This will seem like blasphemy, but we once had a Porter served in a pub in New Zealand during their winter season (our summer) that was topped with a sprinkle of nutmeg and cinnamon on the foam and, well, it was damn good. So if you want to intensify the spice or are feeling lazy and want to skip the spice additions altogether, add a sprinkle of spice to your glass when you serve it.

PROFESSIONAL BEERS TO ASPIRE TO

Cocoa Porter Winter Warmer: Tommyknocker Brewery, Idaho Springs, Colorado. Traditional Porter style brewed with pure cocoa powder and honey. Big malty notes with a hint of sweetness; 5.7% ABV.

Anchor Christmas Ale: Anchor Brewing, San Francisco, California. A dark spiced holiday Ale whose top secret recipe changes every year, as does the tree on the label. Notes of coffee, chocolate, ginger, licorice, and nutmeg; 5.5% ABV.

Old Fezziwig Ale: Samuel Adams/Boston Beer Co., Boston, Massachusetts. Big sweet malt character with notes of toffee, caramel, and chocolate. Brewed with cinnamon, ginger, and orange peel; 5.8% ABV.

Gift That Beer!

It's that time again when you run through the list of generic gift ideas, arriving at choices that will mildly please or, more likely, disappoint your friends and family. Trust us when we tell you that a bottle or two of homebrew, made with love by you, will stand out among the gift cards, earrings, and ties. Here are some tips for giving the gift of your homebrew:

- Make a cool label. There are so many places online now to make great beer labels. Our favorite is www.myownlabels.com/beer_labels. You'll look like a pro!
- Wrap in tissue paper. Italian craft brewers often wrap their beer in beautifully designed tissue paper. Find something stylish and tie with a bow, no reason beer can't be beautiful.

- Gift the proper vessel. Give a set of the appropriate glassware to go with the style of your homebrew; you don't want them guzzling your masterpiece from the bottle!
- Tie a note on your brew with a list of the ingredients, description of the flavor profile, and some food pairing suggestions for your gift receiver.
- Add a complementary food to your homebrew gift package:
  - Pecan Pie Brown Ale + Beer Nutz (page 148)
  - Christmas Spiced Porter + homemade gingerbread cookies
  - Fig and Clove Dubbel + Fig and Clove Dubbel Chutney (page 183)
- And for nascent homebrewers, buy them the ingredients you used in the respective homebrew you are giving and encourage them to give it a go! Give a man a beer, he'll enjoy the pint; teach a man to brew . . .

DECEMBER HOMEBREW 2

Fig and Clove Dubbel

MAKE THIS BEER IF YOU LIKE: Dark fruit. Bold spices. Earthy notes. Belgian beers. A religious experience.

PAIRS WELL WITH: Moroccan dishes, Roquefort, brandied figs, smoked meats, glazed ham, and samosas.

STYLE AND BREWING NOTES

Dubbels are Belgian Ales that typically offer notes of dark fruit and spices like clove, cinnamon, and licorice. They were originally brewed by monks, who had been brewing beer to sustain them during fasting (yes, they drank beer while eating no food at all!). The beer they brewed was flavorful, drinkable, but low in alcohol. Their more seasonal and specialty beers were often stronger and offered different flavor profiles; one of these became the Dubbel. The name is thought to refer to being almost double in overall intensity than their personal session Ale used for sustenance. Dubbels are not necessarily double the strength of the Monks' personal brew (though they may have twice the amount of malt), but are certainly higher in alcohol and darker than a Belgian Pale Ale. They sometimes have subtle notes of brown sugar and rum and a complex yeast character. They can be fairly dry or not at all; however, Dubbels are never thought of as bitter beers as traditional Belgian brewing uses hops as a balancing agent, not a dominating flavor.

Cloves are a flower bud from an Indonesian evergreen tree. The strength of their flavor defines many festive foods: cookies, pie, chutneys, and many curries. There is a spicy character to cloves that affects the palate much like ginger or cinnamon. In fact, cloves actually contain capsaicin, which is an active ingredient in cayenne pepper. In beer, cloves offer a spicy nose, which parallels the notes you often smell in Dubbels. Figs are a romantic fruit that call to mind paintings of Adam and Eve and earthy flavors from ancient trees. Drinking Dubbels always makes us think of the complex flavor that exists within a fig—that rum-soaked raisin rolled-in-dirt sensation. This Dubbel will pair perfectly with the festive flavors of the holiday season. We also used it in our chutney recipe (see page 183), a nice Belgian twist on a traditional Indian food.

The recipe calls for fig puree. It's important to use fig puree free of any preservatives or other ingredients. Organic fig puree is easy to find online but is sometimes available at specialty stores that sell organic produce. It will be added in the secondary vessel.

BREW IT: FIG AND CLOVE DUBBEL

DIFFICULTY LEVEL: **Promiscuous**

TYPE OF BREWING: **Extract with specialty grains**

SPECIALTY/EXTRA EQUIPMENT: **Blow-off tube**

TARGET OG: **1.067**

TARGET FG: **1.011**

IBUs: **22**

TARGET ABV: **7.4**

PROPER GLASS: **Tulip**

SHOPPING LIST

1 packet Wyeast Trappist High Gravity Ale yeast
   3787

2 ounces Special B malt—milled

2 ounces Belgian Aromatic malt—milled

3 pounds Pilsner liquid malt extract

12 ounces Amber dry malt extract

0.5 ounce Hallertauer hop pellets

0.4 ounce Saaz hop pellets

4 ounces Belgian dark candi sugar
   (see page 86)

6 ounces granulated sugar

5 whole cloves

2 pounds organic fig puree (see "Style and Brewing
   Notes" for this recipe)

Makes about 2.5 gallons

PREP

■ *Prepare your yeast (at least 3 hours before you brew):* Crack your packet of Trappist High Gravity Ale Yeast and let it warm up to room temperature. You can do this the day before you brew as well.

STEEP/MASH

■ Heat 2 quarts of water. Attach a thermometer, and heat the brew pot until it reaches 160°F. Turn off the heat.

■ Put the specialty grains (Special B and Belgian Aromatic malts) in the grain bag (tying the ends) and place it in the brew pot. Cover with a lid and rest for 30 minutes.

■ Prepare your sparge water by heating 3 quarts of water to 170°F in a separate small pot.

SPARGE

■ After 30 minutes, remove the grain bag from the brew pot. Put a large fine-mesh strainer over the brew pot. Put the grain bag in the strainer, open the grain bag, and slowly run the hot sparge water through it, making sure to cover all of the grains with water. Do not squeeze the grain bag! Remove the grain bag and discard.

■ Add an additional 2 gallons of water to the brew pot.

■ Reheat your brew pot to 155°F; turn off the heat and add the Pilsner liquid malt extract. Gently stir to make sure the extract doesn't stick to the bottom of the pot. Add the Amber dry malt extract; be careful the dry extract doesn't clump.

THE BOIL

■ As soon as the pot comes to a boil, add your first hop addition, the Hallertauer hops and set your timer for 60 minutes. The hops will dissolve immediately. Stir occasionally, skimming off the big solids with a slotted spoon and looking out for the dreaded boilover!

■ At 50 minutes (that is, with 10 minutes left in the boil), add your second hop addition, the Saaz hops, and the Belgian candi sugar.

■ At 55 minutes (that is, with 5 minutes left in the boil), stir in the granulated sugar and cloves.

PITCH THE YEAST

- *Prepare your ice bath:* In your sink or another vessel, prepare an ice bath to cool the beer down in.
- *Cool your wort:* Remove the pot from the heat and place it into your ice bath. Place a sanitized thermometer in the wort and let cool until it reaches 70°F or below.
- *Clean your stuff:* Sanitize anything that will come into contact with your beer.
- *Transfer your wort:* Pour the wort through a sanitized strainer into a 3- or 5-gallon plastic fermenting bucket or through a sanitized strainer and funnel into a 3- or 5-gallon glass carboy.
- *Pitch your yeast:* Shake your packet of prepared yeast, sanitize the outside, tear it open, and throw all of its contents into the cooled wort in the fermenter

PRIMARY FERMENTATION

- For this brew, use the blow-off tube method (see Chapter 2).
- Keep the container in a dark and relatively cool place (ideal fermentation temperature for this style is between 64° and 78°F) for 7 to 10 days.

SECONDARY AND FIG ADDITION

- Pour the fig puree into a 3- to 5-gallon sanitized bucket or glass carboy. Transfer the beer from the primary fermenter to the secondary container with a sanitized tube siphon. (Make sure to leave the sediment behind.)
- Put an airlock on the secondary container and let the beer sit for 14 days.
- When transferring the beer to the bottling bucket, pass the auto-siphoned beer through your strainer to remove excess fig puree. Try to leave the sediment at the bottom of the secondary container.
- Bottle for 14 days as described in Chapter 2. Then refrigerate and enjoy!

RULE BREAKERS AND TIPS

- If you want to substitute the figs for something a bit easier, chuck 1 to 2 pounds of organic raisins into your secondary instead.
- If you can't find fig puree, you can substitute organic fig juice, free of any preservatives or added sugar.

PROFESSIONAL BEERS TO ASPIRE TO

Grimbergen Dubbel: Brouwerij Alken-Maes, Alken, Belgium. Sweet, complex malt profile with notes of cherry, figs, and raisins. Fairly smooth with a tangy dry finish; 6.5% ABV.

He'brew Jewbelation Fifteen: Shmaltz Brewing Co., San Francisco, California, and New York, New York. Big, malty beer with notes of currants, figs, dates, molasses, brown sugar, and vanilla. A touch of bitter chocolate on the finish; 15% ABV.

Monk's Blood: 21st Amendment Brewery, San Francisco, California. Black cherries, dates, figs, brown sugar, and light hints of caramel with a nice maltiness. A good hint of cinnamon and a touch of vanilla. There is a light but pleasant hint of booziness; 8.3% ABV.

DECEMBER HOMEBREW 3

Alpine Juniper Braggot

BREW THIS STYLE IF YOU LIKE: *The Canterbury Tales*. Winter solstice. Gin. Rosemary. Vikings. Renaissance fairs. Honey.

PAIRS WELL WITH: Swedish meatballs, venison, choucroute garnie, Italian pan-roasted lamb, wild grouse, and roasted game hens with orange.

STYLE AND BREWING NOTES

We were first turned onto the Braggot style by Mark Jilg who made a wonderful Sour Braggot at Craftsman Brewing Co. in Pasadena, California. It's a very old, almost extinct style in the United States but has just started to gain some attention among brewers and craft beer drinkers looking for something different. It's actually a combination of mead (an alcoholic beverage made from honey) and a centuries-old style of Ale, flavored with local spices and herbs.

Mark also gave us the idea of using juniper berries. On a visit to his brewery, he pulled out a bucket of handpicked fresh juniper berries and marveled at the powerful pine and fruit aromatics. Juniper is an evergreen that is native to the Northern Hemisphere and is common in Scandinavia, where it's often used in their cuisine. It harks back to their winter festivals in the days of yore when great Yule logs were burned, and people celebrated by drinking mead and Braggot flavored with local herbs and spices. Very *Lord of the Rings*.

Our Alpine Juniper Braggot was made specifically with winter solstice in mind and completely inspired by Mark Jilg and the Craftsman Brewing Co. It's rich and spicy with a pleasant astringency and pairs wonderfully with Scandinavian dishes, wild birds, and game.

BREW IT: ALPINE JUNIPER BRAGGOT

DIFFICULTY LEVEL: **Promiscuous**

TYPE OF BREWING: **Extract and honey with specialty grains**

BREWING NOTE: **Champagne yeast, long fermentation and aging times**

SPECIALTY/EXTRA EQUIPMENT: **Two mason jars**

TARGET OG: **1.079**

TARGET FG: **1.003**

IBUs: **12.6**

TARGET ABV: **10%**

2 grams Wyeast Champagne yeast 4021

6 grams Safale Ale dry yeast

2 ounces Carafa II malt—milled

2 pounds Extra-Light dry malt extract

0.3 ounce Cascade hop pellets

2 ounces dried juniper berries

2 pounds clover honey

½ Whirlfloc tablet

Makes about 2.0 gallons

PREP

■ Prepare the yeast: Sanitize two mason jars and add the Champagne dry yeast to one and the Safale Ale dry yeast to the other. Add ¼ cup warm water (95° to 105°F) to each jar. Put the lids on the jars and rest 15 minutes. After 15 minutes, test the yeasts by adding ¼ teaspoon of the Extra-Light dry malt extract to each jar. Replace the lids and put the jars in a warm place (out of direct sunlight). After 30 minutes your yeasts should be foaming and will be ready to pitch into your beer later.

■ *Prepare the juniper berries:* Put the juniper berries in a resealable plastic bag and whack them with a rolling pin or a hammer to crack them.

STEEP/MASH

■ *Steep your grains:* Heat 1 cup of water. Attach a thermometer and heat the saucepan until it reaches 155°F. Turn off the heat. Add the Carafa II malt, put a lid on the saucepan, and rest 30 minutes.

■ Heat 3.5 gallons of water. Attach a thermometer and heat the brew pot until it reaches 160°F.

■ Prepare your sparge water by heating 1 to 1½ cups of water to 170°F in a separate small pot.

SPARGE

▪ After 30 minutes strain the Carafa II malt through a fine mesh strainer into the brew pot, reserving the grains. Slowly run the hot sparge water through the strainer, making sure to cover all the grains. Remove the strainer and discard the grains.

▪ Reheat your brew pot water to 155°F; turn off the heat and add the Extra-Light dry malt extract. Gently stir to make sure the extract doesn't stick to the bottom of the pot; be careful it doesn't clump.

THE BOIL

▪ Bring the pot to a boil.

▪ As soon as the pot comes to a boil, add the Cascade hops and set your timer for 60 minutes. The hops will dissolve immediately. Stir occasionally, skimming off the big solids with a slotted spoon and looking out for the dreaded boilover!

▪ At 30 minutes (that is, with 30 minutes left in the boil), empty the bag of cracked juniper berries into the brew pot.

▪ At 45 minutes (that is, with 15 minutes left in the boil), add the honey and stir to dissolve, being careful not to let it scorch on the bottom of the brew pot.

▪ At 55 minutes (that is, with 5 minutes left in the boil), add the half tablet of Whirlfloc and stir to dissolve.

PITCH THE YEAST

▪ *Prepare your ice bath:* In your sink or another vessel, prepare an ice bath to cool the beer down in.

▪ *Cool your wort:* Remove the pot from the heat and place it into your ice bath. Place a sanitized thermometer in the wort and let cool until it reaches 70°F or below.

▪ *Clean your stuff:* Sanitize anything that will come into contact with your beer.

- *Transfer your wort:* Pour the wort through a sanitized strainer into a 3- or 5-gallon plastic fermenting bucket or through a sanitized strainer and funnel into a 3- or 5-gallon glass carboy.
- *Pitch your yeast:* Pour the rehydrated yeasts from the mason jars into the fermenter.

PRIMARY FERMENTATION

- Place an airtight lid equipped with your airlock (filled with vodka) and stopper on the plastic bucket or place the airlock and stopper on a glass carboy. Or use the blow-off tube method (see Chapter 2).
- Keep the container in a dark and relatively cool place (ideal fermentation temperature for this style is between 68° and 72°F) for 4 weeks.

SECONDARY

- Transfer the beer from the primary fermenter to a 3- to 5-gallon bucket or glass carboy with a sanitized tube siphon. (Make sure to leave the sediment behind.)
- Put an airlock on the secondary container and let the beer sit at cooler temperatures (ideally 50° to 55°F) for 6 to 8 weeks. You'll know that the Braggot is ready when it's good and clear. You should be able to read newsprint through the carboy.
- Bottle for 3 months to (gulp!) a year as described in Chapter 2, filtering out any remaining juniper berries through a strainer when you transfer the beer into the bottling bucket. Then refrigerate and enjoy!

RULE BREAKERS AND TIPS

- Go ahead and taste some along the way to see how it develops (we can never resist). You'll taste the difference the age puts on this style; and look on the bright side—you'll have a perfectly aged Alpine Juniper Braggot just in time for next year's winter solstice.

The Simplest Mead of All Time

Tired of this whole process? Just make mead in five simple steps by leaving the grains out:

Heat 1 gallon of spring water to a boil to kill any bacteria. Turn off the heat and stir in 3 pounds of honey.

Cool in an ice bath to 70°F, transfer to a 1-gallon glass carboy and add yeast (use a sweet or dry mead yeast from White Labs or Wyeast).

Stir it for 5 minutes.

Put an airlock and stopper on the carboy and ferment and age the mead at 65° to 75°F for 6 to 12 months.

Bottle, chill, and enjoy.

PROFESSIONAL BREWS TO ASPIRE TO

Crafstman Spring Braggot: Craftsman Brewing Co., Pasadena, California. Light malty sweetness with characteristics reminiscent of stone fruit and honeysuckle. Well balanced and soft with the smallest bit of honey sweetness at the end; 7.5% ABV.

Old Danish Braggot: Ørbæk Bryggeri, Ørbæk, Denmark. Brewed based on an 18th-century recipe, according to old Danish mead and Braggot making traditions. Sweet with fresh honey and toffee notes. Bready, spicy, and a light toast in the finish; 10.1% ABV.

Crabtree Braggot: Crabtree Brewing, Greeley, Colorado. This Braggot is a really interesting blend of an Imperial Stout and an English mild Ale brewed with hops and tons of honey. The result is big sweetness in the beginning followed by a long toffee and molasses finish; 7.85% ABV.

Fig and Clove Dubbel Chutney

Jar this for a lovely holiday gift!

3–4 tart apples, such as Granny Smith, peeled,
    cored and cut into ¼-inch cubes

1 small red onion, chopped fine

2 garlic cloves, minced

1 teaspoon minced or grated gingerroot

¾ cup Fig and Clove Dubbel

½ cup apple cider vinegar

½ cup packed brown sugar

¼ cup chopped dried figs

1½ teaspoons garam masala

½ teaspoon whole brown mustard seeds

½ teaspoon turmeric

¼ teaspoon ground ginger

¼ teaspoon red chili flakes

¼ teaspoon salt

Makes about 1 (12-ounce) jar

In a medium saucepan, bring all the ingredients to a boil. Cover the pan; turn the heat to medium low, and simmer for 1 hour, stirring occasionally. Cool and refrigerate in a sealed container.

Serve on a cheese plate or with Indian dishes and a glass of Fig and Clove Dubbel!

TEN

January

NEW YEAR'S RESOLUTIONS ◯ ICE AND SNOW ◯ REFLECTION ◯ BAKED
APPLES ◯ HOT STEW ◯ NEW AND DIFFERENT EXPERIENCES

Your January Homebrew
> BERLINER WEISSE: Sour with a crisp light citrus bite, emulating
> the classic Berlin style
> ZEE RUSSIAN IMPERIAL STOUT: Espresso, bitter chocolate, warm-
> ing alcohol
> SCANDALOUS HARD APPLE CIDER: Slightly frizzante, dry and
> complex, made with tart apples

To Eat
> Zee Russian Imperial Stout Affogato

Ugh . . . January brings about the pressures of a new year. What
will be different, how can we lose those bad habits? Can we become better homebrewers? Time to dig deep and resolve to improve
your brewing technique and your beer-tasting palate. It's way better
than resolving to eat fewer plates of pasta. Our resolutions are always

beer related. Whether to brew more beer or to brew a wider variety of styles or to enter more homebrewing competitions, we always have a goal for the year.

We have two very different beers in this chapter. They have distinctive flavors. One, a Berliner Weisse, is light-bodied, tart, and sour, and the other is creamy, full-bodied, and dark with smoky, coffee notes—a luscious Russian Imperial Stout. We also have something scandalous to brew in January! It's actually not beer at all. It's a *cider*; a beverage we both used to hate because, well, we're Beer Chicks. But our recipe harkens to Europe and the shores of Normandy, where cider has had a long and respected tradition, and has enough complexity to please our beer-loving palates.

YOUR JANUARY HOMEBREW 1

Berliner Weisse

BREW THIS BEER IF YOU LIKE: Puckery sourness. Beer cocktails. Bacteria. Lactic acid.

PAIRS WELL WITH: Chèvre, chicken piccata, fines herbes salad, and pickled herring.

STYLE AND BREWING NOTES

We usually introduce people to sour beers through one of the lightest, the Berliner Weisse. It has been well-known in Gemany and, of course, Berlin, but has had little popularity in the American market, until the resurgence of craft beers that is, and in particular the cult trend of sour beers. Berliner Weisse is different from your usual German Weisse. They are lemony and super light-bodied, usually with an ABV around 3%—yeah, that light. Berliner Weisse is also fermented with lactic bacteria called *Lactobacillus* that gives this beer style some super mouth-puckering sour lactic acidity, much like the acidic zing found in wine. Now, you're probably thinking what we did as first, which was, "We're not comfortable with the idea of bacterial fermentation in the home and is *Lactobacillus* contagious?" Do not be afraid. You can find this bacteria in the homebrew store right next to the yeast. In fact it's made by the same popular companies that make yeast and is sold in similar packaging. No hazmat suit required.

Because these beers are distinctly sour, Berliner Weisses are traditionally served with one of two sweet syrups, one green and one red. The green one is called Waldmeister, and it's made using a grassy and lemony green herb called woodruff. The red one is called Himbeer, which is raspberry syrup. We actually made our own syrup to accompany this beer, using some beautiful seasonal pomegranate juice we found at the farmers' market. This Berliner Weisse is fast (with a 15-minute boil) and easy (extract only)! Better than that, it's delicious, especially with the pomegranate syrup. Think of it as a beer cocktail.

BREW IT: BERLINER WEISSE

DIFFICULTY LEVEL: Neophyte

TYPE OF BREWING: Extract

SPECIALTY/EXTRA EQUIPMENT: None

TARGET OG: 1.039

TARGET FG: 1.012

IBUs: 5.8

TARGET ABV: 3.5%

PROPER GLASS: Goblet

SHOPPING LIST

1 tube White Labs European Ale yeast WLP011

1 packet Wyeast *Lactobacillus delbrueckii* 4335

1 pound 6 ounces Pilsner liquid malt extract

1 pound 6 ounces Wheat liquid malt extract (typically a blend of Wheat and Pale malts; check the
ingredients when you purchase)

0.5 ounce Liberty hop pellets

Makes about 2.5 gallons

PREP

▪ *Prepare your yeast and* Lactobacillus *(at least 3 hours before you brew):* Crack your packet of *Lactobacillus* and let it warm up to room temperature. You can do this the day before you brew as well. Let the tube of European Ale yeast warm up to room temperature, allow 3 to 6 hours before you brew.

STEEP/MASH

▪ Heat 3.5 gallons of water. Attach a thermometer and heat the brew pot until it reaches 155°F. Turn off the heat.

▪ Add the Pilsner liquid and Wheat liquid malt extracts to the brew pot. Stir constantly to dissolve and to make sure the extracts don't stick to the bottom of the pot.

THE BOIL

▪ Bring the pot to a boil.

▪ As soon as the pot comes to a boil, set your timer for 15 minutes.

▪ At 5 minutes (that is, with 10 minutes left in the boil), add the Liberty hops and stir to dissolve.

PITCH THE YEAST AND *LACTOBACILLUS*

▪ *Prepare your ice bath:* In your sink or another vessel, prepare an ice bath to cool the beer down in.

▪ *Cool your wort:* Remove the pot from the heat and place it into your ice bath. Place a sanitized thermometer in the wort and let cool until it reaches 70°F or below.

- *Clean your stuff:* Sanitize anything that will come into contact with your beer.
- *Transfer your wort:* Pour the wort through a sanitized strainer into a 3- or 5-gallon plastic fermenting bucket or through a sanitized strainer and funnel into a 3- or 5-gallon glass carboy.
- *Pitch your yeast:* Sanitize the outside of the tube of yeast and packet of *Lactobacillus deibrueckii*. Shake your tube of yeast, crack it open, and throw all of its contents into the cooled wort in the fermenter.
- Cut open the *Lactobacillus delbrueckii* and throw all the contents of that package in as well. Swirl the fermenter around a bit to get some aeration for better yeast health.

PRIMARY FERMENTATION

- Place an airtight lid equipped with your airlock (filled with vodka) and stopper on the plastic bucket or place the airlock and stopper on a glass carboy. Or use the blow-off tube method (see Chapter 2).
- Keep the container in a dark and relatively cool place (ideal fermentation temperature for this style is between 60° and 70°F) for 10 to 14 days.
- Bottle for 14 days as described in Chapter 2. Then refrigerate and enjoy alone or with pomegranate syrup (page 189).

RULE BREAKERS AND TIPS

- The biggest challenge to making a good Berliner Weisse is making a light, clean base beer and then souring it rapidly with bacteria. You need to do this fairly quickly and at fairly high temperatures because the gravity of this style is quite low, meaning, there's not a lot of alcohol to act as a preservative.

Spicy-Tart Berliner Weisse Syrup

 As we mentioned, in Berlin Berliner Weisse is traditionally served with syrup, usually made with woodruff or raspberries. But sometimes, Berliner Weisse is flavored with other syrups, fruits, wines, and liqueurs. The most popular one other than the red and green is called kümmel, which is a clear sweet-flavored liqueur made with cumin, caraway seed, and fennel. We've always been inspired by these innovative beer additions and decided to get creative and make our own syrup. We went to the farmers' market and found some freshly made 100% pomegranate juice made from seasonal fruit and put our bartending/cooking skills to work. The result was a tart syrup with a hint of spice that works perfectly in the Berliner Weisse. It also makes a nice beer aperitif for your next party.

POMEGRANATE SYRUP

2 cups pomegranate juice (100% juice, no preservatives or additives)

1 cup sugar

2 teaspoons freshly squeezed lemon juice

2–3 drops Tabasco sauce

In a saucepan, simmer the pomegranate juice and the sugar until they've reduced by half. Remove the pan from the heat and add the lemon juice and Tabasco to taste.

Add this to your Berliner Weisse in small amounts until you have the taste you like. We like to have a balance between the sweetness from the syrup and the sourness from the beer. A great combination and new twist on a classic from Berlin.

Hottenroth Berliner Weisse: The Bruery, Placentia, California. Big *Lactobacillus* and a nice dry sourness and a touch of barnyard funk. Behind that is just a hint of estery banana. Very representative of this classic German style; 3.1% ABV.

Craftsman Berliner Weisse: Craftsman Brewing Co., Pasadena, California. Very traditional, light bodied, refreshing, and crisp with bright lemon notes and a balanced sour finish; 3.5% abv.

Berliner Kindl Weisse: Berliner Kindl Brauerei, Berlin, Germany. Three words: Acidic. Sour. Tart. Has a little bit of citrus and a crisp pucker finish that makes you thirsty again even before you finish your sip; 3% ABV.

JANUARY HOMEBREW 2

Zee Russian Imperial Stout

BREW THIS BEER IF YOU LIKE: Big, strong Ales. Freshly pulled espresso. Cocoa nibs. Bitter beers. Russian poetry. Big ABVs.

PAIRS WELL WITH: Truffles, aged cheeses, gelato, chocolate-covered cherries, and brownies.

STYLE AND BREWING NOTES

So, the story goes like this: The popular Stouts made by the British were shipped over to the Russian court, and alas, they were going bad and freezing along the way. So the British upped the hops for their preservative value and upped the alcohol content, so the beer wouldn't freeze and thus the Russian Imperial Stout (RIS) was born. The Russian court apparently couldn't get enough of the stuff—who wouldn't want a high-octane brew with notes of freshly brewed espresso, bitter baking chocolate, and roasted barley on a chilly Russian evening? Catherine the Great was said to have loved it, and we admire a woman who can handle a formidable brew. Today in Russia you will be hard-pressed to find this style, as the ever-dominant mass-produced light Pilsner has taken over, but the cultlike love for this style in the United States has brought it back to the forefront of the craft beer world.

The typical Alcohol by Volume for the Russian Imperial Stout is any-where from 7% to 10%, and the notes typically have that bitter espresso with roasted barley and sometimes even complex rum and dark berry notes. Russian Imperial Stouts are often aged in wood and do well with the background of oak, bourbon, vanilla, whiskey, or whatever the bar-rel imparts. RIS also does well with certain specialty ingredients, like coffee, vanilla bean, and dark chocolate. It has a variety of bitternesses as well, definitely meant to finish dry but can be downright bitter. There's a lot of leeway on this front, and you may want to adjust our recipe to create the bitterness and bite you like.

We first tasted this style in the form of North Coast Brewing's famous Old Rasputin Russian Imperial Stout. We were serving it on the nitro tap when we were bartending together, and it immediately rose to one of our top 10 favorite beers. The combination of espresso and bitter chocolate notes with the creamy mouthfeel and an ABV that made us feel "relaxed" led us to describe this style of beer with one word: *seductive*. There's just something sexy about it. Just like an espresso with a silky *crema*. Serve this as a nightcap in lieu of coffee or Port and every-one will feel "relaxed."

BREW IT: ZEE RUSSIAN IMPERIAL STOUT

DIFFICULTY LEVEL: Sophomore

TYPE OF BREWING: Extract with specialty grains

SPECIALTY/EXTRA EQUIPMENT: None

TARGET OG: 1.094

TARGET FG: 1.021

IBUs: 84

TARGET ABV: 9.7%

PROPER GLASS: Pint or teardrop

SHOPPING LIST

1 packet Wyeast American Ale yeast 1056

4 ounces roasted barley—milled

3 ounces Chocolate malt—milled

4 ounces Carafa II malt—milled

2 ounces Caramel/Crystal 30 L malt—milled

4 pounds Pale liquid malt extract

2 pounds Briess Dark dry malt extract

1 ounce Cluster hop pellets

0.9 ounce Centennial hop pellets

0.6 ounce Northern Brewer hop pellets

Makes about 2.5 gallons

PREP

■ *Prepare your yeast (at least 3 hours before you brew):* Crack your packet of American Ale yeast and let it warm up to room temperature. You can do this the day before you brew as well.

STEEP/MASH

■ Heat 3 quarts of water. Attach a thermometer, and heat the brew pot until it reaches 160°F. Turn off the heat.

- Put the specialty grains (roasted barley and Chocolate, Carafa II, and Caramel/Crystal 30 L malts) in the grain bag (tying the ends) and place it in the brew pot. Cover with a lid and rest for 30 minutes.
- Prepare your sparge water by heating 3 quarts of water to 170°F in a separate small pot.

SPARGE

- After 30 minutes, remove the grain bag from the brew pot. Put a large fine-mesh strainer over the brew pot. Put the grain bag in the strainer, open the grain bag, and slowly run the hot sparge water through it, making sure to cover all of the grains with water. Do not squeeze the grain bag! Remove the grain bag and discard.
- Add an additional 2 gallons of water to the brew pot.
- Reheat your brew pot to 155°F; turn off the heat and add the Pale liquid malt extract. Gently stir to make sure the extract doesn't stick to the bottom of the pot. Add the Briess Dark dry malt extract; be careful it doesn't clump.

THE BOIL

- Bring the pot to a boil.
- As soon as the pot comes to a boil, add your first hop addition, the Cluster hops and set your timer for 60 minutes. The hops will dissolve immediately. Stir occasionally, skimming off the big solids with a slotted spoon and looking out for the dreaded boilover!
- At 30 minutes (that is, with 30 minutes left in the boil), add your second hop addition, the Centennial hops.
- At 45 minutes (that is, with 15 minutes left in the boil), add your third hop addition, the Northern Brewer hops.

PITCH THE YEAST

- *Prepare your ice bath:* In your sink or another vessel, prepare an ice bath to cool the beer down in.

- *Cool your wort:* Remove the pot from the heat and place it into your ice bath. Place a sanitized thermometer in the wort and let cool until it reaches 70°F or below.
- *Clean your stuff:* Sanitize anything that will come into contact with your beer.
- *Transfer your wort:* Pour the wort through a sanitized strainer into a 3- or 5-gallon plastic fermenting bucket or through a sanitized strainer and funnel into a 3- or 5-gallon glass carboy.
- *Pitch your yeast:* Shake your packet of prepared yeast, sanitize the outside, tear it open, and throw all of its contents into the cooled wort in the fermenter.

PRIMARY FERMENTATION

- Place an airtight lid equipped with your airlock (filled with vodka) and stopper on the plastic bucket or place the airlock and stopper on a glass carboy. Or use the blow-off tube method (see Chapter 2).
- Keep the container in a dark and relatively cool place (ideal fermentation temperature for this style is between 60° and 72°F) for 7 to 10 days if using secondary or 12 to 14 days if not.

RECOMMENDED: SECONDARY

- Transfer the beer from the primary fermenter to a 3- to 5-gallon bucket or glass carboy with a sanitized tube siphon. (Make sure to leave the sediment behind.)
- Put an airlock on the secondary and let the beer sit for 14 more days or more.
- Bottle for 14 days as described in Chapter 2. Then refrigerate and enjoy!

RULE BREAKERS AND TIPS

- For increased alcohol, add some granulated sugar to the boil. We'd start with about 1 pound.

- To barrel-age your Russian Imperial Stout, add some oak chips to the secondary vessel. The longer you let it sit, the more oak and vanilla flavor you will get.

PROFESSIONAL BEERS TO ASPIRE TO

Old Rasputin Russian Imperial Stout: North Coast Brewing Company, Fort Bragg, California. One of our favorite brews; deep bitter espresso and dark, dark chocolate. A perfect nightcap, and great poured over vanilla bean gelato; 9% ABV.

The Abyss: Deschutes Brewery, Bend, Oregon. A highly sought-after RIS; seasonal and rare. Ages in French oak bourbon barrels; notes of molasses, licorice, and dark fruit; 11% ABV.

AleSmith Speedway Stout: AleSmith Brewing Co., San Diego, California. A big Stout brewed with a ton of coffee. Dark chocolate notes with a rich toasted caramel. There is a rare barrel-aged version that adds notes of oak and bourbon; 12% ABV.

JANUARY HOMEBREW 3

Scandalous Hard Apple Cider

BREW THIS CIDER IF YOU LIKE: Not beer. Apple pie. A new challenge. Fruity drinks.

PAIRS WELL WITH: Vanilla ice cream, Wisconsin Cheddar cheese, apple-wood-smoked bacon, quiche Lorraine, crème caramel, and buckwheat pancakes.

STYLE AND BREWING NOTES

No. It's not beer. Beer is a fermented beverage made from malted grains. Cider is fermented fruit. Scandalous! When we first entered the craft beer world, we scoffed at anyone who was drinking a cider. We saw it as an übersweet, easy alternative for people who claimed, "I'm not a beer drinker." We viewed serving a cider as a way to sidestep the sometimes challenging art of breaking through people's misconceptions about beer. An easy out. But now we're a bit wiser and realize we were mistaken. With the rise of craft beer, a new generation of artisanal cider makers has arisen, producing with great care, a beverage that is every bit as complex and storied as beer. Cider as a DIY beverage had the same fate as beer: People were drinking poorly made mass-produced cider just to get wasted, instead of appreciating it as a standalone, quality artisanal drink. But cider, just like beer, has been a staple of human consumption documented as far back as Julius Caesar's time.

So why the hell is it in a beer-making book?!? Bottom line, we really enjoy making cider. It's fun, it's relatively easy, *and* it's a gluten-free alternative, which is great for our anti-gluten eaters out here in Los Angeles. And sometimes it's the only way to get a true brut cider because those available at the local market often resemble apple-flavored wine coolers. Cider should not simply be sweet but also tart, earthy, and sometimes dry.

So here's the thing about cider making. You can go all the way DIY and buy something like 20 pounds of cider apples that you then have to mature, juice or process, strain, and pasteurize all for 1 gallon of hard cider. *Or* you can do what we do. It's so much easier and just as delicious to buy apple cider from the local farmers' market and ferment it with some Champagne yeast! We make sure to buy organic cider that is free of all preservatives or added chemicals. Most important, if it's been pasteurized (we prefer nonpasteurized), we make sure it was a cold pasteurization process, which eliminates any bacteria present but does not change the taste of the cider the way heated pasteurization can.

BREW IT: SCANDALOUS HARD APPLE CIDER

DIFFICULTY LEVEL: Neophyte

TYPE OF BREWING: Cider

SPECIALTY/EXTRA EQUIPMENT: None

TARGET OG: 1.054

TARGET FG: 0.988

IBUs: 0

TARGET ABV: 8.7%

PROPER GLASS: Tulip or pint

SHOPPING LIST

1 packet Wyeast Champagne yeast 4021

2.5 gallons fresh pressed organic apple cider (no
preservatives, 100% apples, nonpasteurized)

4 ounces organic brown sugar (weighed
not packed)

6 ounces wildflower honey

Makes about 2.5 gallons

PREP

■ *Prepare your yeast (at least 3 hours before you brew):* Crack your packet of Wyeast Champagne yeast and let it warm up to room temperature. You can do this the day before you brew as well.

■ *Heat the cider:* Attach a thermometer and heat the brew pot until it reaches 160°F. Turn off the heat.

■ Add the brown sugar and the honey. Stir to dissolve and make sure that nothing sticks to the bottom of the pot.

■ Reheat your brew pot and keep the temperature between 160° and 170°F for 30 minutes. *Do not boil* the must (must in cider making = wort in beer making). Boiling will break down the pectins in the fruit and create a cloudy cider.

PITCH THE YEAST

- *Prepare your ice bath:* In your sink or another vessel, prepare an ice bath to cool the cider down in.
- *Cool your must:* Remove the pot from the heat and place it into your ice bath. Place a sanitized thermometer in the must and let cool until it reaches 70°F or below.
- *Clean your stuff:* Sanitize anything that will come into contact with your cider.
- *Transfer your must:* Pour the must through a sanitized strainer into a 3- or 5-gallon plastic fermenting bucket or through a sanitized strainer and funnel into a 3- or 5-gallon glass carboy. Try to aerate the must as much as you can in the process.
- *Pitch your yeast:* Shake your packet of prepared yeast, sanitize the outside, tear it open, and throw all of its contents into the cooled must in the fermenter.

PRIMARY FERMENTATION

- Place an airtight lid equipped with your airlock (filled with vodka) and stopper on the plastic bucket or place the airlock and stopper on a glass carboy. Or use the blow-off tube method (see Chapter 2).
- Keep the container in a dark and relatively cool place (ideal fermentation temperature for this style is between 55° and 75°F) for 14 days.

SECONDARY

- Transfer the cider from the primary fermenter to a 3- to 5-gallon bucket or glass carboy with a sanitized tube siphon. (Make sure to leave the sediment behind.)
- Put an airlock on the secondary container and let the cider ferment for 4 weeks.
- Bottle as described in Chapter 2. Refrigerate the bottles for 7 to 10 days. Enjoy your homemade hard apple cider with friends!

RULE BREAKERS AND TIPS

- You could try fermenting your cider without heating it. The heating up of the cider kills the natural yeasts that may exist in the cider already. But we've been pretty successful with cider by just putting it in the carboy with the sugar, shaking it up, pitching the yeast, placing the airlock, and watching it go! You could actually end up with some complex cider if any complementary wild yeasts existed in the cider. It could also go terribly wrong. It's a risk; you could lose the whole batch. But sometimes you gotta risk big to win big. Your choice. (This is easier with a 1-gallon batch.)

- Get creative in the secondary vessel. You can add a cinnamon stick, lemon peel, orange peel, cloves, raisins, chilies, or nutmeg, for example. The possibilities are endless. Experiment with amounts and lengths on 1-gallon batches.

- If you just want to make 1 gallon of hard cider, buy a cider that comes in a 1-gallon glass jug that you can just use as the fermenting carboy. Just fasten a rubber stopper and airlock on the jug and, voilà!, instant fermenter.

- If you want a sweeter rather than dryer cider, replace the Champagne yeast with Wyeast Cider yeast 4766.

PROFESSIONAL HARD CIDERS TO ASPIRE TO

Woodchuck Granny Smith Cider: Vermont Hard Cider Co., Middlebury, Vermont. A single-variety cider using only delicious Granny Smith apples. Nice and balanced, dry, tart, and tangy; 5% ABV.

Julian Hard Cider: Julian Hard Cider, Julian, California. Originating from the old British styles of cider, this lightly carbonated pure apple cider is bright with tartness and acidity. Finishes clean and dry; 7.27% ABV.

Weston's Special Reserve Cider: H. Weston's & Sons Ltd., Much Marcle, United Kingdom. A vintage cider that uses cider apples from a single year. Aged in oak casks (some over 200 years old). This high-ABV cider has a full body and a long lingering bitter-sweet finish; 8.2% ABV.

TO EAT

Zee Russian Imperial Stout Beer Affogato

2 small scoops of vanilla bean gelato (other flavors
we love: salted caramel, cherry, coffee)
¼ cup Zee Russian Imperial Stout

Serves 1

Put the gelato in a decorative bowl or martini glass, pour over the Stout. Serve immediately with a spoon.

Additional possible toppings: Real maraschino cherries, a touch of port, a pinch of nutmeg, grated orange zest, or candied bacon.

ELEVEN

February

A HEART-SHAPED BOX OF CHOCOLATES ☽ THE GLORY OF LOVE
☽ DRINKING YOUR DESSERT ☽ COFFEE IN NEW ORLEANS ☽
A WELL-MADE SAZERAC ☽ TAKING VOWS

Your February Homebrew

STUPID CUPID'S BITTERSWEET CHOCOLATE STOUT: An American-style Stout brewed with bittersweet chocolate

CRESCENT CITY CAFÉ AU LAIT STOUT: A Milk Stout brewed with chicory coffee and fermented with Sazerac rye and French oak

GROOM'S SCOTCH WHISKY WEE HEAVY: Scotch-style Wee Heavy Ale aged on Hungarian oak soaked in Highland Park 18-year Scotch whisky

To Eat

Crescent City Café au Lait Stout Braised Pork

All of our February beers are celebratory. Two celebrate February holidays and one the beautiful wedding of some dear friends. The first beer is a bittersweet elixir that's perfect for Valentine's Day. Now, one of us hates Valentine's Day. The other one loves it. But however much we disagree about February 14, we agree that beer is the perfect gift to give (to your loved one or to yourself). And what's a more appropriate beer to brew for Valentine's Day than a Chocolate Stout?

Our second delectable beer was inspired by a trip to New Orleans, where we shot our special *Eat This, Drink That* for the Cooking Channel. We fell in love with the food-centric culture steeped in French and American history. We closed our eyes and uttered *mmmmm*'s as we drank their famous coffee laced with chicory, and shared big high fives at the Carousel Bar quaffing the perfectly balanced, herbaceous Sazerac, the "Official Cocktail of New Orleans." What better month to brew a beer celebrating NOLA than February, when the Crescent City comes alive with Mardi Gras.

The last recipe was born as a wedding gift. We were commissioned by our friend to make a beer for her future husband for their wedding day. We came up with a Scotch Ale that represented his culture and personality. We enjoyed the beer so much that we wanted to share it with you.

Stupid Cupid's Bittersweet Chocolate Stout

BREW THIS BEER IF YOU LIKE: No, really like chocolate. Making extracts. Drinking to get through Valentine's Day. The bitter and the sweet in life.

PAIRS WELL WITH: Macaroons, pollo con mole, salty sweet potato fries, and Luxardo maraschino cherries.

STYLE AND BREWING NOTES

As we mentioned in the Porter recipe (page 166), *Stout* was originally a general term for a strong dark beer stemming from Porters that were so popular that the English started making Extra-Stout Porters, which eventually became known simply as Stouts. These beers are Black Ales that use deeply roasted barley for their toasty character and dark color. Stouts vary greatly in alcohol content, sweetness, and bitterness. Though these attributes change from Stout to Stout, the richness of the roasted barley is the common thread. Generally American Stouts have roasted coffee and dark chocolate qualities with a low hop presence and a medium to full body. For Stupid Cupid, we are going to get into double trouble by extending the natural chocolate flavors of the dark malt by actually adding roasted and crushed Valrhona cocoa nibs—aka chocolate—to the beer in the secondary vessel. We've also added just a smidge of flaked oats, which adds to the body, resulting in a lusciously rich, beautifully balanced, bittersweet Chocolate Stout. So whether you're bitter or sweet on V-day—this Ale will be an appropriate beverage.

BREW IT: STUPID CUPID'S BITTERSWEET CHOCOLATE STOUT

DIFFICULTY LEVEL: Promiscuous

TYPE OF BREWING: Partial mash

SPECIALTY/EXTRA EQUIPMENT: Mason jar

TARGET OG: 1.053

TARGET FG: 1.012

IBUs: 42

TARGET ABV: 5.4%

PROPER GLASS: Pint

SHOPPING LIST

1 packet of Wyeast Denny's Favorite yeast 1450

0.5 pound flaked oats

0.5 pound American Chocolate malt—milled

0.5 pound Caramel/Crystal 80 L malt—milled

3.5 pounds Alexanders Pale liquid malt extract

0.8 ounce Mt. Hood hop pellets

1.5 ounce cocoa powder

1 ounce Fuggle hop pellets

½ Whirlfloc tablet

3 whole vanilla beans

4 ounces roasted and crushed Valrhona cocoa nibs

4–6 ounces vodka

Makes about 2.5 gallons

PREP

▪ *Prepare your yeast (at least 3 hours before you brew):* Crack your packet of Denny's Favorite yeast and let it warm up to room temperature. You can do this the day before you brew as well.

STEEP/MASH

▪ Heat 3.5 gallons of water. Attach a thermometer and heat the brew pot until it reaches 160°F. Turn off the heat.

▪ Put the specialty grains (oats and American Chocolate and Caramel/Crystal 80 L malts) in the grain bag (tying the ends) and place it in the brew pot. Cover with a lid, and rest for 60 minutes at 152° to 154°F; you may have to turn the heat on and off periodically to hold the temperature.

▪ After 60 minutes, simply lift the grain bag out of the brew pot. Put a large fine-mesh strainer over the brew pot. Put the grain bag in the strainer and let liquid in the bag drain into the brew pot. (This is like a mini version of the brew-in-a-bag method used in all-grain brewing; see Chapter 13.) Do not squeeze the grain bag! Remove the grain bag and discard.

▪ Gently stir in the Alexanders Pale liquid extract, making sure not to aerate the liquid. Make sure the extract doesn't stick to the bottom or sides of the pot and let it fully dissolve.

THE BOIL

- Bring the pot to a boil.

- As soon as the pot comes to a boil, add your first hop addition, the Mt. Hood hops, and set your timer for 60 minutes. Stir occasionally, skimming the big solids with a slotted spoon and looking out for the dreaded boilover!

- At 45 minutes (that is, with 15 minutes left in the boil), add your first chocolate addition, the cocoa powder. (We want this beer to be very chocolaty, so we're adding chocolate twice.)

- At 50 minutes (that is, with 10 minutes left in the boil), add your second hop addition, the Fuggle hops.

- At 55 minutes (that is, with 5 minutes left in the boil), add the half tablet of Whirlfloc and stir to dissolve.

PITCH THE YEAST

- *Prepare your ice bath:* In your sink or another vessel, prepare an ice bath to cool the beer down in.

- *Cool your wort:* Remove the pot from the heat and place it into your ice bath. Place a sanitized thermometer in the wort and let cool until it reaches 70°F or below.

- *Clean your stuff:* Sanitize anything that will come into contact with your beer.

- *Transfer your wort:* Pour the wort through a sanitized strainer into a 3- or 5-gallon plastic fermenting bucket or through a sanitized strainer and funnel into a 3- or 5-gallon glass carboy.

- *Pitch your yeast:* Shake your packet of prepared yeast, sanitize the outside, tear it open, and throw all of its contents into the cooled wort in the fermenter.

PRIMARY FERMENTATION

■ Place an airtight lid equipped with your airlock (filled with vodka) and stopper on the plastic bucket or place the airlock and stopper on a glass carboy. Or use the blow-off tube method (see Chapter 2).

■ Keep the container in a dark and relatively cool place (ideal fermentation temperature for this style is between 60° and 70°F) for 7 to 10 days.

■ Prepare the second chocolate addition (7 to 10 days before secondary): Cut the vanilla beans in half lengthwise and widthwise (basically quartering the vanilla beans) with a sharp paring knife. Put the beans along with the Valrhona cocoa nibs into a glass mason jar. Pour in the vodka, screw the lid on tight, and give it a shake to make sure all is coated in the vodka. Put the jar in a cool, dark place and let it steep. This will be added to the beer in the secondary vessel to provide a rich and bittersweet double-chocolate flavor!

SECONDARY AND SECOND CHOCOLATE ADDITION

■ Transfer the beer from the primary fermenter to a 3- to 5-gallon bucket or glass carboy with a sanitized tube siphon. (Make sure to leave the sediment behind.)

■ Add your second chocolate addition by gently stirring in the contents of the mason jar, trying not to aerate the beer too much.

■ Put an airlock on the secondary container and let the beer sit for at least 2 weeks, but we think it's even better after 4 weeks.

■ When transferring the beer to the bottling bucket, pass the autosiphoned beer through your strainer to remove the vanilla beans and Valrhona cocoa nibs.

■ Bottle for 14 days as described in Chapter 2. Then refrigerate and enjoy!

RULE BREAKERS AND TIPS

- You can skip the first chocolate addition of cocoa powder if you feel like it. You'll still get a nice chocolate characteristic from the cocoa nibs.

- It may help, just a bit, with head retention if you put the mason jar mixture in the freezer. The oils from the cocoa nibs will float to the top, and you'll be able to skim some of them off. Oil is known to kill head retention, so you may want to try that if you're having bubble troubles.

PROFESSIONAL BEERS TO ASPIRE TO

Bison Chocolate Stout: Bison Brewing Co., Berkeley, California. Pitch black and delicious, this organic roasted, dry Stout with nice bittersweet chocolate uses cocoa powder in the mash; 6.1% ABV.

Young's Double Chocolate Stout: Wells & Young's Ltd., Bedford, United Kingdom. Sweet, rich, double-dark chocolate milk shake flavors; a perfect dessert and a perfect beer for Valentine's Day; 5.2% ABV.

Rogue Chocolate Stout: Rouge Ales, Newport, Oregon. Talk about balance—this beer blends the flavors so that you can't tell where the chocolate malts end and the real chocolate begins! Black with a rich creamy head and a velvety mouthfeel supplied by the oatmeal malts; 6% ABV.

YOUR FEBRUARY HOMEBREW 2

Crescent City Café au Lait Stout

BREW THIS BEER IF YOU LIKE: The Big Easy. Jazz in the afternoon. Whiskey and rye. French culture. The good times rolling. The Saints.

PAIRS WELL WITH: Beignets, boudin sausage, smoked duck, red beans and rice, bananas Foster, jambalaya.

STYLE AND BREWING NOTES

When we returned home to L.A. from our adventures in New Orleans, we decided that we wanted to make a beer that celebrated our trip, but we needed a beer style that could capture the intense flavors of New Orleans. After several semisuccessful attempts using various Stout styles, we finally moved away from the dryer versions and tried a Sweet Stout, also known as a Milk Stout. This style is so named because it is often sweetened with a bit of milk sugar or lactose, unfermentable sugars that provide a creamy mouthfeel and residual sweetness in beer. (Lactose is not fermentable in beer, so it won't add to the alcohol content or to the CO_2.)

This beer style, which is lower in bitterness, fuller in body, and slightly roasty, turned out to be just the ticket for our needs. We added roasted chicory coffee to remind us of the earthy goodness of coffee at Café du Monde and threw in some French oak wood cubes that had been soaked in Sazerac rye whiskey. The end product was a Sweet Stout that was dark, creamy, and smoky, with a lingering but balanced finish, reminding us of our time in the Crescent City. It's New Orleans in a glass. Who dat?

The Sazerac

Our first cocktail in New Orleans—the birthplace of the cocktail—was the famed Sazerac cocktail at the spinning Carousel Bar. It's a historic cocktail dating back to the 1870s. It's an old-world kind of cocktail, balanced and demure and without the cloying sweetness that accompanies some cocktails today. And, it's strong, which we like.

Besides Sazerac rye, this cocktail uses Peychaud's Bitters, developed in the mid-1800s by New Orleans apothecary Antoine Amedie

Peychaud. The Sazerac also originally used absinthe (which we prefer), but because it was outlawed, other anise liqueurs, most frequently Herbsaint, were used. If you can't find Sazerac rye, then use another rye. If you can't find Peychaud's Bitters, use Angostura; if you can't find Herbsaint or absinthe—go for Pernod or Chartreuse. The Sazerac is a great cocktail to sip while brewing our NOLA-inspired beer.

1 tablespoon Herbsaint (or Lucid absinthe)
1.5 ounces Sazerac 18-year rye whiskey
½ teaspoon simple syrup
4–5 healthy dashes Peychaud's Bitters
1 thick lemon peel (no pith)

Pour the Herbsaint into an old-fashioned or rocks glass and swirl to coat the inside; then throw the excess liquor away. (We know, but that's the way they do it.) Then fill the same glass with ice to chill while you make the rest of the cocktail.

Fill a cocktail shaker with more ice and add the rye, simple syrup, and bitters. Stir for a few seconds. Now, discard the ice from your coated glass and strain your shaker into it. Rub the rim of the glass with the lemon twist, float it in the glass, and drink immediately. You're welcome.

BREW IT: CRESCENT CITY CAFÉ AU LAIT STOUT RECIPE
DIFFICULTY LEVEL: Devout
TYPE OF BREWING: Extract with specialty grains
SPECIALTY/EXTRA EQUIPMENT: Mason jar
TARGET OG: 1.049
TARGET FG: 1.010
IBUs: 32.8
ABV: 5.1%
PROPER GLASS: Pint or teardrop

SHOPPING LIST

1 tube White Labs Irish Stout yeast WLP004

2 ounces roasted barley—milled

4 ounces Caramel/Crystal 80 L malt—milled

4 ounces Chocolate malt—milled

3.25 pounds Alexanders Pale liquid malt extract

0.5 ounce Northern Brewer hop pellets

0.5 ounce Fuggles hop pellets

7 ounces lactose (milk sugar)

½ Whirlfloc tablet

1 ounce French oak cubes, medium roast

6–8 ounces Sazerac 18-year rye whiskey

4 ounces espresso beans

2 ounces ground roasted chicory root

Makes about 2.5 gallons

PREP

▪ *Prepare your yeast (at least 3 hours before you brew):* Let the tube of Irish Stout yeast warm up to room temperature.

STEEP/MASH

▪ Heat 3 quarts of water. Attach a thermometer and heat the brew pot until it reaches 160°F. Turn off the heat.

▪ Put the specialty grains (roasted barley and Caramel/Crystal 80 L and Chocolate malts) in the grain bag (tying the ends) and place it in the brew pot. Cover with a lid, and rest for 30 minutes.

▪ Prepare your sparge water by heating 3 quarts of water to 170°F in a separate small pot.

SPARGE

▪ After 30 minutes, remove the grain bag from the brew pot. Put a large fine-mesh strainer over the brew pot. Put the grain bag in the strainer, open the grain bag, and slowly run the hot sparge water through it, making sure to cover all of the grains with water. Do not squeeze the grain bag! Remove the grain bag and discard.

- Add an additional 2 gallons of water to the brew pot.
- Reheat your brew pot water to 155°F; turn off the heat and add the Alexanders Pale liquid malt extract. Gently stir to make sure the extract doesn't stick to the bottom of the pot.

THE BOIL

- Bring the pot to a boil.
- As soon as the pot comes to a boil, add your first hop addition, the Northern Brewer hops, and set your timer for 60 minutes. The hops will dissolve immediately. Stir occasionally, skimming off the big solids with a slotted spoon and looking out for the dreaded boil-over!
- At 45 minutes (that is, with 15 minutes left in the boil), add your second hop addition, the Fuggles hops along with the lactose; stir to dissolve.
- At 55 minutes (that is, with 5 minutes left in the boil), add the half tablet of Whirlfloc, stirring to dissolve.

PITCH THE YEAST

- *Prepare your ice bath:* In your sink or another vessel, prepare an ice bath to cool the beer down in.
- *Cool your wort:* Remove the pot from the heat and place it into your ice bath. Place a sanitized thermometer in the wort and let cool until it reaches 70°F or below.
- *Clean your stuff:* Sanitize anything that will come into contact with your beer.
- *Transfer your wort:* Pour the wort through a sanitized strainer into a 3- or 5-gallon plastic fermenting bucket or through a sanitized strainer and funnel into a 3- or 5-gallon glass carboy.

- *Pitch your yeast:* Shake your tube of yeast, sanitize the outside of the tube, crack it open, and throw all of its contents into the cooled wort in the fermenter.

PRIMARY FERMENTATION

- Place an airtight lid equipped with your airlock (filled with vodka) and stopper on the plastic bucket or place the airlock and stopper on a glass carboy. Or use the blow-off tube method (see Chapter 2).
- Keep the container in a dark and relatively cool place (ideal fermentation temperature for this style is between 62° and 72°F) for 7 to 10 days.
- *Prepare the Sazerac rye whiskey French oak barrel* (7 to 10 days before the transfer into secondary): Put the oak cubes in a mason jar, pour in the Sazerac, screw on the lid, and let the cubes soak in the rye in a dark, cool place for 7 to 10 days, or while your beer is in the primary fermentation.

SECONDARY AND OAK ADDITION

- Transfer the beer from the primary fermenter to a 3- to 5-gallon bucket or glass carboy with a sanitized tube siphon. (Make sure to leave the sediment behind.)
- Strain the oak cubes from the rye, reserving them both. Add the oak cubes to the secondary container, stirring gently to combine while trying not to aerate the beer too much. Pour the reserved rye into the beer a bit at a time—stirring and tasting in between (with a spoon that has been sanitized between each taste)—until you get the taste you want. Remember, we want the flavor of the Sazerac to be in the background, just a subtle spiciness.
- Put an airlock on the secondary container and let the beer sit and age for 2 to 4 weeks.

- *Prepare the chicory coffee* (2 to 4 hours before bottling): Grind the espresso beans and mix them with the ground chicory. Use this mixture to make 8 cups of very strong chicory coffee.
- After gently siphoning the beer into the bottling bucket. slowly add the chicory coffee, gently stirring and tasting in between (with a spoon that has been sanitized between each taste).
- Bottle for 14 days as described in Chapter 2. Then refrigerate and enjoy!

RULE BREAKERS AND TIPS

- If you can't find Sazerac rye, substitute one of our other favorite ryes: Van Winkle Family Reserve rye, Rittenhouse 100 proof rye, or Old Overholt straight rye whiskey. Also Wild Turkey rye is surprisingly delicious.
- Instead of blending your own chicory coffee, you can also buy a commercial blend, such as Café du Monde French Market chicory coffee.

PROFESSIONAL BEERS TO ASPIRE TO

Hitachino Nest Sweet Stout: Kiuchi Brewery, Ibaraki-ken Naka-gun, Japan. This beer is a bomb in the nose with dark chocolate, milk chocolate, caramel, and dark fruit. The taste is a blend of sweet creaminess from lactose, caramel, and milk chocolate finished by roasty coffee notes; 3.9% ABV.

Left Hand Milk Stout: Left Hand Brewing Co., Longmont, Colorado. Roasty chocolate and coffee are predominant in this beer followed by the milky sweetness of the lactose. More of a beer cappuccino, if you will; 6% ABV.

Samuel Adams Cream Stout: Samuel Adams/Boston Beer Co., Boston, Massachusetts. An English-style Cream Stout brewed with English malts, roasted chocolate, and caramel malts. The addition of unmalted barley creates an even-fuller body. Finishes roasty and malty; 4.9% ABV.

Groom's Scotch Whisky Wee Heavy

BREW THIS BEER IF YOU LIKE: Holy matrimony. The Highlands of Scotland. Woolen sweaters. A wee dram. The Orkney Islands. Personal customization. Hungarian oak.

PAIRS WELL WITH: A roaring fire, a smooth cigar, lobster bisque, lamb chops, razor clams, and fish-and-chips.

STYLE AND BREWING NOTES

Sometimes we get asked to brew a special beer for weddings (which is rad!), and our friend Mila asked us to do one for her fiancé, Martin. We love the creativity that flows when we get to customize our beer for the big day. We consider the circumstances and which beer style would best represent the people and/or the place, the time past and present. Martin, the dapper groom, is a gregarious Scotsman from Glasgow who also happens to be—God bless him—a scotch whisky expert. Our first thought was, "Let's make a Scottish style of beer!" (which we freely admit, was no great feat of creativity). Our second thought (equally mind-wrenching) was, "There had better be some damn whisky in this beer!"

We decided on the lovely Scottish style called a Wee Heavy, known for its rich, malty, and typically sweet, roasted flavors. We added one of our favorite malts (the dark, toasty and slightly smoky Carafa), caramelized honey, and Scottish Ale yeast. For that whisky touch, we decided to soak some medium-roast oak cubes in one of Martin's favorite scotches—Highland Park 18-year single malt—for a week and then add them to the beer in the secondary vessel, aging the brew for 2 months leading up to the wedding—the perfect Scotch Ale aged in "whisky barrels" for our Scottish groom. It was a hit with the wedding goers, so make it for a scotch-lover in your life.

BREW IT: GROOM'S SCOTCH WHISKY WEE HEAVY

DIFFICULTY LEVEL: Devout

TYPE OF BREWING: Extract with specialty grains

SPECIALTY/EXTRA EQUIPMENT: Mason jar

TARGET OG: 1.086

TARGET FG: 1.020

IBUs: 30

TARGET ABV: 8.8%

PROPER GLASS: Pint

SHOPPING LIST

1 packet Wyeast Scottish Ale yeast 1728

8 ounces Caraston malt—milled

8 ounces Munich malt—milled

4 ounces Carafa I—milled

5 pounds Pale liquid malt extract

0.5 ounce Northdown hop pellets

0.25 ounce Willamette hop pellets

6 ounces caramelized honey

½ Whirlfloc tablet

1 ounce Hungarian oak chips, medium roast

8 ounces Highland Park 18-year single malt scotch whisky

Makes about 2.5 gallons

PREP

- *Prepare your yeast (at least 3 hours before you brew):* Crack your packet of Wyeast Scottish Ale yeast and let it warm up to room temperature. You can do this the day before you brew as well.

STEEP/MASH

- Heat 3 quarts of water. Attach a thermometer and heat the brew pot until it reaches 160°F. Turn off the heat.
- Put the specialty grains (Caraston, Munich, and Carafa I malts) in the grain bag (tying the ends) and place it in the brew pot. Cover with a lid, and rest for 30 minutes.
- Prepare your sparge water by heating 3 quarts of water to 170°F in a separate small pot.

SPARGE

- After 30 minutes, remove the grain bag from the brew pot. Put a large fine-mesh strainer over the brew pot. Put the grain bag in the strainer, open the grain bag, and slowly run the hot sparge water through it, making sure to cover all of the grains with water. Do not squeeze the grain bag! Remove the grain bag and discard.
- Add an additional 2 gallons of water to the brew pot.
- Reheat your brew pot to 155°F; turn off the heat and add the Pale liquid malt extract. Gently stir to make sure the extract doesn't stick to the bottom of the pot.

THE BOIL

- Bring the pot to a boil.
- As soon as the pot comes to a boil, add your first hop addition, the Northdown hops, and set your timer for 60 minutes. The hops will dissolve immediately. Stir occasionally, skimming off the big solids with a slotted spoon and looking out for the dreaded boilover!
- At 30 minutes (that is, with 30 minutes left in the boil), add your second hop addition, the Willamette hops.

- At 55 minutes (that is, with 5 minutes left in the boil), add the caramelized honey. Stir to dissolve and be careful not to let it stick to the bottom of the brew pot. When the honey is dissolved, add the half tablet of Whirlfloc; stir to dissolve.

PITCH THE YEAST

- *Prepare your ice bath:* In your sink or another vessel, prepare an ice bath to cool the beer down in.
- *Cool your wort:* Remove the pot from the heat and place it into your ice bath. Place a sanitized thermometer in the wort and let cool until it reaches 70°F or below.
- *Clean your stuff:* Sanitize anything that will come into contact with your beer.
- *Transfer your wort:* Pour the wort through a sanitized strainer into a 3- or 5-gallon plastic fermenting bucket or through a sanitized strainer and funnel into a 3- or 5-gallon glass carboy.
- *Pitch your yeast:* Shake your packet of prepared yeast, sanitize the outside, tear it open, and throw all of its contents into the cooled wort in the fermenter.

PRIMARY FERMENTATION

- Place an airtight lid equipped with your airlock (filled with vodka) and stopper on the plastic bucket or place the airlock and stopper on a glass carboy. Or use the blow-off tube method (see Chapter 2).
- Keep the container in a dark and relatively cool place (ideal fermentation temperature for this style is between 55° and 75°F) for 7 to 10 days.
- *Prepare the "whisky barrel"* (7 to 10 days before transferring to the secondary vessel): Put the oak cubes in a mason jar, pour in the scotch, screw on the lid, and let the cubes soak in the scotch in a dark, cool place for 7 to 10 days, or while your beer is in the primary fermentation.

SECONDARY AND OAK AND SCOTCH ADDITION

▪ Transfer the beer from the primary fermenter to 3- to 5-gallon bucket or glass carboy with a sanitized tube siphon. (Make sure to leave the sediment behind.)

▪ Strain the oak cubes from the scotch, reserving them both. Add the oak cubes to the secondary container, stirring gently to combine while trying not to aerate the beer too much. Pour the reserved scotch into the beer a bit at a time—stirring and tasting in between (with a spoon that has been sanitized between each taste)—until you get the taste you want. There should be some whisky notes, but the scotch should not overpower the beer. (We ended up adding about 6 ounces and drinking the rest of the scotch with a splash of water—cheers!)

▪ Put an airlock on the secondary container and let the beer sit and age for at least 2 weeks; we went with 4 weeks.

▪ Bottle for 14 days as described in Chapter 2. Then refrigerate and enjoy! We toasted Martin and Mila at their wedding with a totally distinct beer, perfectly customized for the groom.

RULE BREAKERS AND TIPS

- If you're not a scotch fan, you can always leave the whisky out and just pitch the oak cubes alone into the secondary container (make sure to steam them to sanitize first).
- Or leave the oak cubes and whisky out completely and have a great Wee Heavy closer to what they drink in bonny old Scotland.

PROFESSIONAL BEERS TO ASPIRE TO

AleSmith Barrel Aged Wee Heavy: AleSmith Brewing Co., San Diego, California. A great example of an American-made Scottish Wee Heavy. Rich, toasty, and malty with a waft of smokiness. A perfect amount of hops provides the perfect balance to the maltiness. A big beer, aged for a year in bourbon barrels; 10% ABV.

Founders Backwoods Bastard: Founders Brewing Co., Grand Rapids, Michigan. Lovely, primary flavors of single malt scotch and bourbon barrels with notes of vanilla, peat, sweet caramel, and roasty, toasty malts. This full-bodied beer finishes with a bit of spice and earth and dark old-world fruit; 10.2% ABV.

Belhaven Wee Heavy: Belhaven Brewery Co., East Lothian, Scotland. A quintessential Wee Heavy. Caramel and toffee notes with a hint of peat and wood. Malty sweet and balanced, with just the right amount of bittering hops; 6.5% ABV.

TO EAT

Crescent City Café au Lait Stout Braised Pork

One 5- to 6-pound bone-in pork butt roast

DRY RUB

3 tablespoons light brown sugar

2 teaspoons kosher salt

1 teaspoon smoked paprika

½ teaspoon ground cinnamon

½ teaspoon ground ginger

½ teaspoon onion powder

½ teaspoon ancho chili powder

BRAISING LIQUID

2 cups Crescent City Café au Lait Stout

3 tablespoons apple cider vinegar

2 tablespoons Worcestershire sauce

2 tablespoons maple syrup

1 tablespoon hot sauce

Serves 8 to 10

Rinse and dry the pork roast.

Combine all the dry rub ingredients and pat onto the pork roast. Put the roast in a resealable plastic bag and refrigerate for at least 2 hours and up to 12 hours; the longer the better.

Place the roast in a slow cooker and add all the braising liquid ingredients. Set the cooker on high and cook for 6 to 8 hours, or until the meat falls apart with gentle pressure. Turn the cooker to low if the liquid begins to boil.

Remove the roast and set aside.

Carefully strain all the liquid from the slow cooker into a saucepan. Skim off the fat and simmer liquid until it has reduced to a thick sauce, about 45 minutes.

Using two forks, shred the pork. Toss the meat with the sauce to taste.

Serve with a pint of Crescent City Café au Lait Stout!

TWELVE

March

ST. PATTY'S DAY ◌ SPRING SKIING ◌ SPRING BREAK ◌ DREAMS
OF FRESH PIÑA COLADAS AND HAWAIIAN BREEZES

Your March Homebrew

DRY IRISH STOUT: **Bitter chocolate, dark coffee, roasted grain**

TROPICAL BELGIAN-STYLE IPA: **A dry-hopped Belgian-style IPA
with big pineapple notes**

BIÈRE DE MARS: **Rustic farmhouse style with some mild esters and
a *lot* of dryness**

To Eat

Dry Irish Stout Oatmeal Cookies

March used to be about spring break and trying to kiss Irish boys. But that was a long, long, long time ago (*for us*). Nowadays we try our best not to go anywhere for vacation during spring break, lest we wind up watching a college kid puke on the beach. And on St. Patty's Day we nurse a few pints and sing some Irish songs but politely decline the Irish Car Bombs and try not to kiss anyone we don't know.

We're getting older, true, but we still celebrate St. Patrick's Day, only now we do it right. We'll wear a lot of green, but we won't drink the green food-colored beer, that's for sure. Instead we like to brew up a classic Dry Irish Stout; a chalky beer with a balance of chocolate and roasted coffee and a waft of smoke. Come March 17, we're pairing this beer with dense Irish soda bread, corned beef and cabbage, and Irish lamb stew and adding it to our Dry Irish Stout Oatmeal Cookies (page 237).

Because spring break no longer applies to our lives, we interpret the idea of spring break with a beer that conjures up days of piña coladas and cheap beers on the beach without any notion of responsibility. Instead of piña coladas and cheap beer, however, we make a beer that humbly imitates one of our favorite Belgian IPAs. Our twist is dry-hopping the crap out of it with Amarillo and Citra hops—both pack a tropical, pineapple aromatic punch. This will make you think of Hawaiian beaches for sure, without having to join the spring break madness.

Finally, we've included one of our favorite styles, Bière de Mars, which translates to "March Beer." We created this recipe because we love this earthy, rustic, and frankly, weird style and because it's relatively hard to find. If you can't find it, brew it yourself!

MARCH HOMEBREW 1

Dry Irish Stout

MAKE THIS BEER IF YOU LIKE: Porters and Stouts. The luck of the Irish. Black coffee and straight espresso. Tradition. Singing in pubs.

PAIRS WELL WITH: Irish stew, meat pie, oysters, flourless chocolate cake, and sharp Irish Cheddar.

STYLE AND BREWING NOTES

The first dark beer most people taste is Guinness. It is the most widely distributed Stout, and because of its Irish fame, it has become the beer of choice on St. Patrick's Day. Draught Guinness in Ireland is just over 3% ABV, while the version we often drink here is 5% to 6%. Most people think they are drinking a beer that's more like 10% ABV. This leads to a misconception that we tried to debunk in *The Naked Pint*: You can't judge a beer by its color! Guinness, as with most Irish Stouts, is not a particularly strong beer. It's not "a meal," so please don't replace your lunch with Guinness. It is the rich flavors and dry finish set inside a dark black beer that leads to this misconception.

Dry Stouts are called such because of their dry finish and lack of sweetness. Instead, there is a rich toasty, often bitter coffee flavor with a hint of cocoa nibs. This recipe is straight up, no unusual ingredients (though this would be lovely with some coffee or chocolate added to the brew). You'll marvel at the depth of character that comes from the toasty specialty grains that give it that true Stout character.

BREW IT: DRY IRISH STOUT

DIFFICULTY LEVEL: **Sophomore**
TYPE OF BREWING: **Extract with specialty grains**
SPECIALTY/EXTRA EQUIPMENT: **None**
TARGET OG: **1.044**
TARGET FG: **1.012**
IBUs: **38**
TARGET ABV: **4.2%**
PROPER GLASS: **Pint**

SHOPPING LIST

1 tube White Labs WL004 Irish Stout yeast
5 ounces black roasted barley—milled
4 ounces Chocolate malt—milled

4 ounces Black Patent malt—milled

4 ounces CaraFoam malt—milled

2 pounds Pilsner liquid malt extract

12 ounces dry Dark malt extract

0.5 ounce Fuggles hop pellets

0.5 ounce East Kent Goldings hop pellets

0.5 ounce Fuggles hop pellets

½ Whirlfloc tablet

Makes about 2.5 gallons

PREP

▪ *Prepare your yeast (at least 3 hours before you brew):* Let the tube of Irish Ale yeast warm up to room temperature. This can be done the day before you brew as well.

STEEP/MASH

▪ Heat 3 quarts of water. Attach a thermometer and heat the brew pot until it reaches 160°F. Turn off the heat.

▪ Put the specialty grains (roasted barley and Chocolate, Black Patent, and CaraFoam malts) in the grain bag (tying the ends) and place it in the brewpot. Cover with a lid and rest for 30 minutes.

▪ Prepare your sparge water by heating 3 quarts of water to 170°F in a separate small pot.

SPARGE

▪ After 30 minutes, remove the grain bag from the brew pot. Put a large fine-mesh strainer over the brew pot. Put the grain bag in the strainer, open the grain bag, and slowly run the hot sparge water through it, making sure to cover all of the grains with water. Do not squeeze the grain bag! Remove the grain bag and discard.

▪ Add an additional 2 gallons of water to the brew pot.

Reheat your brew pot to 155°F; turn off the heat and add the Pilsner liquid malt extract. Gently stir to make sure the extract doesn't stick to the bottom of the pot. Add the dry Dark malt extract; be careful it doesn't clump.

THE BOIL

Bring the pot to a boil.

As soon as the pot comes to a boil, add your first hop addition, 0.5 ounce of Fuggles and 0.5 of East Kent Goldings hops, and set your timer for 60 minutes. The hops will dissolve immediately. Stir occasionally, skimming off the big solids with a slotted spoon and looking out for the dreaded boilover!

At 55 minutes (that is, with 5 minutes left in the boil), add your second hop addition, 0.5 ounce Fuggles hops. Also add the half tablet of Whirlfloc; stir to dissolve.

PITCH THE YEAST

Prepare your ice bath: In your sink or another vessel, prepare an ice bath to cool the beer down in.

Cool your wort: Remove the pot from the heat and place it into your ice bath. Place a sanitized thermometer in the wort and let cool until it reaches 70°F or below.

Clean your stuff: Sanitize anything that will come into contact with your beer.

Transfer your wort: Pour the wort through a sanitized strainer into a 3- or 5-gallon plastic fermenting bucket or through a sanitized strainer and funnel into a 3- or 5-gallon glass carboy.

Pitch your yeast: Shake your tube of yeast, sanitize the outside of the tube, crack it open, and throw all of its contents into the cooled wort in the fermenter.

PRIMARY FERMENTATION

■ Place an airtight lid equipped with your airlock (filled with vodka) and stopper on the plastic bucket or place the airlock and stopper on a glass carboy. Or use the blow-off tube method (see Chapter 2).

■ Keep the container in a dark and relatively cool place (ideal fermentation temperature for this style is between 65° and 68°F) for 7 to 10 days if using secondary or 12 to 14 days if not.

OPTION: SECONDARY

■ Transfer the beer from the primary fermenter to a 3- to 5-gallon bucket or glass carboy with a sanitized tube siphon. (Make sure to leave the sediment behind.)

■ Put an airlock on the secondary container and let the beer sit for at least 14 days.

■ Bottle for 14 days as described in Chapter 2. Then refrigerate and enjoy!

RULE BREAKERS AND TIPS

• You can substitute White Labs California Ale yeast for the Irish Ale yeast if you are fermenting at a much warmer or cooler temperature than called for in the recipe. This will help the beer attenuate better.

PROFESSIONAL BEERS TO ASPIRE TO

Guinness Extra Stout: Guinness Ltd., Dublin, Ireland. Perhaps the most beloved beer of all time. A classic dry Irish Stout. Best in Ireland; 6% ABV.

Murphy's Irish Stout: Murphy's Brewery Ireland Ltd., Cork, Ireland. A lighter and sweeter dry Stout. Flavors of roasted coffee and chocolate with some sourness toward the finish. Finishes fairly clean and dry with a light bitterness; 4.3% ABV.

Dragoons Dry Irish Stout: Moylan's Brewery, Novato, California. Dry, roasty, and incredibly rich in flavor, this Stout is made with a unique blend of imported hops and malted barley from the United Kingdom; 8% ABV.

MARCH HOMEBREW 2

Tropical Belgian-Style IPA

MAKE THIS BEER IF YOU LIKE: Tropical drinks. Cultures blending. American craft beer influence on Belgians. Complexity and bitterness. The thought of pineapple.

PAIRS WELL WITH: Seared scallops, Maine lobster rolls, fish tacos, spicy sushi, and coconut gelato.

STYLE AND BREWING NOTES

When we tasted our first Belgian IPA (Allagash's Hugh Malone) we danced a little jig because this style fulfilled a dream that we had. It was a beer style that offered the best of all worlds in one glass. We had actually kind of been doing this already in our beer drinking. We started making "beer cocktails" if you will: mixing this cloyingly malty and highly alcoholic beer with that super-hoppy smack-you-across-the-face hop bomb, just for something different. Through these tasting trials, we found that we loved a complex Belgian-style beer, with its high candy sweetness and estery fruitness, mixed with an IPA that provided a big hop backbone. It was kind of frowned on to mix craft beers at that time, but we liked the freedom and idea of being beer mixologists.

Our desire to mix styles is not unique; the craft beer world brings cultures together and new beer styles are constantly being invented and traditional beer styles are constantly evolving (some faster than others). The Belgian IPA is a new style of beer that is a result of Belgian brewers who loved big, hoppy American beers. They too wanted the best of both worlds and so invented a new beer style.

The inspiration for this beer came from one particular Belgian IPA, called Houblon Chouffe Dobbelen IPA Tripel, an amalgam if there ever was one. It's a super-dry and hoppy, grassy, and grainy beer that tastes like a third citrusy Tripel, a third earthy Saison, and a third West Coast IPA. We wanted to get a bit more fruit in the beer, so we dry-hopped with the beer-cult favorite aromatic hops of the hour: Amarillo and Citra, which offer big tropical notes. The result is a wonderfully hopped beer with definite Belgian characteristics and a big pineapple nose and finish. Pineapple is not the easiest thing to brew with, so we decided to evoke the pineapple note with these delicious aroma hops. You'll be surprised at how much the aroma from dry hopping can have you dreaming of tropical fruit and spring break beach days gone by.

BREW IT: TROPICAL BELGIAN-STYLE IPA

DIFFICULTY LEVEL: Devout

TYPE OF BREWING: Extract

SPECIALTY/EXTRA EQUIPMENT: Room in the fridge;
    large stainless-steel tea ball

TARGET OG: 1.079

TARGET FG: 1.010

IBUs: 33

TARGET ABV: 9.1%

PROPER GLASS: Teardrop or tulip

SHOPPING LIST

1 packet Wyeast Belgian Ardennes yeast 3522

1 pound Pilsner liquid malt extract

1 pound 2 ounces cane or beet sugar

0.4 ounce Columbus/Tomahawk hop leaves

0.2 ounce Columbus/Tomahawk hop leaves

3 pounds Pilsner liquid malt extract

0.5 ounce Czech Saaz hop leaves

½ Whirlfloc tablet

0.3 ounce Amarillo hop leaves—dry-hopped

0.3 ounce Citra hop leaves—dry-hopped

2 pineapples, skinned, cored, cubed, and crushed,
    optional

Makes about 2.5 gallons

PREP

■ *Prepare your yeast (at least 3 hours before you brew):* Crack your packet of Belgian Ardennes yeast and let it warm up to room temperature. You can do this the day before you brew as well.

STEEP/MASH

■ Heat 3.5 gallons of water. Attach a thermometer and heat the brew pot until it reaches 155°F. Turn off the heat.

■ Add 1 pound of the Pilsner liquid malt extract and the sugar; stir to dissolve.

THE BOIL

■ Bring the pot to a boil.

■ As soon as the pot comes to a boil, add your first hop addition, 0.4 ounce of Columbus/Tomahawk hops, and set your timer for 60 minutes. The hops will dissolve immediately. Stir occasionally, skimming off the big solids with a slotted spoon and looking out for the dreaded boilover!

■ At 40 minutes (that is, with 20 minutes left in the boil), add your second hop addition, 0.2 ounce of Columbus/Tomahawk hops.

■ At 45 minutes (that is, with 15 minutes left in the boil), carefully add the remaining 3 pounds of the Pilsner liquid malt extract and stir to dissolve, making sure it doesn't stick to the bottom of the pot. Bring the pot back up to a boil if the temperature has dropped. If the temperature drops below a boil, stop the clock until the boil begins again. When it does, add your third hop addition, the Czech Saaz hops.

- At 55 minutes (that is, with 5 minutes left in the boil), add the half tablet of Whirlfloc, stirring to dissolve.

PITCH THE YEAST

- *Prepare your ice bath:* In your sink or another vessel, prepare an ice bath to cool the beer down in.
- *Cool your wort:* Remove the pot from the heat and place it into your ice bath. Place a sanitized thermometer in the wort and let cool until it reaches 70°F or below.
- *Clean your stuff:* Sanitize anything that will come into contact with your beer.
- *Transfer your wort:* Pour the wort through a sanitized strainer into a 3- or 5-gallon plastic fermenting bucket or through a sanitized strainer and funnel into a 3- or 5-gallon glass carboy.
- *Pitch your yeast:* Shake your packet of prepared yeast, sanitize the outside, tear it open, and throw all of its contents into the cooled wort in the fermenter.

PRIMARY FERMENTATION

- Place an airtight lid equipped with your airlock (filled with vodka) and stopper on the plastic bucket or place the airlock and stopper on a glass carboy. Or use the blow-off tube method (see Chapter 2).
- Keep the container in a dark and relatively cool place (ideal fermentation temperature for this style is between 65° and 76°F) for 7 to 10 days.

SECONDARY AND DRY HOPPING

- Transfer the beer from the primary fermenter to a 3- to 5-gallon bucket or glass carboy with a sanitized tube siphon. (Make sure to leave the sediment behind.)
- *Prepare your dry hops:* Fill a sanitized stainless-steel tea ball with the Amarillo and Citra hops. Tie some dental floss to the tea ball and tie the other end of the floss to the fermentation container's handle (or MacGyver it with duct tape to the outside of the container) so you can remove the hops without affecting the lid's seal. Put an airlock on the secondary container.
- Place your fermenter in the refrigerator and lager the beer (ideally at around 36°F, although most refrigerators are set to 41°F) for 2 weeks. Be sure to taste the beer periodically and let your taste preference be the guide as to when it's time to pull out the hops.
- Bottle for 14 days as described in Chapter 2, filtering out the hops through a strainer when you transfer the beer into the bottling bucket. Then refrigerate and enjoy!

RULE BREAKERS AND TIPS

- Pineapples are in season in March. If you can't find the Amarillo or Citra hops, which are super popular right now and in high demand, or if you just want to up the tropical ante, dry-hop with some Simcoe or Summit hops and then throw two skinned, cored, cubed, and crushed pineapples into the fermenter during secondary for 7 to 10 days.
- An even easier shortcut to preparing fresh pineapple would be to take two 16-ounce cans of crushed pineapple (in 100% pure juice) and throw them into secondary for 7 to 10 days. Rack the beer off the pineapple for bottling and lager for 2 weeks in the fridge.

PROFESSIONAL BEERS TO ASPIRE TO

Houblon Chouffe Dobbelen IPA Tripel: Brasserie d'Achouffe, Achouffe, Belgium. Citrusy and bready, a hint of spice, with a big dose of hop bitterness; 9% ABV.

Hugh Malone: Allagash Brewing Co., Portland, Maine. A complex beer with complex malty notes, intense hop aromas, and a bitter, dry finish; 7.8% ABV

Le Freak: Green Flash Brewing Co., Vista California. A Belgian-style IPA that mixes American Imperial IPAs with Belgian Trippels. Dry-hopped and bottle-conditioned. Big bitterness and fresh fruit; 9.2% ABV

MARCH HOMEBREW 3

Bière de Mars

MAKE THIS BEER IF YOU LIKE: Farms in northern France. Springtime. A balanced maturity. Soft, bready notes. Tradition.

PAIRS WELL WITH: French onion soup, triple crème cheese, croque madame or monsieur.

STYLE AND BREWING NOTES

Bière de Garde is one of the oldest traditions in French beer making and, according to the *Oxford Companion to Beer* by Garrett Oliver, "the only widely acknowledged French contribution to specialty brewing." Originally a style from the Pas-de-Calais region of France, *Bière de Garde* literally translates as "beer for keeping." The style was originally brewed in the winter to store or keep, so there would be beer available for drinking in the months when it was too warm to brew.

Modern Bière de Garde is earthy and rustic, with a malty and sweet-but-not-too-sweet complexity. Herbal and woody notes dominate and a subtle spicy hop character balances on the finish. This style has several substyles, one of which is Bière de Mars, or March Beer. This particular style was meant to be offered in March, when the world was thawing out from a long dark winter. These beers are typically a little bit bigger on both the malts and hop notes and usually come in around 6% to 7% ABV.

Our Bière de Mars blends a few base malts to re-create a rustic farmhouse quality and uses a French Ale yeast from Wyeast that helps achieve that certain *je ne sais quoi* estery farmhouse funk. The result is a well-balanced, slightly spicy, super-dry elegant March Beer.

BREW IT: BIÈRE DE MARS
DIFFICULTY LEVEL: Devout
TYPE OF BREWING: Partial mash
SPECIALTY/EXTRA EQUIPMENT: None
TARGET OG: 1.066
TARGET FG: 1.012

IBUs: 20
TARGET ABV: 7.1%
PROPER GLASS: Tulip

SHOPPING LIST
1 packet Wyeast French Saison yeast 3711
5.1 ounces flaked barley
5.6 ounces Wheat malt—milled
6 ounces Special B malt—milled
4.5 pounds Pilsner liquid malt extract
0.5 ounce German Hallertauer hop pellets
0.3 ounce French Strisselspalt hop pellets

0.3 ounce French Strisselspalt hop pellets

3 ounces cane or beet sugar or Homemade Belgian
Candi Sugar (page 86)

Makes about 2.5 gallons

PREP

■ *Prepare your yeast (at least 3 hours before you brew):* Crack your packet of French Saison yeast and let it warm up to room temperature. You can do this the day before you brew as well.

STEEP/MASH

■ Heat 1.5 quarts of water. Attach a thermometer and heat the brew pot until it reaches 160°F. Turn off the heat.

■ Put the specialty grains (flaked barely and Wheat and Special B malts) in the grain bag (tying the ends) and place it in the brew pot. Cover with a lid, and maintain a temperature of 152° to 154°F for 60 minutes. You may have to turn the heat on periodically to keep the temperature.

■ Prepare your sparge water by heating 4 quarts of water to 170°F in a separate small pot.

SPARGE

■ After 60 minutes, remove the grain bag from the brew pot. Put a large fine-mesh strainer over the brew pot. Put the grain bag in the strainer, open the grain bag, and slowly run the hot sparge water through it, making sure to cover all of the grains with water. Do not squeeze the grain bag! Remove the grain bag and discard.

■ Add an additional 1.75 gallons of room-temperature water to the brew pot. Reheat your brew pot water to 155°F; turn off the heat and add the Pilsner liquid malt extract. Gently stir to make sure the extract doesn't stick to the bottom of the pot.

THE BOIL

■ Bring the pot to a boil.

■ As soon as the pot comes to a boil, add your first hop addition, the Hallertauer hops, and set your timer for 60 minutes. The hops will dissolve immediately. Stir occasionally, skimming off the big solids with a slotted spoon and looking out for the dreaded boilover!

■ At 30 minutes (that is, with 30 minutes left in the boil), add your second hop addition, 0.3 ounce of Strisslespalt hops.

■ At 55 minutes (that is, with 5 minutes left in the boil), add your third hop addition, the remaining 0.3 ounce Strisselespalt hops.

■ At flameout (that is, when the boil has finished and you've turned off the heat), add the sugar; stir to dissolve.

PITCH THE YEAST

■ *Prepare your ice bath:* In your sink or another vessel, prepare an ice bath to cool the beer down in.

■ *Cool your wort:* Remove the pot from the heat and place it into your ice bath. Place a sanitized thermometer in the wort and let cool until it reaches 70°F or below.

■ *Clean your stuff:* Sanitize anything that will come into contact with your beer.

■ *Transfer your wort:* Pour the wort through a sanitized strainer into a 3- or 5-gallon plastic fermenting bucket or through a sanitized strainer and funnel into a 3- or 5-gallon glass carboy.

■ *Pitch your yeast:* Shake your packet of prepared yeast, sanitize the outside, tear it open, and throw all of its contents into the cooled wort in the fermenter.

PRIMARY FERMENTATION

■ Place an airtight lid equipped with your airlock (filled with vodka) and stopper on the plastic bucket or place the airlock and stopper on a glass carboy. Or use the blow-off tube method (see Chapter 2).

- Keep the container in a dark and relatively cool place (ideal fermentation temperature for this style is between 65° and 77°F) for 2 weeks.

NECESSARY: SECONDARY

- This highly attenuated, aged beer style needs to be in a secondary vessel—for a while! Transferring the beer off the yeast and into a new fermenter will greatly improve the flavors of your beer.
- Transfer the beer from the primary fermenter to a 3- to 5-gallon bucket or glass carboy with a sanitized tube siphon. (Make sure to leave the sediment behind.)
- Put an airlock on the secondary container and let the beer sit for at least 1 month.
- Bottle for 2 to 3 months at lagering temperatures (or in the fridge) as described in Chapter 2. Then open and enjoy! This beer hits its prime at 6 months.

RULE BREAKERS AND TIPS

- You can skip secondary in the bucket/carboy if you wish and just prime, rack, and bottle the Bière de Mars all in one shot right after the primary fermentation. If you do this, then you should store your bottles for about 3 months of bottle conditioning and maturation in a nice warm spot (73° to 77°F). Cool the beer down to 50°F to serve.
- You can also use White Labs French Ale yeast WLP072 or Wyeast European Ale yeast 1338 as a substitute if the other yeast isn't available.

PROFESSIONAL BEERS TO ASPIRE TO

LA-31 Bière de Mars: Bayou Teche Brewery, Arnaudville, Louisiana. Notes of biscuit malt with herbaceous hops and a gentle bitter finish; 5% ABV.

Bière de Mars: Jolly Pumpkin Artisan Ales, Dexter, Michigan. Sweet caramel notes with a sour punch. Hints of cherry, plum, oak, and vanilla with a tart, spicy finish; 7% ABV.

Lips of Faith Bière de Mars: New Belgium Brewing Co., Ft. Collins, Colorado. Earthy flavors with notes of mango and lemon verbena. Brewed with barley, oats, and wheat and bottle-conditioned; 6.2% ABV.

TO EAT

Dry Irish Stout Oatmeal Cookies

1 (12-ounce) bottle Dry Irish Stout plus ½ cup for
    soaking raisins

1½ teaspoons honey

1 cup raisins

¼ cup unsalted butter, room temperature

1 cup sugar

2 eggs

1¾ cups all-purpose flour

1 teaspoon baking soda

1½ teaspoons salt

1 teaspoon cinnamon

2 cups old-fashioned rolled oats

Makes 2 dozen cookies

Place the Stout and honey in a small saucepan and bring to a low boil and boil until reduced to 6 tablespoons, 30 to 40 minutes.

Preheat the oven to 400°F. Line cookie sheets with parchment paper.

In a small bowl, combine raisins with ½ cup of Stout. Microwave on high for 30 seconds. Set aside to soak.

In a large bowl, cream the butter and sugar. Add the beer reduction. Add eggs, one at a time, beating until incorporated. In another large bowl, combine flour, baking soda, salt, and cinnamon. Slowly add the dry ingredients to the creamed mixture; combine thoroughly. Drain the raisins and fold them into the dough, along with the rolled oats.

Roll the dough into large balls about the size of a tablespoon and place them on the prepared cookie sheets, about 4 inches apart. Press each ball to flatten slightly. Bake 10 to 15 minutes, or until lightly browned.

Cool on a cooling rack, then serve.

Variation: Make ice cream sandwiches using your favorite ice cream. Makes 1 dozen sandwiches.

Dip the cookies into a glass of Dry Irish Stout!

April

TAXES ○ FLOWERS ○ DANDELION GREENS ○
MORELS ○ CHOCOLATE BUNNIES ○ APRIL SHOWERS

Your April Homebrew

SAISON CLASSIQUE AVEC MIELE: **Earth, citrus, and pepper notes
with a touch of honey**

ROSEMARY LAUREL SAVORY SAISON: **Savory, herbaceous notes with
a rustic backbone**

DARK AND STORMY WITBIER: **April Fools! A Black White Ale
that's spicy, malty, and grainy with a hint of tangerine**

To Eat

Mussels Steamed in Classique Saison avec Miele

When April hits, spring is in full effect, the daisies and sweet peas
are blooming. We love the showers and thunderstorms that
April brings. A true chance to hunker down with a book and a satisfying beer. April also means tax day is here, which warrants quite a bit
of beer drinking itself for obvious reasons. What most thrills us about

April, however, is the fact that many breweries' seasonal Saisons are released in this month. It's a time of earthy and complex, fresh and grassy beers. It's starting to get warm during the day, but there's still quite a chill at night. It's a time when we want to drink a light, dry, crisp, but complex beer.

Our first recipe is a classic Saison like you'd get in Belgium, made with buckwheat honey. The second is also a Saison (we do love us some Saison), this time flavored with the herbs of spring; rosemary and laurel bring an interesting savory feeling to the beer. And finally our third beer of the month is a bit of an oxymoron. It is a Black Witbier, or a Black White Ale; we used some dark malts and some dark rum as an homage to the famous Dark and Stormy classic cocktail!

Saison Classique avec Miele

MAKE THIS BEER IF YOU LIKE: Sleeping in a farmhouse. Lemon and pepper. Idyllic countryside settings. Complex flavors.

PAIRS WELL WITH: Scallops in a lemon butter caper sauce, arugula and Parmesan salad, shrimp garnished with cilantro, and grilled artichokes.

STYLE AND BREWING NOTES

Saisons are often called Farmhouse Ales, due to their rustic heritage. The farmers of Wallonia in French-speaking Belgium would brew this Ale with whatever was in season (*saison* translates to "season"), so traditionally Saisons vary greatly in their recipes. Barley, wheat, oats, spelt, buckwheat, honey, sugar, dried orange peel, and different spices like black pepper and coriander have all been used. Sort of a kitchen sink approach for rustic farmers in Belgium. The focus of this beer, however, is the yeast. The Saison yeast has a bold peppery note that makes the beer a perfect pairing for most foods. The yeast is often thought of as a cousin to red wine yeast and can handle a very high fermentation temperature, around 85° to above 90°F.

We rank Saisons among our favorite styles of beer. It is often our go-to style if we're attending a friend's dinner party without knowing the menu. Saisons have a blend of citrus and pepper with an earthy, dry, somewhat tart finish. When you think of most foods, lemon and pepper go well with just about anything you can put on a plate, and the dryness of the Saison can handle most dishes without interfering with the flavors. The first Saison we had was Saison DuPont, and it often stands as the litmus test for the style. It is direct from Belgium, and the brewery produces brews deeply connected to the history of the Farmhouse beers. It is still a beer we use in our beer pairing dinners and to impress wine-only drinkers. Our recipe incorporates honey for a touch of the sweet.

BREW IT: SAISON CLASSIQUE AVEC MIELE

DIFFICULTY LEVEL: Devout

TYPE OF BREWING: Extract with specialty grains

SPECIALTY/EXTRA EQUIPMENT: None

TARGET OG: 1.062

TARGET FG: 1.010

IBUs: 30

TARGET ABV: 6.9%

PROPER GLASS: Tulip

SHOPPING LIST

1 packet Wyeast Belgian Saison yeast 3724

4 ounces CaraMunich malt—milled

8 ounces Caravienne malt—milled

2 pounds Pilsner liquid malt extract

1 pound Amber dry malt extract

6 ounces Wheat dry malt extract

0.7 ounce Styrian Goldings hop pellets

0.25 ounce East Kent Goldings hop pellets

0.25 ounce Styrian Goldings hop pellets

0.25 ounce coriander seeds, lightly crushed

½ Whirlfloc tablet

4 ounces honey—buckwheat, if possible

4 ounces granulated sugar

Makes about 2.5 gallons

PREP

- *Prepare your yeast (at least 3 hours before you brew):* Crack your packet of Belgian Saison yeast and let it warm up to room temperature. You can do this the day before you brew as well.

STEEP/MASH

- Heat 3 quarts of water. Attach a thermometer and heat the brew pot until it reaches 160°F. Turn off the heat.
- Put the specialty grains (CaraMunich and Caravienne malts) in the grain bag (tying the ends) and place it in the brew pot. Cover with a lid, and rest for 30 minutes.
- Prepare your sparge water by heating 3 quarts of water to 170°F in a separate small pot.

SPARGE

- After 30 minutes, remove the grain bag from the brew pot. Put a large fine-mesh strainer over the brew pot. Put the grain bag in the strainer, open the grain bag, and slowly run the hot sparge water through it, making sure to cover all of the grains with water. Do not squeeze the grain bag! Remove the grain bag and discard.
- Add an additional 2 gallons of water to the brew pot.

Reheat your brew pot to 155°F; turn off the heat and add the Pilsner liquid malt extract. Gently stir to make sure the extract doesn't stick to the bottom of the pot. Add the Amber and Wheat dry malt extracts; be careful they don't clump.

THE BOIL

Bring the pot to a boil.

As soon as the pot comes to a boil, add your first hop addition, 0.7 ounce Styrian Goldings hops, and set your timer for 60 minutes. The hops will dissolve immediately. Stir occasionally, skimming off the big solids with a slotted spoon and looking out for the dreaded boilover!

At 45 minutes (that is, with 15 minutes left in the boil), add your second hop addition, the East Kent Goldings hops.

At 55 minutes (that is, with 5 minutes left in the boil), add your third hop addition, the remaining 0.25 ounce Styrian Goldings hops. Also add the coriander seeds and the half tablet of Whirlfloc; stir to dissolve.

At flameout (that is, at the end of the boil when you turn off the heat), add the honey and sugar. Be sure to stir well, so it doesn't stick to the bottom of the pot.

PITCH THE YEAST

Prepare your ice bath: In your sink or another vessel, prepare an ice bath to cool the beer down in.

Cool your wort: Remove the pot from the heat and place it into your ice bath. Place a sanitized thermometer in the wort and let cool until it reaches 70°F or below.

Clean your stuff: Sanitize anything that will come into contact with your beer.

Transfer your wort: Pour the wort through a sanitized strainer into a 3- or 5-gallon plastic fermenting bucket or through a sanitized strainer and funnel into a 3- or 5-gallon glass carboy.

- *Pitch your yeast*: Shake your packet of prepared yeast, sanitize the outside, tear it open, and throw all of its contents into the cooled wort in the fermenter

PRIMARY FERMENTATION

- Place an airtight lid equipped with your airlock (filled with vodka) and stopper on the plastic bucket or place the airlock and stopper on a glass carboy. Or use the blow-off tube method (see Chapter 2).
- Keep the container in a dark and relatively cool place (ideal fermentation temperature for this style is between 70° and 95°F) for 7 to 10 days if using secondary or for 12 to 14 days if not. You may need to experiment with fermenting at higher temperatures.

OPTION: SECONDARY

- Transfer the beer from the primary fermenter to a 3- to 5-gallon bucket or glass carboy with a sanitized tube siphon. (Make sure to leave the sediment behind.)
- Put an airlock on the secondary container and let the beer sit for at least 14days.
- Bottle for 14 days as described in Chapter 2. Then refrigerate and enjoy!

RULE BREAKERS AND TIPS

- Not so much a rule breaker, but a note that Saison yeast works well at warm temperatures up to 80° to 90°F. You may want to experiment with fermenting this beer in a warm room or during the summer.

PROFESSIONAL BEERS TO ASPIRE TO

Saison DuPont: Brasserie DuPont, Tourpes-Leuze, Belgium. The most famous and often most favorite Belgian Saison or Farmhouse

Ale. Dry and peppery, with a touch of earthy sourness and citrus; 6.5% ABV.

Hennepin: Brewery Ommegang, Cooperstown, New York. Earthy, dry, nutty, and grassy. Good hop presence with more bitter than sweet notes; 7.5% ABV.

Fantôme Saison: Brasserie Fantôme, Soy, Belgium. Fruity, complex Saison beer from the Ardennes Forest from a small farmhouse brewery. Some drinkers call this beer the "Nectar of the Gods"; 8% ABV.

APRIL HOMEBREW 2

Rosemary Laurel Savory Saison

MAKE THIS BEER IF YOU LIKE: Variations on a theme. Savory drinks. Rustic aromatics. Complex beers.

PAIRS WELL WITH: Rosemary rubbed goat cheese, herb-roasted chicken, Gorgonzola cream sauce, and pizza.

STYLE AND BREWING NOTES

Beer doesn't have to be refreshing or bitter or sweet; it can act like a sauce to your food, an ingredient in the dinner. Rosemary and bay leaf are fantastic with big rustic dishes, and so we wanted to create a recipe that skewed savory. After all, Saisons are often called Farmhouse Ales, and the aroma of rosemary and bay leaf evokes that scenery.

Laurel, or bay leaf, is best known for crowning Olympians in ancient Greece. Today we use it primarily to flavor soups. Oh, how the mighty laurel has fallen. Our soup will be the wort in this recipe, and the bay will add a touch of a bitter, herbaceous note. Rosemary is an evergreen shrub related to mint that is often used in grand, rustic meat dishes. It is one of our most favorite herbs, with an elegant pine-like aroma, strong slightly bitter flavor, and impressive resilience in all weather. California, with its drought issues, is home to many rosemary bushes, which require very little care and watering. There are nights in L.A. when your walks are filled with the scent of rosemary. The aromas of this Saison remind us of those evenings.

BREW IT: ROSEMARY LAUREL SAVORY SAISON

DIFFICULTY LEVEL: Devout

TYPE OF BREWING: Extract with specialty grains

SPECIALTY/EXTRA EQUIPMENT: None

TARGET OG: 1.062

TARGET FG: 1.010

IBUs: 30

TARGET ABV: 6.9%

PROPER GLASS: Tulip

SHOPPING LIST

1 packet Wyeast Belgian Saison yeast 3724

4 ounces CaraMunich malt—milled

8 ounces Caravienne malt—milled

2 pounds Pilsner liquid malt extract

1 pound Amber dry malt extract

6 ounces Wheat dry malt extract

0.7 ounce Styrian Goldings hop pellets

0.25 ounce East Kent Goldings hop pellets

0.25 ounce Styrian Goldings hop pellets

0.25 ounce coriander seeds, lightly crushed

½ Whirlfloc tablet

4 ounces honey, buckwheat if possible

4 ounces granulated sugar

2 dried bay leaves

10–12 fresh rosemary leaves (about 1 sprig)

Makes about 2.5 gallons

PREP

■ *Prepare your yeast (at least 3 hours before you brew):* Crack your packet of Belgian Saison yeast and let it warm up to room temperature. You can do this the day before you brew as well.

STEEP/MASH

■ Heat 3 quarts of water. Attach a thermometer and heat the brew pot until it reaches 160°F. Turn off the heat.

■ Put the specialty grains (CaraMunich and Caravienne malts) in the grain bag (tying the ends) and place it in the brew pot. Cover with a lid and rest for 30 minutes.

■ Prepare your sparge water by heating 3 quarts of water to 170°F in a separate small pot.

SPARGE

■ After 30 minutes, remove the grain bag from the brew pot. Put a large fine-mesh strainer over the brew pot. Put the grain bag in the strainer, open the grain bag, and slowly run the hot sparge water through it, making sure to cover all of the grains with water. Do not squeeze the grain bag! Remove the grain bag and discard.

■ Add an additional 2 gallons of water to the brew pot.

■ Reheat your brew pot to 155°F; turn off the heat and add the Pilsner liquid malt extract. Gently stir to make sure the extract doesn't stick to the bottom of the pot. Add the Amber and Wheat dry malt extracts; be careful they don't clump.

THE BOIL

- Bring the pot to a boil.

- As soon as the pot comes to a boil, add your first hop addition, 0.7 ounce Styrian Goldings hops, and set your timer for 60 minutes. The hops will dissolve immediately. Stir occasionally, skimming off the big solids with a slotted spoon and looking out for the dreaded boilover!

- At 45 minutes (that is, with 15 minutes left in the boil), add your second hop addition, the East Kent Goldings hops.

- At 55 minutes (that is, with 5 minutes left in the boil), add your third hop addition, the remaining 0.25 ounce of Styrian Goldings hops. Also add the coriander seeds and the half tablet of Whirlfloc; stir to dissolve.

- At flameout (that is, at the end of the boil when you turn off the heat), add the honey, sugar, bay leaf, and rosemary. Be sure to stir well, so the honey doesn't stick to the bottom of the pot.

PITCH THE YEAST

- *Prepare your ice bath:* In your sink or another vessel, prepare an ice bath to cool the beer down in.

- *Cool your wort:* Remove the pot from the heat and place it into your ice bath. Place a sanitized thermometer in the wort and let cool until it reaches 70°F or below.

- *Clean your stuff:* Sanitize anything that will come into contact with your beer.

- *Transfer your wort:* Pour the wort through a sanitized strainer into a 3- or 5-gallon plastic fermenting bucket or through a sanitized strainer and funnel into a 3- or 5-gallon glass carboy.

- *Pitch your yeast:* Shake your packet of prepared yeast, sanitize the outside, tear it open, and throw all of its contents into the cooled wort in the fermenter.

PRIMARY FERMENTATION

- Place an airtight lid equipped with your airlock (filled with vodka) and stopper on the plastic bucket or place the airlock and stopper on a glass carboy. Or use the blow-off tube method (see Chapter 2).

- Keep the container in a dark and relatively cool place (ideal fermentation temperature for this style is between 70° and 95°F) for 7 to 10 days if using secondary or for 12 to 14 days if not. You may need to experiment with fermenting at higher temperatures.

RECOMMENDED: SECONDARY

- Transfer the beer from the primary fermenter to a 3- to 5-gallon bucket or glass carboy with a sanitized tube siphon. (Make sure to leave the sediment behind.)

- Put an airlock on the secondary container and let the beer sit for at least 14 days.

- Bottle for 14 days as described in Chapter 2. Then refrigerate and enjoy!

RULE BREAKERS AND TIPS

- Not so much a rule breaker, but note that Saison yeast works well at warm temperatures up to 80° to 90°F. You may want to experiment with fermenting this beer in a warm room or during the summer.

- Dried rosemary isn't quite the same as fresh, but if it's all you have, you can add 1 teaspoon at flameout.

- Experiment with the rosemary and bay leaf amounts until you get the herbaceousness you desire.

PROFESSIONAL BEERS TO ASPIRE TO

Trip XI: New Belgium Brewing Co., Fort Collins, Colorado, and Elysian Brewing Co., Seattle, Washington. Brewed with rosemary and sage. Flavors of citrus and earth with a hint of fruit and bread. Sage and rosemary on the finish; 8.5% ABV.

Saison Athene: Saint Somewhere Brewing Co., Tarpon Springs, Florida. A bottle-conditioned Saison brewed with chamomile, fresh rosemary, and black pepper. Super complex with a touch of funk from the addition of a wild yeast; 7.5% ABV.

Utah Sage Saison: Epic Brewing Co., Salt Lake City, Utah. Big aromas of rosemary, thyme, and sage. Finishes with earthy hops; 7.6% ABV.

Dark and Stormy Witbier

BREW THIS BEER IF YOU LIKE: Contradiction. Practical jokes. Nina Simone's voice. Rainy days. Dark rum. Sailors' drinks.

PAIRS WELL WITH: Smoked pork belly, charcuterie, truffled mac and cheese, and miso-glazed sea bass.

STYLE AND BREWING NOTES

We call this beer a Black White Ale. Meaning, it's a Belgian-style Witbier made with dark malts. Now that's not a real style. It's actually inspired by a beer that we can't get anymore. Until recently, the Bruery, one of our favorite breweries out of Southern California, made a sublime beer called Black Orchard, which we called a Black Wit, but which they described as an "unfiltered, Belgian-style black wheat beer brewed with chamomile, coriander and citrus." Man, that beer was good. Well, for whatever reason, they stopped making it. Sadly, that's sometimes how it goes in the craft beer world. Nothing lasts forever. But that's one of the great advantages of homebrewing. If you can't get it, brew it! So we did. We came up with this recipe, which is quite

different from Black Orchard. We could never claim to be able to imi-
tate that beer, but ours hits the spot in the way that the Bruery's beer
did. Our Dark and Stormy Wit has a touch of smoke from the Carafa
malt, a touch of rustic Farmhouse charm from the yeast, and a pop of
citrus and spice from the tangerines and coriander. As a final little tip
of the hat to the famous cocktail of the same name, we've added a
bit of dark rum in the secondary vessel. You can take that or leave it.
We really liked it, but you can have a perfectly delicious Dark and
Stormy Witbier without it.

BREW IT: DARK AND STORMY WITBIER

DIFFICULTY LEVEL: Devout

TYPE OF BREWING: Partial mash with specialty
grains

SPECIALTY/EXTRA EQUIPMENT: None

TARGET OG: 1.048

TARGET FG: 1.010

IBUs: 20

TARGET ABV: 5%

PROPER GLASS: Teardrop or tulip

SHOPPING LIST

1 tube White Labs Belgian Wit Ale yeast
WLP400

4 ounces roasted barley—milled

1 ounce Carafa malt—milled

2 ounces Carapils malt—milled

4 ounces CaraWheat malt—milled

2.5 pounds Wheat liquid malt extract (typically a
blend of Wheat and Pale malts; check the
ingredients when you purchase)

8 ounces Pilsner liquid malt extract

0.4 ounce Tettnang hop pellets

0.2 ounce Saaz hop pellets

0.2 ounce Saaz hop pellets

0.75 ounce fresh tangerine zest (no pith)

0.2 ounce coriander seeds—lightly crushed

4 ounces dark or caramelized honey

2–6 ounces of black rum (Gosling Black Seal or
   Cruzan Black Strap), optional

Makes about 2.5 gallons

PREP

■ *Prepare your yeast (at least 3 hours before you brew):* Let the tube of Belgian Wit Ale yeast warm up to room temperature.

STEEP/MASH

■ Heat 3 quarts of water. Attach a thermometer and heat the brew pot until it reaches 160°F. Turn off the heat.

■ Put the specialty grains (roasted barley, Carafa, Carapils, and Cara-Wheat malts) in the grain bag (tying the ends) and place it in the brew pot. Cover with a lid and rest for 30 minutes.

■ Prepare your sparge water by heating 3 quarts of water to 170°F in a separate small pot.

SPARGE

■ After 30 minutes, remove the grain bag from the brew pot. Put a large fine-mesh strainer over the brew pot. Put the grain bag in the strainer, open the grain bag, and slowly run the hot sparge water through it, making sure to cover all of the grains with water. Do not squeeze the grain bag! Remove the grain bag and discard.

■ Add an additional 2 gallons of water to the brew pot.

■ Reheat your brew pot to 155°F; turn off the heat and add the Wheat and Pilsner liquid malt extracts. Gently stir to make sure the extracts don't stick to the bottom of the pot.

THE BOIL

- Bring the pot to the heat and bring the water to a boil.
- As soon as the pot comes to a boil, add your first hop addition, the Tettnang hops and 0.2 ounce of the Saaz hops, and set your timer for 60 minutes. The hops will dissolve immediately. Stir occasionally, skimming off the big solids with a slotted spoon and looking out for the dreaded boilover!
- At 55 minutes (that is, with 5 minutes left in the boil), add your second hop addition, the remaining 0.2 ounce of Saaz hops. Also add the tangerine zest and coriander seeds.
- At flameout (that is, when the boil is finished and you turn off the heat), add the honey. Be sure to stir well, so it doesn't stick to the bottom of the pot.

PITCH THE YEAST

- *Prepare your ice bath:* In your sink or another vessel, prepare an ice bath to cool the beer down in.
- *Cool your wort:* Remove the pot from the heat and place it into your ice bath. Place a sanitized thermometer in the wort and let cool until it reaches 70°F or below.
- *Clean your stuff:* Sanitize anything that will come into contact with your beer.
- *Transfer your wort:* Pour the wort through a sanitized strainer into a 3- or 5-gallon plastic fermenting bucket or through a sanitized strainer and funnel into a 3- or 5-gallon glass carboy.
- *Pitch your yeast:* Shake your tube of yeast, sanitize the outside of the tube, crack it open, and throw all of its contents into the cooled wort in the fermenter.

PRIMARY FERMENTATION

- Place an airtight lid equipped with your airlock (filled with vodka) and stopper on the plastic bucket or place the airlock and stopper on a glass carboy. Or use the blow-off tube method (see Chapter 2).

- Keep the container in a dark and relatively cool place (ideal fermentation temperature for this style is between 67° and 74°F) for 7 to 10 days.

SECONDARY AND RUM ADDITION

- Transfer the beer from the primary fermenter to a 3- to 5-gallon bucket or glass carboy with a sanitized tube siphon. (Make sure to leave the sediment behind.)

- Slowly add the dark rum to the secondary container, starting with a scant 2 ounces and continuing to add in 1-ounce increments—stirring and tasting in between (with a spoon that has been sanitized between each taste)—until you get the taste you like. The beer should be the primary flavor of this brew, the citrus and coriander the secondary flavors, and the rum should come in third.

- Put an airlock on the secondary container and let the beer sit for 14 days.

- Bottle for 14 days as described in Chapter 2. Then refrigerate and enjoy!

RULE BREAKERS AND TIPS

- This *beer* is a rule breaker in and of itself.
- While you're waiting for this beer to brew (or ferment), make a Dark and Stormy cocktail. Put ice in a 12-ounce rocks glass, pour 2 ounces of Goslings dark rum into the glass, squeeze the juice from a ¼ lime wedge into the glass, and drop the wedge in. Add ginger beer to top off, give it a stir, garnish with another lime, and drink. This takes the edge off of waiting for the beer to be ready!

Noire de Chambly: Unibroue, Chambly, Canada. Aromas of wood, smoke, coffee, and licorice. Flavors of roasted grains and spice like cloves, green anise, and mint. Finishes with a hint of chocolate; 6. 2% ABV.

Leffe Brune: Abbaye de Leffe, Dinant, Belgium. Sweet malty notes with a hint of brown sugar and dark fruit. A spicy yeast creates a nice complexity; 6.5% ABV.

Black Velvet Black Witbier: Upstream Brewing Co., Omaha, Nebraska. Carefully spiced with sweet orange, lemon peel, coriander, lemongrass, and rose hips; 5.5% ABV.

TO EAT

Mussels Steamed in Classique Saison avec Miele

½ stick (¼ cup) unsalted butter

4 shallots, finely chopped

1 small onion, chopped (1 cup)

3 garlic cloves, finely chopped

1 tablespoon fresh thyme, chopped

2 small bay leaves

Large pinch of salt

2 cups Classique Saison avec Miele (pour beer slowly
   at an angle to measure, do not measure foam)

2 pounds mussels, scrubbed and debearded

1 teaspoon Dijon mustard

2 tablespoons whipping cream

¼ cup chopped fresh flat-leaf parsley

Serves 4

In a wide 5- to 6-quart heavy pot, heat the butter over medium-high heat until the foam subsides, then cook shallots, onion, garlic, thyme, bay leaves, and salt, stirring occasionally, until softened, about 4 minutes.

Add the beer and bring everything just to a boil. Add the mussels and cook, covered, stirring and shaking occasionally, until the mussels open wide, 4 to 6 minutes. Transfer the mussels to a deep serving platter. (Discard any little bastard mussels that remain unopened.)

Remove pot from the heat. Stir together the mustard and cream in a small bowl, then add mixture along with the parsley to the hot broth in the pot and whisk until combined. Discard the bay leaves. Pour the sauce over mussels and serve with warm freshly baked crusty bread.

Variation: Try the same recipe with the Rosemary Laurel Savory Saison.

Pair with a glass of Saison Classique avec Miele or Rosemary Laurel Savory Saison!

FOURTEEN

May

SERIOUS "YOU'RE ALL GROWN UP" BREWING ○ HORSE
RACES ○ MOTHER'S DAY ○ LILY OF THE VALLEY ○
THE MAY POLE (THAT'S WHAT SHE SAID!)

Your May Homebrew

BRANDIED APRICOT CREAM ALE: **Smooth and crisp "fancy lawn-mower beer" with a little kick.**

DECADENT DUNKELWEIZEN: **Chocolate banana nut bread in a glass. Hint of cloves.**

FRUITY FAUX LAMBIC: **Funky, sour, acidic, and fruity homage to Belgium's Senne Valley.**

To Eat

Roast Duck with Sour Cherry Faux Lambic Sauce

We've reached the last month of our brewing journey
May. And we're going to get serious with this brewi
This month we're going to make the commitment and conce
brewing all-grain. Now don't freak out, don't cry. It's real

hard. In fact, it's pretty easy now that you've been brewing all year. All-grain brewing is a natural progression from extract and partial-mash brewing. In fact, once you cross over, it's kind of difficult for some brewers to go back. Some purists (not us) say that if you're not brewing all-grain, then you're not really a brewer. Being able to say that you're an all-grain brewer is like being able to say that you own instead of rent. The look you get at the homebrew supply store: "Oh . . . you're all-grain, you must be serious."

We must admit, there is a certain amount of extra gratification that comes from actually making beer from nothing more than a pile of grains and some hops, water, and yeast. It opens your mind to the simple wonder that is beer. All-grain brewing helps you understand beer on the most fundamental levels. Did we mention that all-grain brewing is also the least expensive way to brew? Just sayin'.

How Is All-Grain Different from Extract Brewing?

 In all-grain brewing, you don't need to rehydrate the malt extract to get the fermentable sugars in your beer. You're actually doing that step yourself by an additional process called "mashing." The mash is the thick, oatmealy mixture of water and grains. And mashing is the process of letting the water and grains sit at a certain temperature (usually 148° to 154°F) for an amount of time (usually 60 to 90 minutes), during which enzymes that exist naturally in the grain convert the starch in the grains into fermentable sugars. Then the grains are strained and rinsed (sparged), leaving behind the sweet liquidy goodness that you know from your extract and partial-mash brewing as wort. After that you start your boil, do your hop and other additions, cool, and ferment exactly the same way as you do in extract brewing. See, that's not so hard.

It's in the Bag! BIAB

 The BIAB, or the brew-in-a-bag, method is the easiest and cheapest way that we've found to brew all-grain recipes. It's a great baby step into the realm of all-grain for extract brewers. You don't even have to sparge. Compared with other all-grain methods, your volumes are smaller. And it's the equivalent of one-pot cooking in the beer world: one pot to brew in, one pot to clean up. You don't have to buy any additional equipment; the only thing you need is a little extra time and vigilance and a teeny, tiny bit more know-how. Here's how to do it.

THE BREW-IN-A-BAG ALL-GRAIN BREWING METHOD

1. Fill your brew pot with 4 gallons of water. Place it over high heat and bring the water to about 165°F. (In our recipes, we want our mash temperature to be either 150° or 152°F. The temperature will drop to that level when we add our grains.)

2. Fill a 24-by-24-inch grain bag with your milled grains. Turn off the heat and slowly lower the grain bag into the water. Wrap the ends of the bag around the outside of the brew pot and secure the bag to the pot with several metal binder clips (which you can get at any office supply store) or a short Bungee cord with hooks on each end. Stir the grains in the bag gently to make sure that all the grains have been wetted and that there aren't any dry pockets of malt, called "dough balls."

3. Put the lid on the pot and let the mash do its thing for the amount of time (60 to 90 minutes) and at the temperature (148° to 154°F) called for in the recipe. This might require a little bit of noodling and adjusting—turning the heat on and off—to keep the temperature constant. It shouldn't be too strenuous because the covered pot keeps the temperature pretty consistent. Don't worry, you haven't blown it if the temperature drops a couple of degrees below the

optimum for a couple of minutes. Just keep an eye on it and adjust the temperature as necessary throughout the hour.

4. After the mash time required in the recipe is done, take the lid off of the pot, remove the clips or Bungee from the grain bag (holding on to it so the grains don't get loose in the liquid) and slowly lift the grain bag out of the wort. Put a large fine-mesh strainer on top of the brew pot and set the grain bag in the strainer. Let the hot wort drain from the grain bag (which counts as the lautering process, for you beer geeks out there) for 5 to 10 minutes; then discard the grain bag and grains.

5. Now it's time to turn the heat back on and bring the wort to a boil. Make your hop and other additions and cool, ferment, and bottle exactly the same as you do in extract brewing.

Congratulations, you all-grain brewer you!

Tips

1. Get a thermometer that can work outside the pot, so you don't have to constantly lift the lid to take a temperature reading.

2. Put a bucket or a trash bag near you as you end your mash time. Then when you discard the grain bag, you can do it easily instead of racing across the kitchen, dripping very sticky wort as you try to find a place to dispose of it; you probably won't want the spent grains in your normal kitchen trash.

Brandied Apricot Cream Ale

BREW THIS BEER IF YOU LIKE: Lack of lactose. Light beer. A touch of fruit. Corniness.

PAIRS WELL WITH: Eggs Benedict, raw oysters, grilled salmon, and mandarin cake.

STYLE AND BREWING NOTES

The name of this Ale is actually quite deceiving. There's no cream in this beer. It's a style that arose from the light-bodied American Lagers. Craft brewers wanted to make a light- to medium-bodied golden beer that was low in bitterness, with complex, biscuit malts, and a soft, delicate (some say creamy) finish. Oh, and they also wanted a beer that was *good*, instead of the watered-down beer that many of us grew up with. It's a perfect springtime thirst quencher.

This particular Cream Ale recipe is a clone of a beer from Victor Novak of Taps Fish House and Brewery in Brea, California. Victor is an award-winning brewer and, in fact, his Cream Ale won the gold medal at the 2005 and 2001 Great American Beer Festival (the Academy Awards of beer). Victor was kind enough to give us his recipe and we scaled it down to our kind of brewing. This Cream Ale is a straw-colored, light-bodied beer that has just a slight fruitiness, just a touch of corn in the nose, a nice hop presence, and a soft touch of sweetness in the finish. In the homebrew spirit of "What the hell, let's do it," we also added some apricot brandy just before bottling, and it turned out to be a fabulous addition! However, we feel the need to mention that this Cream Ale stands on its own without the addition. And if you're looking for an easy-drinkin' Ale to serve to beer newbies, this is your brew. Try it both ways and see what you prefer.

BREW IT: BRANDIED APRICOT CREAM ALE

DIFFICULTY LEVEL: Devout

TYPE OF BREWING: All-grain BIAB

SPECIALTY/EXTRA EQUIPMENT: Metal binder clips (or a
small Bungee cord), 7.5- to 8-gallon brew pot,
mason jar

TARGET OG: 1.051

TARGET FG: 1.008

IBUs: 10

TARGET ABV: 4.8%

PROPER GLASS: Pint

SHOPPING LIST

1 tube White Labs California Ale yeast
WLP001

4 gallons bottled spring water (not purified) or 2
gallons distilled water

3.75 pounds Pilsner malt—milled

10 ounces corn sugar (dextrose)

0.15 ounce Perle hop pellets

½ Whirlfloc tablet

0.25 ounce Fuggles hop pellets

2–4 ounces homemade apricot brandy (made 6
weeks before brew time; page 265), to taste

Makes about 2.5 gallons

PREP

■ *Prepare your yeast (at least 3 hours before you brew):* Let your tube
of California Ale yeast warm up to room temperature.

STEEP/MASH

▪ Heat 4 gallons of bottled spring water (or 2 gallons of tap water mixed with 2 gallons of distilled water). Attach a thermometer and heat the brew pot until it reaches 165°F. Turn off the heat.

▪ Put the milled grains (Pilsner malt) in the large grain bag. Slowly lower the grain bag into the water. Wrap the ends of the bag around the outside of the brew pot and secure the bag to the pot with several metal binder clips or a short Bungee cord. Stir the grains in the bag gently to make sure that all have been wetted. Cover with a lid and let rest for 60 minutes at 152°F. (You may need to turn the heat on and off to keep the temperature constant.)

▪ After 60 minutes, take the lid off of the pot, remove the clips or cord from the grain bag—being careful to prevent the grains from getting loose in the liquid—and slowly lift the grain bag out of the wort. Put a large fine-mesh strainer over the brew pot, and place the grain bag in the strainer. Let the hot wort drain from the bag for 5 to 10 minutes. Remove the grain bag and grains and discard.

THE BOIL

▪ Bring the pot to a boil.

▪ As soon as the pot comes to a boil, add the corn sugar; stir to dissolve. Immediately after the sugar addition, add your first hop addition, the Perle hops, and set your timer for 60 minutes. Stir occasionally, skimming off the big solids with a slotted spoon and looking out for the dreaded boilover!

▪ At 55 minutes (that is, with 5 minutes left in the boil), add the half tablet of Whirlfloc and stir to dissolve.

▪ At flameout (that is, when the boil is over and you've turned off the heat), immediately add your second hop addition, the Fuggles hops. Stir to dissolve and rest for 5 to 10 minutes.

PITCH THE YEAST

- *Prepare your ice bath:* In your sink or another vessel, prepare an ice bath to cool the beer down in.
- *Cool your wort:* Remove the pot from the heat and place it into your ice bath. Place a sanitized thermometer in the wort and let cool until it reaches 70°F or below.
- *Clean your stuff:* Sanitize anything that will come into contact with your beer.
- *Transfer your wort:* Pour the wort through a sanitized strainer into a 3- or 5-gallon plastic fermenting bucket or through a sanitized strainer and funnel into a 3- or 5-gallon glass carboy.
- *Pitch your yeast:* Shake your tube of yeast, sanitize the outside of the tube, crack it open, and throw all of its contents into the cooled wort in the fermenter.

PRIMARY FERMENTATION

- Place an airtight lid equipped with your airlock (filled with vodka) and stopper on the plastic bucket or place the airlock and stopper on a glass carboy. Or use the blow-off tube method (see Chapter 2).
- Keep the container in a dark and relatively cool place (ideal fermentation temperature for this style is as close to 68°F as you can get) for 2 weeks.
- Transfer to a bottling bucket and add the apricot brandy, stirring gently, so as not to aerate the beer at this point. This beer is very light, so a little apricot brandy will go a long way. Add it 1 tablespoon at a time—stirring and tasting in between (with a spoon that has been sanitized between each taste)—until you get the taste you like.
- Bottle for 14 days described in Chapter 2. Then (this is very important!), condition the bottles by storing them in the fridge for another 2 to 4 weeks before you drink. Then share with friends and enjoy.

Boerenmeisjes: Brandied Apricots

In Denmark, *boerenmeisjes* is a traditional way to preserve fresh apricots. The brandied apricots are served on pancakes and ice cream or with cheese, and the steeping liquor is served as a cordial at special occasions. You can do all those things with this lovely liqueur. Oh, and also, you can add it to the beer we're brewing this month—the Brandied Apricot Cream Ale. Here's our version, which uses dried apricots:

4 cups dried apricots
1 cup organic cane sugar
⅓ cup Riesling (semisweet or sweet)
Zest of 1 lemon (no pith)
1 cup brandy (or cognac)

Rinse the apricots under running water. Place them in a large saucepan, along with the sugar and wine. Soak for 24 hours. The next day, sanitize a 4-quart mason jar (just like you would your brewing equipment). Add the lemon zest to the apricot mixture and bring the saucepan to a boil. When mixture begins boiling, immediately remove the apricots and put them in the mason jar. Reduce the rest of the liquid by half. Remove the pan from the heat, cool slightly, and stir in the brandy. Remove the lemon zest from the saucepan and pour the liquid over the apricots and shake. Screw the lid on the jar and store in a cool, dark place for about 6 weeks.

RULE BREAKERS AND TIPS

- You do not have to add the apricot brandy. You'll still have a wonderfully crisp, smooth, light-bodied and mildly fruity Cream Ale! Or split the batch! Bottle the first 12 bottles with no addition, then add your apricot brandy to taste and bottle the rest.

- You can easily buy apricot brandy at the liquor store if you don't feel like making it.
- You could easily make this recipe all-extract by simply replacing the 2.75 pounds of Pilsner malt for a generous 2 pounds of Pilsner liquid malt extract.
- This style of beer truly benefits from very soft water, which is why we recommended using spring water or half distilled water in this recipe.

PROFESSIONAL BREWS TO ASPIRE TO

Summer Solstice Cerveza Crema: Anderson Brewing Co., Boonville, California. French bread in the nose and a lingering fruitiness in the background. This beer has subdued spicy hops, a light dry bitterness, and lots of creamy carbonation; 5.6% ABV.

Spotted Cow: New Glarus Brewing Co., New Glarus, Wisconson. A highly sessionable Cream Ale that is well-balanced and has a long, smooth finish and Wisconsin sweet corn notes with a dry finish; 4.8% ABV.

Nuptiale Cream Ale: Ninkasi Brewing Co., Eugene, Oregon. Straw hued, rich and creamy mouthfeel, balanced with thirst-quenching drinkability; 5.7% ABV.

YOUR MAY HOMEBREW 2

Decadent Dunkelweizen

MAKE THIS BEER IF YOU LIKE: Your nana's famous banana bread. Clouds in your coffee. Bananas dipped in chocolate. Skor bars.

PAIRS WELL WITH: Fried plantains, ricotta cheesecake, bananas Foster, and smoked rabbit and veal sausage.

STYLE AND BREWING NOTES

It's dark, it's decadent, it's Dunkelweizen. *Dunkel* is German for "dark" and *Weizen* is German for "wheat." It's a beer that is totally under-rated, in our humble opinion, and way underbrewed. Dunkelweizens have the same banana and clove notes that Hefeweizens have, but they use darker Chocolate, Caramel, and Munich malts that give this beer style a coffee and toffee quality. And, you guessed it, this beer is a style that, like a Hefeweizen, uses a substantial amount of wheat as part of its malt profile. The wheat gives the beer a breadiness that is reminiscent of banana bread or bananas Foster. Have you ever put chocolate chips into your banana bread? That is what this beer will taste like. Sounds good, right? And that is how you should describe it to a new beer drinking friend who may be afraid of darker beers. Who doesn't like bananas and chocolate?

This is an easy beer to brew. Yes, it's in the slightly advanced BIAB all-grain method, but you don't have to worry about secondary be-cause clarity isn't an issue. Dunkelweizens are meant to be a cloudy beer. Our very traditional version is a style of beer that really shines with all-grain brewing.

BREW IT: DECADENT DUNKELWEIZEN

DIFFICULTY LEVEL: **Promiscuous**

TYPE OF BREWING: **All-grain, BIAB**

SPECIALTY/EXTRA EQUIPMENT: **Metal binder clips (or small Bungee cord), 7.5- or 8-gallon brew pot**

TARGET OG: **1.058**

TARGET FG: **1.011**

IBUs: **26**

TARGET ABV: **6.1%**

PROPER GLASS: **Pint**

1 packet Wyeast Weihenstephaner Weizen
   yeast 3068

3 pounds 8 ounces flaked wheat

1 pound 8 ounces Munich malt—milled

1 pound Pilsner 2-row malt—milled

4 ounces Caramel/Crystal 40 L malt—milled

0.8 ounce Chocolate malt—milled

2 ounces Hallertauer Hersbrucker hop
   pellets

Makes about 2.5 gallons

PREP

■ *Prepare your yeast (at least 3 hours before you brew):* Crack your packet of Weihenstephaner Weizen yeast and let it warm up to room temperature. You can do this the day before you brew as well.

STEEP/MASH

■ Heat 4 gallons of water. Attach a thermometer and heat the brew pot until reaches 170°F. Turn off the heat.

■ Put the milled grains (flaked wheat and Munich, Pilsner 2-row, Caramel/Crystal 40 L, and Chocolate malts) in the large grain bag. Slowly lower the grain bag into the water. Wrap the ends of the bag around the outside of the brew pot and secure the bag to the pot with several metal binder clips or a short Bungee cord. Stir the grains in the bag gently to make sure that all have been wetted. Cover with a lid and let rest for 75 minutes at 150°F. (You may need to turn the heat on and off to keep the temperature constant.)

■ After 75 minutes, take the lid off of the pot, remove the clips or cord from the grain bag—being careful to prevent the grains from getting loose in the liquid—and slowly lift the grain bag out of the wort. Put a large fine-mesh strainer over the brew pot, and place the grain bag in the strainer. Let the hot wort drain from the bag for 5 to 10 minutes. Remove the grain bag and grains and discard.

THE BOIL

- Bring the pot to a boil.
- As soon as the pot comes to a boil, add the Hallertauer Hersbrucker hops, and set your timer for 60 minutes. The hops will dissolve immediately. Stir occasionally, skimming off the big solids with a slotted spoon and looking out for the dreaded boilover!

PITCH THE YEAST

- *Prepare your ice bath:* In your sink or another vessel, prepare an ice bath to cool the beer down in.
- *Cool your wort:* Remove the pot from the heat and place it into your ice bath. Place a sanitized thermometer in the wort and let cool until it reaches 70°F or below.
- *Clean your stuff:* Sanitize anything that will come into contact with your beer.
- *Transfer your wort:* Pour the wort through a sanitized strainer into a 3- or 5-gallon plastic fermenting bucket or through a sanitized strainer and funnel into a 3- or 5-gallon glass carboy.
- *Pitch your yeast:* Shake your packet of prepared yeast, sanitize the outside, tear it open, and throw all of its contents into the cooled wort in the fermenter.

PRIMARY FERMENTATION

- Place an airtight lid equipped with your airlock (filled with vodka) and stopper on the plastic bucket or place the airlock and stopper on a glass carboy. Or use the blow-off tube method (see Chapter 2).
- Keep the container in a dark and relatively cool place (ideal fermentation temperature for this style is between 64° and 75°F) for 10 to 14 days.

- Bottle for 14 days as described in Chapter 2. Then refrigerate and enjoy!

RULE BREAKER AND TIPS

- You can easily change this beer to an extract with specialty grains recipe. Just replace the flaked wheat with 2.6 pounds of Dark Wheat liquid malt extract and replace the Munich and Pilsner malts with 2 pounds of Munich liquid malt extract. Steep the rest of the grains (Chocolate and Caramel/Crystal) as specialty grains in 3 quarts of water for 30 minutes and follow the hop schedule in the recipe.

PROFESSIONAL BREWS TO ASPIRE TO

Dunkel Weiss: Great Divide Brewing Co., Denver, Colorado. Dark wheat bread with hints of cocoa, hazelnuts, banana, and clove; a hint of Weizen sourness in the middle is followed by a cocoa and bready finish; 6.4% ABV.

Weihenstephaner Hefeweissbier Dunkel: Bayerische Staatsbrauerei Weihenstephan, Freising, Germany. A medium-bodied classic Dunkelweizen with big clean banana notes and secondary spicy, clovey, and fruity characteristics; 5.3% ABV.

Franziskaner Hefe-Weissbier Dunkel: Spaten-Franziskaner-Bräu, Munich, Germany. A great Dunkelweizen, this complex brew has notes of banana and maraschino cherry. A bigger-feeling Dunkel, it is balanced by a bit of acidity; 5.5% ABV.

Fruity Faux Lambic

BREW THIS BEER IF YOU LIKE: Funky things. Having patience. Greek yogurt. Good bacteria. Sour acidity. Leaving things alone.

PAIRS WELL WITH: Pastrami Reuben, roasted duck, braised lamb, Gruyère cheese.

STYLE AND BREWING NOTES

Lambics are, without a doubt, considered the most difficult beers to brew. Traditionally, they are sour beers that come from the village of Lembeek in the Senne Valley in Belgium. They are wild-fermented beers that are naturally fermented by yeasts that exist in the air of the Senne Valley. These beers are considered some of the most complex, funky, strange, sour, acidic, dry beers in the world. We were very intimidated ourselves when we saw recipes with a complex turbid mashing processes and super-long low-temperature boils, steps that are difficult for even experienced brewers. We also decided to drink it young instead of waiting for a year for the beer, as many professional brewers do (we can't wait that long).

So we make kind of a fake Lambic. One that celebrates the sour, funky qualities of Lambics, using a Belgian Ale yeast as well as a Lambic yeast blend that, in addition to yeast, also contains bacteria cultures (like *Lactobacillus*, *Brettanomyces*, and *Pediococcus*), which are essential to the production of the spontaneously fermented, sour beers of the Lambic region. But we do just a single mash for 90 minutes at 150°F, which no Lambic brewer would consider respectable (their process is quite a bit more complicated). So we're not calling this beer a Lambic, we're calling it a Fauxbic, a Lambaux, a Fakebic, a Faux Lambic (OK, we're done). The Faux Lambic is a lighter, faster

Lambic style, if you will. A starter sour to get you into appreciating the interesting qualities of these funky-tasting beers.

Even though our Lambic is a little faux, we do use fruit as an addition to this beer, which is very traditional with Lambics. We have a cherry addition in secondary that balances the tart, acidic quality of the beer. It's delicious with our duck recipe (page 277) and a wonderful flavor for beer drinkers who prefer fruit-forward profiles.

Age Your Own Hops

Lambic beer styles are brewed with aged hops. What does that mean? Exactly that. These hops are old. They're months and years old. Brewers use aged hops in Lambics because they want the preservative quality that hops provide but they don't want any of the flavor or bitterness or aroma from the hops. Due to sour beer's popularity, it's pretty easy nowadays to buy aged hops at your local homebrew supply store or to order aged hops online. However, these hops are still somewhat limited and are often sold out. We have two solutions: a long one and a short one (that's what she said!). You can actually age hops yourself by putting them in a paper bag, stowing them away someplace warm and dry, and then waiting— for about 6 months to a couple of years (that would be the long-term solution). Or you can do our preferred method we learned from a fellow homebrew club member. He taught us how to fake-age our hops by baking them in the oven. Simply spread out your hops on a cookie sheet and bake them at 200°F for about 30 minutes. Let them cool and use them in your brew as per the recipe. Fake-aged hops definitely go with a Faux Lambic!

BREW IT: FRUITY FAUX LAMBIC

DIFFICULTY LEVEL: **Promiscuous**

TYPE OF BREWING: **All-grain BIAB**

SPECIALTY/EXTRA EQUIPMENT: **Metal binder clips (or
small Bungee cord), 7.5- or 8-gallon brew pot**

TARGET OG: **1.054**

TARGET FG: **1.010**

IBUs: **5.6**

TARGET ABV: **5%**

PROPER GLASS: **Flute**

SHOPPING LIST

1 tube White Labs Belgian Ale yeast WLP550

2.5 pounds Pilsner 2-row malt—milled

2 pounds Torrified Wheat malt—milled (or flaked
wheat)

8 ounces Carapils malt—milled

0.5 ounce aged Hallertauer hop cones

1 packet Wyeast Belgian Lambic Blend yeast 3278

3 pounds frozen and thawed sour cherries, pits in
(or other seasonal fruit)

2.5 ounces corn sugar (dextrose)

8 grams dry yeast

Makes about 2.5 gallons

PREP

■ *Prepare your first yeast (at least 3 hours before you brew):* Allow
your tube of Belgian Ale yeast to warm up to room temperature.

STEEP/MASH

■ Heat 4.5 gallons of water. Attach a thermometer and heat the brew
pot until reaches 170°F. Turn off the heat.

- Put the grains (Pilsner 2-row, Torrified Wheat, and Carapils malts) in the large grain bag. Slowly lower the grain bag into the water. Wrap the ends of the bag around the outside of the brew pot and secure the bag to the pot with several metal binder clips or a short Bungee cord. Stir the grains in the bag gently to make sure that all have been wetted. Cover with a lid and let rest for 90 minutes at 150°F. (You may need to turn the heat on and off to keep the temperature constant.)

- After 90 minutes, take the lid off of the pot, remove the clips or cord from the grain bag—being careful to prevent the grains from getting loose in the liquid—and slowly lift the grain bag out of the wort. Put a large fine-mesh strainer over the brew pot, and place the grain bag in the strainer. Let the hot wort drain from the bag for 5 to 10 minutes. Remove the grain bag and grains and discard.

THE BOIL

- Bring the pot to a boil.

- As soon as the pot comes to a boil, add the aged Hallertauer hops, and set your timer for 90 minutes. Stir occasionally, skimming off the big solids with a slotted spoon and looking out for the dreaded boil-over!

PITCH THE YEAST

- *Prepare your ice bath:* In your sink or another vessel, prepare an ice bath to cool the beer down in.

- *Cool your wort:* Remove the pot from the heat and place it into your ice bath. Place a sanitized thermometer in the wort and let cool until it reaches 70°F or below.

- *Clean your stuff:* Sanitize anything that will come into contact with your beer.

- *Transfer your wort:* Pour the wort through a sanitized strainer and funnel into a 3- or 5-gallon glass carboy (use glass with this one; plastic is too porous for the amount of time this beer will be sitting in the fermenter).

- *Pitch your first yeast:* Shake the tube of Belgian Ale yeast, crack it open, and dump it into the fermenter.

PRIMARY FERMENTATION

- Place an airtight lid equipped with your airlock (filled with vodka) and stopper on the plastic bucket or place the airlock and stopper on a glass carboy. Or use the blow-off tube method (see Chapter 2).
- Keep the container in a dark and relatively warm place (ideal fermentation temperature for this style is between 68° and 78°F) for 5 to 7 days.
- *After 5 to 7 days, prepare your second yeast (at least 3 hours before pitching):* Crack your packet of Belgian Lambic Blend yeast and allow it to warm up to room temperature.

PITCH YOUR SECOND YEAST

- Don't worry about transferring this beer to a different container. Lambic rules (or lack thereof) are a little different. Just throw the second yeast in the beer, and reseal with the airlock and stopper. Keep the container between 63° and 75°F for 4 to 6 weeks.

ADD YOUR FRUIT

- After 4 to 6 weeks, add the thawed cherries and reseal with the airlock and stopper. Keep the container around 70°F for another 4 to 6 weeks.
- Transfer the beer from the primary fermenter to a 3- to 5-gallon bucket or glass carboy with a sanitized tube siphon, aerating the beer as little as possible. (Make sure to leave the sediment behind.) If there's something floating in your Lambic—don't worry about it, just work around it; it's supposed to be there. Bottle as described in Chapter 2, adding the corn sugar and dry yeast to the bottling bucket.
- Condition the bottles in a dark closet for 2 to 12 months, tasting at intervals. That's right, you heard us. What might be undrinkable in 2 months could be an award-winning Lambic in 12.

RULE BREAKERS AND TIPS

- You can make this beer as an extract base instead of an all-grain. Replace the grains with 2.5 pounds of Wheat liquid malt extract and 3 pounds of Pilsner liquid malt extract.
- Instead of frozen fruit, you can use a fruit puree, such as those by Oregon Fruit Products. These are 100% fruit with no pits or seeds. Use ½ to 1 (49-ounce) can per 2.5-gallon batch of beer. The purees come in raspberry, cherry, apricot, and peach. You can get them at your local homebrew supply store or order straight from the source at www.fruitforbrewing.com.
- Let this beer go for as long as you can. Try it, as recommended, after 2 months, but this beer really should be given 6 months to a year (or longer—yikes!). Hide a few bottles where you'll never remember them, so when you find them again you'll have a pleasant surprise waiting for you!

PROFESSIONAL BREWS TO ASPIRE TO

Cantillon Kriek: Brasserie Cantillon, Brussels, Belgium. This is an amazing beer from an amazing brewery. Sour and puckery tart cherries balanced with a funky middle and crisp acidic finish. A smack on the palate; 5% ABV.

Wisconsin Belgian Red: New Glarus Brewing Co., New Glarus, Wisconsin. One of our absolute favorite Lambic-style beers, but only available in Wisconsin. This smuggle-worthy beer is fermented with over a pound of Door County cherries in each bottle, making it intensely cherried; 5.1% ABV.

Selin's Grove Phoenix Kriek: Selin's Grove Brewing Co., Selinsgrove, Pennsylvania. Rich with balanced sour and sweet cherries. Nice warmth with a touch of vanilla; 8% ABV.

Roast Duck with Sour Cherry Lambic Sauce

1 (4–5-pound) duck, neck and giblets removed, ex-
    cess fat trimmed, cut into six pieces (breasts,
    wings, and leg quarters)
Salt and freshly ground black pepper to taste

SAUCE
1½ cups Fruity Faux Lambic
⅛ cup dried tart cherries, halved
1½ teaspoons minced shallot

Serves 4

In a large stock pot with a lid, bring 2 inches of water to a boil. Reduce the heat to medium low, place duck pieces into steamer insert in the pot, and steam, covered, for 45 minutes, replenishing water, if necessary.

Meanwhile, make the sauce. Bring the beer, cherries, and shallot to a boil in small saucepan; reduce the heat to a bare simmer, and cook uncovered until the liquid is reduced to about ⅓ cup, about 40 minutes. Cover to keep warm.

Preheat oven to 450°F. Allow a large cast-iron skillet or heavy roasting pan to heat up in the oven.

Season the steamed duck generously with salt and pepper. Place the leg quarters and wings, skin side down, in the hot pan and roast 15 minutes. Turn the duck pieces skin side up and add the breast pieces to pan, skin side down. Roast another 10 to 12 minutes, or until the skin is deep brown and crispy.

Pour hot cherry Faux Lambic sauce over duck and serve.

   Tip: Reserve the duck fat that accumulated from steaming and roasting. You can make some seriously sexy roasted root vegetables by using just a few tablespoons of that.

Serve with a flute of Fruity Faux Lambic!

Glossary

ABV (Alcohol by Volume) Standard measurement of the amount of alcohol present in a beverage.

ABW (alcohol by weight) Alternative to ABV for measuring alcohol content. Beware, these two measures are not created equal. To convert from ABW to ABV, multiply the ABW by 1.25.

Adjunct (1) Unmalted grain (such as oats, rye, or wheat) and other sugar sources added as a supplement to malted barley for brewing. (2) A starch used in brewing other than malted barley, sometimes used for flavor, sometimes for mouthfeel, sometimes instead of an amount of malt, making the beer cheaper to make.

Airlock and stopper Device used during fermentation to allow the escape of carbon dioxide from the fermentation vessel, while preventing inflow of air and potential contaminants.

Ale Beer made with top-fermenting yeast at warm temperatures.

All-grain or full mash A brew made with all grains and raw malted barley, instead of malt extracts. This requires space and time and is quite advanced in the brewing world. This is often the practice of professional brewers.

Alpha acids Compounds in hops that cause their characteristic bitterness.

Alt Old German; refers to a German style of beer similar to a Pale Ale.

Aroma hops Added last to the boil, meant to lend hop aromas without bitterness or flavor.

Attenuation Amount of fermentation that has occurred and how much the Original Gravity has decreased. Refers to the final ABV.

Auto-siphon Siphoning hose attached to a one-way valve for easy transfer of liquid between containers.

Bacteria Single-celled organisms responsible for a vast diversity of human experience, from disease to digestion, medicine, cheese making, pickling, and fermentation.

Barrel Traditionally made of wood, a cylindrical vessel with a 31-gallon capacity (this capacity is particular to barrels intended for beer). Can also be filled with monkeys.

Base malt Malt used as the main source of sugar for fermentation.

Bavarian From the German state of Bavaria, an area thickly populated with breweries.

Beer geek Us. And possibly you.

Beer snob One who uses his or her knowledge of beer to exclude, alienate, and judge, rather than share, guide, and spread the love.

Bittering hops Used early in the boil to bitter the beer, not for aroma.

Blow-off tube Large tube attached to the top of a carboy as an alternative to an airlock; very useful in the case of overflows during fermentation.

Bottle conditioned Carbonated by living yeast in the bottle.

Brettanomyces Genus of yeast often employed in brewing.

Campden tablets Used for removal of chlorine and undesirable wild yeast and bacteria from wort.

Caramel/Crystal malt Malt that is heated while wet to caramelize its starches.

Carboy Glass or plastic narrow-mouthed container, usually with a 3- to 5-gallon capacity, used for primary fermentation and as a secondary vessel.

Cask Wooden barrel used to ferment or mature beer, wine, and other potent potables.

Cask conditioned Carbonated by a second fermentation in the barrel.

Chill haze Cloudy appearance of beer caused by proteins and tannins clumping together at cold temperatures.

CO$_2$ Carbon dioxide.

Cold break Sediment that settles to the bottom of the vessel when wort is cooled.

Cold crash Refrigeration of a brew to force suspended particles to sink to the bottom, resulting in a clearer beer.

Coupler Connecter that joins a tap to a keg.

Decoction Mashing technique by which a portion of the mash is removed and boiled, then returned to the whole to raise the temperature.

Devout Believer in beer. In this book: A brewer who's really into it and ready for slightly more advanced recipes.

Dextrins Unfermentable sugars that contribute to sweetness and mouthfeel.

Diacetyl Volatile compound produced during fermentation that in very low doses provides a slick mouthfeel and in larger doses a buttery or off-flavor. Acceptable in some beer styles, incorrect in others.

Dry hopping Process of adding hops after fermentation to lend supplementary hoppy character.

Dunkel German for "dark."

Esters Compounds responsible for most fruity aromas in beer.

Fermentation Metabolic process by which yeast converts sugars to alcohol and carbon dioxide.

Fermenter Vessel in which fermentation occurs; usually a large lidded bucket or glass carboy with an airlock.

Final Gravity Measurement of the density of the wort after fermentation. By comparing the Original Gravity and Final Gravity, you can calculate the ABV.

Flavor hops Used later in the boil to add some aroma and flavor.

Flavorings Extras added to some beers solely for flavor, such as fruits, some spices, and coffee.

Flocculation Clumping together of yeast into sediment toward the end of fermentation.

Gluten Protein present in many grains, such as wheat and barley.

Grain bag Fine-mesh bag for containing grain during boiling or steeping.

Grain bill All the grains that will go into the mash.

Gravity Measure of the amount of sugar and dissolved solids in beer.

Grist Mixture of grains that are crushed in a mill and prepared for mashing.

Growler Take-home container for beer, allowing for the transport of beer from pubs or breweries for home consumption.

Gruit Medieval herb blend used to flavor beer before the widespread use of hops.

Half-barrel Vessel with the standard capacity of 15.5 gallons of beer.

Hefe German for "yeast."

Helles or heller German for "pale."

Hop pellets Little things that look like gross vitamins, used by most homebrewers in lieu of dried or fresh hops.

Hophead A person addicted to the bitterness characteristic of hoppy beers.

Hops Flower cones of the hop plant, used in brewing for their aroma and bitterness. They also have a preservative quality.

Hot break Sediment that settles to the bottom of the vessel while wort is hot.

Humulus lupulus Scientific name of hops.

Hydrometer Device that measures the density of a liquid against the density of water. You will need to take an initial measurement of the density of the beer before and after fermentation. This will help you figure out the ABV of your beer.

IBU (International Bitterness Units) Scale for the measurement of bitterness in beer.

Iodophor Sanitizer commonly used by homebrewers.

Irish moss Variety of red algae used as a clarifying agent in beer.

Kolner Stangen or Stange German for "stick" or "rod." Refers to the traditional glass used to drink Kölsch.

Kraeusen Foam layer produced by yeast during fermentation.

Lactobacillus Common bacteria sometimes used to add sourness to beer, though some strains can be responsible for beer spoilage.

Lager Beer made with bottom-fermenting yeast at cold temperatures. The term *lagering* traditionally refers to a prolonged, cold-storage maturation.

Lightstruck Term used to describe a beer that has off-flavors caused by exposure to light.

Lovibond Scale used to measure degrees of color, such as in roasted grain or beer.

Malt Grain (usually barley) that has germinated and been dried or roasted.

Malt extract Concentrated liquid formed from wort that contains the sugars needed for brewing. This is what most homebrewers use as an alternative to all-grain brewing.

Maltose Sugar produced by enzymes from malted barley starch.

Mash Process in which the crushed grains are mixed into hot water and enzymes change the starch into fermentable (sometimes unfermentable) sugars for the yeast to eat.

Mash tun Vessel that contains the mash during all-grain brewing.

Microbrew The product of a brewery that produces less than 15,000 barrels per year.

Mouthfeel Sensation in the mouth exclusive of flavor, as texture, body, and carbonation.

Neophyte Beer newbie. In this book: a brewer who's totally new to brewing and needs to start out slowly.

Nitrogen tap Tap system that introduces nitrogen into beer during the pour, resulting in a creamy texture and weighty mouthfeel.

Noble hops Refers collectively to four hop varieties from central Europe: Hallertauer Mittelfruh, Tetramer, Saaz, and Spalter.

Original Gravity Measurement of the density of the liquid wort before fermentation, important for later ABV determination.

Oxidation Degradation of beer caused by exposure to oxygen over time.

Partial mash A wort made partially from grain and partially from malt extract.

Pasteurization Process of terminating microbial growth by means of heat.

Phenols Compounds producing certain flavors and aromas, sometimes desirable (as in the clove notes imparted by certain yeast), sometimes undesirable (as in the medicinal/plastic flavors imparted by contaminants like chlorine).

Pitch Term for adding the yeast to the cooled wort, as in "time to pitch the yeast!"

Primary fermentation The initial stage of fermentation, in which yeast converts the sugar in the wort into alcohol and CO_2.

Priming Addition of sugar (priming sugar) to beer that has already fermented. This occurs as the beer is being bottled to promote more flavor nuances and/or alcohol and carbonation.

Priming sugar Sugar added to beer in the bottling phase, to activate yeast for production of CO_2.

Prohibition The bad time.

Promiscuous Experimenting with beer. In this book: a brewer who's up for anything and ready for advanced recipes.

Rack Process of moving beer at different stages of homebrewing.

Rauch German for "smoke"; usually refers to smoked malts.

Roasted malt Malt that has been toasted until brown to produce color and flavor in beer.

Saccharomyces cerevisiae Yeast employed in brewing. Also known as brewer's yeast.

Schwarz German for "black"; usually refers to a very dark Lager.

Secondary Additional aging process for beer that has been separated from the trub after primary fermentation.

Session or sessionable Beer with moderate to low alcohol content, suitable for drinking in quantity over a leisurely stretch of time.

Sophomore The newly initiated. In this book: a brewer who's moving up in the homebrew world and ready for recipes just above the neophyte brewer's level.

Sparge Rinsing of grains to extract remaining wort and flavors.

Specialty malts Small amounts of malt used for flavoring and nuance. These can be steeped like tea instead of turned into a mash.

Specific gravity A measure of sugar content, and therefore, ultimately the alcohol content of beer.

Spent grain Grain left behind after the mashing process is completed.

SRM (standard reference method) A measurement of beer and malt color much like Lovibond.

Starch Carbohydrate present in grains that is converted to sugar by enzymes.

Star San Sanitizer commonly used by homebrewers.

Steeping grains Used to add flavor, nuance, and/or color for brewers using a malt extract. These do not need to be converted to sugar and can be steeped like tea.

Strike water Water added to malted grains in the formation of mash.

Tannin Bitter or astringent chemical.

Trub Sediment that accumulates at the bottom of the boiling vessel, and later the fermenter, composed mostly of grain and hop particles, yeast and protein.

Weisse German for "white"; refers to a Wheat beer. See also *Weizen*.

Weizen German for "wheat"; refers to a Wheat beer. See also *Weisse*.

Wet hopped Beer made with the addition of fresh, undried hops.

Whirlfloc tablet Easy-to-use tablet composed of Irish moss and carrageenan, used for clarifying beer.

Wit Flemish for "white"; usually refers to Belgian-style Wheat beer.

Wort Gross name chosen for the liquid that is extracted from the mash. Pronounced "wert."

Yeast Single-celled fungi responsible for the fermentation process.

Yeast Smack-pack Style of yeast packaging in which a small pouch of nutrients is broken open inside of a larger pack of yeast to awaken the yeast.

Yeast starter Kind of mini wort solution of malt extract and water, used to encourage a large viable colony of yeast.

Homebrew Resources: Your Lifeline

We all need a lot of help when we brew. We need inspiration, community, love, criticism, connection, suggestion, and some good hard numbers. The following are resources we know and love; they will help you air your frustration, gather answers, share the joy of homebrewing, advance your brew recipes, and find ingredients and equipment for your new favorite hobby. We highly recommend joining your local homebrew club and getting to know the brewers at your local brewery, both will be important advisers and resources.

- **Brewing software:** This software has been indispensable to us as we created our own beer recipes. Usable directly online or as downloadable software, these tools help you calculate your beers potential ABV, color, bitterness, and so on and help you keep your beer on style—if that is what you desire!

  Beersmith: www.beersmith.com
  BeerTools: www.beertools.com

Hopville: www.hopville.com
ProMash: www.promash.com

- **Websites:** The series of tubes known as the Internet has been a huge step forward in spreading beer knowledge to the people. With discussions and expert instruction on style, nuance, brand, how to brew, and what to look for in a beer, these websites have been invaluable to us as our learning progresses:

  American Homebrewers Association: www.homebrewersasso ciation.com
  Beer Advocate: www.beeradvocate.com
  Beer Judge Certification Program (BJCP): www.bjcp.org
  Brew Your Own: www.byo.com
  Cicerone Certification Program: www.cicerone.org
  Homebrew Talk: www.homebrewtalk.com
  Rate Beer: www.ratebeer.com

- **Suppliers of ingredients** (also check at your local farmers' market):

  Culver City/Eagle Rock Homebrew Supply: www.brewsupply.com
  Midwestsupplies.com
  Morebeer.com
  Northernbrewer.com
  Spicestationsilverlake.com
  Wholefoodsmarket.com

- **Other books** that are great resources:

  Sam Calagione, *Extreme Brewing: An Enthusiast's Guide to Brewing Craft Beer at Home* (Gloucester, Mass.: Quarry Books, 2006).
  Ray Daniels, *Designing Great Beers* (Boulder, Co.: Brewers Publications, 1998).

Randy Mosher, *Radical Brewing* (Boulder, Co.: Brewers Publications, 2004).

Garrett Oliver, *The Oxford Companion to Beer* (New York: Oxford University Press, 2011).

John Palmer, *How to Brew* (Boulder, Co.: Brewers Publications, 2006).

Charlie Papazian, *The Complete Joy of Homebrewing* (New York: William Morrow, 2003).

Christina Perozzi and Hallie Beaune, *The Naked Pint* (New York: Perigee, 2009) (shameless plug).

Jamil Zainasheff and John Palmer, *Brewing Classic Styles* (Boulder, Co.: Brewers Publications, 2007).

- **Magazines:**

  All About Beer
  Beer Advocate
  Beer West
  Brew Your Own: The How-To Homebrew Beer Magazine
  Celebrator
  DRAFT Magazine
  Zymurgy

- **Blogs:**

  Brookston Beer Bulletin: http://brookstonbeerbulletin.com
  Hot Knives: www.urbanhonking.com/hotknives
  The Beer Chicks: www.thebeerchicks.com (shameless plug)
  The Mad Fermentationist: www.themadfermentationist.com

- **Radio Shows and Podcasts:**

  Brewstrong: http://thebrewingnetwork.com/shows/Brew-Strong
  The Sunday Session: http://thebrewingnetwork.com/shows/The -Sunday-Session

The Jamil Show: http://thebrewingnetwork.com/shows/The
-Jamil-Show

Basic Brewing Radio: www.basicbrewing.com/index.php?page=
radio

Beer O'Clock: http://beergoddess.com/beer_o_clock

Hop Chart

Here's a reference chart that will help you get to know the different varieties of hops. The flavors and alpha acid content greatly affect your brew. There are many different types of hops that can and will keep you experimenting in homebrew recipes for the rest of your life. Here are some of the characteristics of commonly used hops, including the hops used in this book.

Hop	Alpha Acid (%)	Use	Flavor/Aroma
Amarillo	8–11	Aroma, can be used as bittering and flavor	Citrus, floral
Cascade	4.5–7.5	Bittering, aroma	Grapefruit, citrus, floral
Centennial	9–11.5	Bittering, aroma	Spicy, citrus,
Challenger	6.5–8	Bittering, flavor, aroma	Spicy, clean
Chinook	11–14	Bittering	Bold, spicy
Cluster	5.5–8.5	Bittering, flavor, aroma	Clean, spicy
Columbus	12–16	Bittering, flavor, aroma	Herbal
East Kent Golding	4–7	Bittering, aroma	Spicy, earthy, floral
Fuggles	4–5.5	Aroma	Grassy, mild
Galena	12–14	Bittering	Strong
Hallertauer	3–5	Aroma	Earthy, spicy, noble, herbal
Liberty	3–5	Aroma	Mild, spice, clean
Mt. Hood	3–8	Aroma	Mild, clean
Northdown	7–9.5	Bittering	Clean
Northern Brewer	6–10	Bittering	Dry
Nugget	12–14.5	Bittering, aroma	Herbal, spicy
Perle	6–9.5	Bittering	Mint, spice
Pioneer	8–10	Bittering, aroma	Citrus notes
Saaz	2–5	Aroma	Floral, mild
Simcoe	12–14	Bittering, flavor, aroma	Citrus, grapefruit, tropical fruit
Sorachi Ace	10–12	Bittering	Lemon, citrus
Sterling	6–9	Bittering, flavor, aroma	Spice, herbal, citrus
Styrian Golding	4.5–6.5	Bittering, aroma	Mild, spicy
Target	8–12	Bittering, flavor	Herbal
Tettnanger	3.5–6	Aroma	Spice
Ultra	2–4.5	Aroma	Floral, spicy, mild
Warrior	15–17	Bittering	Clean, bitter
Willamette	3.5–7	Aroma	Floral, spicy, grassy
Zeus	13–17	Aroma	Aromatic

Malt Chart

Here are some of the most common kinds of malt used in brewing. The base malts serve as the base of many beers and provide the majority of the sugars for the yeast to eat as well as some flavor and color (*in extract-only brewing, these are replaced by malt extract*). The specialty malts can provide sugars as well but predominantly provide flavor and color.

Base Malts (Used for Mashing, Not Typically Steeped)

American 2-Row	Barley with two rows on the stem; solid base for most beers, offers a lot of fermentable sugars
English Pale	Nutty, toasty
Marris Otter malt	Rich and toasty, nutty, a bit bigger than English Pale
Pilsner malt	Light, mellow flavor
Rye malt	Can be added to other base malts. Spicy rye character
Wheat malt	Can be added to other base malts; adds body to a beer

Kilned and/or Roasted Specialty Malts (Can Be Mashed or Steeped)

Aromatic	Intense malty aroma and flavor
Biscuit	Big biscuit, bready, pie crust notes
Black barley	Coffee, chocolate notes with more of a burned flavor
Black Patent	Bold notes of bitter espresso and chocolate with an acrid, ash flavor
Brown malt	Toasted bread and biscuit notes
Carafa malts	Smooth roasted coffee notes
Caramel/Crystal malt	Comes in many different roast levels; offers sweet caramel, toffee, and honey notes
CaraMunich	Rich toasty sweetness slightly bigger than Caravienne
Carapils	Not used for flavor but provides good head retention and body
Caravienne	Caramel, toasty toffee notes
Chocolate malt	Chocolate notes (obviously), cocoa, vanilla, caramel
Honey malt	Big honey notes; hint of bread too
Munich	Rich malty flavor; toast and toffee notes
Rauch malt	Malt that has been smoked over wood; tastes like smoke and bacon
Roasted barley	Big coffee, chocolate flavors
Special B	Provides big notes of fig, raisin, plum, nutty, caramel in Belgian Dubbels
Special Roast	Biscuit flavor and orange color
Victory	Biscuity, nutty flavor
Vienna	Toasty sweet notes (can be used as a base malt)

Malt Extracts: Popular Choices (Replace the Mashing of the Base Malt in All-Grain or Partial-Mash Brewing)

Amber liquid malt extract	Darker than Pale extract, toasty flavors
Dark malt extract	Rich dark color used as a base for dark beers
Dry Amber malt extract	Made with crystal malt, amber in color
Dry Light malt extract	Great for light-colored beers, helps raise gravity levels
Golden syrup	Good for head retention
Light liquid malt extract	Light color and malty base
Munich liquid malt extract	Rich, toasty flavor; made with Munich and Pilsner malt
Pale liquid malt extract	The base of most extract beers, malt flavors
Pilsner Light liquid malt extract	Super-light, good clean base flavor, offers good head retention
Rauch liquid malt extract	Very hard to find, made from dark smoked malt
Wheat malt extract	Made from wheat and barley, used for many Wheat beer styles

Yeast Chart

This chart lists every yeast we use in this book and in which recipe(s) it appears. Each yeast has different qualities and is best for a different variety of styles.

Yeast	Characteristics	Alternative	Styles	Used In
Wyeast London Ale yeast 1028; temperature range: 60°–72°F	Minerally, bold, crisp, and fruity	White Labs London Ale yeast WLP013	Mild, English Brown Ale, dry Stouts, Russian Imperial Stouts, Porters, Barleywine	Summer English Pale (page 54)
Wyeast American Ale yeast 1056; temperature range: 60°–72°F	Clean, crisp, mild fruit and citrus; allows malt and hop character to shine through	White Labs California yeast WLP001; Wyeast American Ale II yeast 1272	American Pale, American Amber, American Brown, Irish Red, IPAs, Russian Imperial Stout, Scotch Ale, Barleywine	West Coast Hopped-Up Pale (page 59), Black Smoke Pale (page 63), Zee Russian Imperial Stout (page 190)
Wyeast Weihenstephaner Weizen yeast 3068; temperature range: 64°–75°F	Banana and clove notes	White Labs Hefeweizen Yeast WLP300	German Hefeweizen, Dunkelweizen, Weizenbock	Traditional Bavarian Hefeweizen (page 71), Decadent Dunkelweizen (page 266)
White Labs Belgian Wit Ale liquid yeast WLP400; temperature range: 67°–74°F	Slightly tart, fruit notes	White Labs Belgian Wit II Ale liquid yeast WLP410	Witbiers, Belgian Ales, German-style Wheat, spiced Ales	Poor Man's Provence Lavender Wit (page 76), Dark and Stormy Witbier (page 250)
Wyeast Trappist High Gravity yeast 3787; temperature range: 64°–78°F	Balanced fruit notes	White Labs Abbey Ale Yeast WLP566	Dubbel, Tripel, Golden Strong, Bière de Garde	Sisters of Summer Tripel (page 81), Fig and Clove Dubbel (page 172)
Wyeast Kölsch yeast 2565; temperature range: 56°–70°F	Touch of fruit with a clean finish; ferments well at cold temperatures	White Labs WLP011 European Ale yeast	Kölsch, American Wheat or Rye, Berlinerweiss, Cream Ale, spiced/fruited beer	Crisp Summer Kölsch (page 90), Der Nackte Brauer Festbier (page 129)
Wyeast Northwest Ale yeast 1332; temperature range: 65°–75°F	Malty, mild fruit notes with nice complexity	White Labs British Ale yeast WLP005	American Pale Ale, IPA, American Brown, American Stout, American Red, Barleywine, Blonde Ale, spiced/fruited Ale	Honey Chamomile Blonde (page 96)
Wyeast American Wheat yeast 1010; temperature range: 58°–74°F	Dry finish, crisp, touch of tartness	White Labs American Hefeweizen Ale yeast WLP320	American Wheat, Cream Ale, Kölsch, Altbier	Lemon Verbena Basil Wheat (page 101)

Yeast	Characteristics	Alternative	Styles	Used In
White Labs California Ale yeast WLP001; temperature range: 68°–73°F	Clean flavors, balanced, versatile, accentuates hop flavors	Wyeast American Ale yeast 1056	American Cream Ale, American Wheat, herbed/spiced Ales, honey Ales, smoked beers, American Pale Ale, IPA, American Brown, American Amber, Barleywine	Just One Hop Simcoe IPA (page 109), Just One Hop Cascade IPA (page 114), East India Pale Ale (page 118), Imperial Blood Red (page 134), Brandied Apricot Cream Ale (page 261)
Wyeast Whitbread Ale yeast 1099; temperature range: 64°–75°F	Touch of malt and fruit, clean finish, not too dry	White Labs Bedford British Ale yeast WLP006	English IPA, Blonde Ale, Southern English Brown, Special Bitter, Oatmeal Stout	Pecan Pie Brown Ale (page 147), Controversial Pumpkin Ale (page 138)
Wyeast Belgian Ardennes yeast 3522; temperature range: 65°–76°F	Fruit and spice, balanced, versatile	White Labs Belgian Ale yeast WLP550	Belgian Pale Ale, Dubbel, Tripel, Strong Golden, Blonde, Flanders Brown	Cranberry Belgian Pale (page 153) Tropical Belgian-Style IPA (page 227)
Wyeast London ESB Ale yeast 1968; temperature range: 64°–72°F	Features the malt notes, sweet finish, touch of fruit	White Labs English Ale yeast WLP002	All British Bitters, mild Ale, Southern English Brown, English IPA, English Barleywine, wood-aged beer, spiced/herbed/fruited Ale, Old Ale	Sage Chestnut ESB (page 158)
Wyeast Ringwood Ale yeast 1187; temperature range: 64°–74°F	Pronounced fruit and malty notes	White Labs British Ale yeast WLP005	American Brown Ale, Porters, mild Ale, sweet Stout, Oatmeal Stout, American IPA, American Stout	Christmas Spiced Porter (page 166)
Wyeast Denny's Favorite yeast 1450; temperature range: 60°–70°F	Great for many beers; caramel, malt, fruit, dry finish, big mouthfeel	White Labs American Ale yeast WLP060	American Amber Ale, Irish Red Ale, Barleywine, American Brown Ale, American IPA, American Pale Ale, Russian Imperial Stout, smoked beer, Scotch Ale, wood-aged beer, spiced/herbed Ale, Dry Stout, Cream Ale, Christmas Ale	Stupid Cupid's Bittersweet Chocolate Stout (page 202)

Yeast	Characteristics	Alternative	Styles	Used In
White Labs Irish Stout yeast WLP004; temperature range: 65–68°F	Light fruit, dry crisp	Wyeast Irish Ale Yeast 1084	Irish Stout, Irish Red, Porters, Brown Ales, English IPA, English Bitters	Crescent City Café au Lait Stout (page 207), Dry Irish Stout (page 222)
Wyeast Scottish Ale yeast 1728; temperature range: 55°–75°F	Clean, neutral finish	White Labs Edinburgh Scottish Ale yeast WLP028	Scottish Ales, Imperial IPA, Imperial Stout, Barleywine, Christmas Ale, Baltic Porter, wood-aged beer, smoked beer	Groom's Scotch Whisky Wee Heavy (page 214)
Wyeast Belgian Abbey Ale yeast 1214; temperature range: 68°–78°F	Spicy notes, good for big alcohol Belgians	White Labs Abbey Ale yeast WLP530	Dubbel, Tripel, Witbier, Christmas Ale, Belgian Dark Strong Ale	Sisters of Summer Tripel (page 81)
White Labs Belgian Ale yeast WLP550; temperature range: 68°–78°F	Spicy flavors, not overly fruity	Wyeast Belgian Abbey Ale Yeast 1214	Saisons, Belgian Ales, Belgian Reds, white beers, Tripel	Fruity Faux Lambic (page 271)
Wyeast French Saison yeast 3711; temperature range: 65°–77°F	Rich mouthfeel, dry, enhances spice additions, pepper, spice and citrus notes	White Labs Belgian Saison I yeast WLP565	Saison, Bière de Garde, Witbier, Belgian Blonde, Belgian Golden and Dark Strong Ales	Bière de Mars (page 232)
Wyeast Belgian Saison yeast 3724; temperature range: 70°–95°F	Complex, spicy, tart, dry, fruit, acidic, does well at high temperatures	White Labs Belgian Saison I yeast WLP565	Saison	Saison Classique avec Miele (page 240), Rosemary Laurel Savory Saison, (page 245)
White Labs European Ale yeast WLP011; temperature range: 65°–70°F	Malty, low fruit esters, clean finish	Wyeast European Ale yeast 1338	Altbiers, Kölsch, English Ales, fruit beers	Berliner Weisse (page 185)
Wyeast *Lactobacillus delbrueckii* 4335; temperature range: 60°–95°F	Bacteria that creates a sour beer	White Labs *Lactobacillus* bacteria WLP677	Lambic, Gueuze, Berlinerweiss, Flander's Red Ale, Flander's Brown Ale, Lambic	Berliner Weisse (page 185)

Yeast	Characteristics	Alternative	Styles	Used In
Wyeast Champagne yeast 4021	Ferments crisp and dry with tiny bubbles	No equivalent	Champagne, Chardonnay, dry mead, Braggot, dry cider	Alpine Juniper Braggot (page 177), Scandalous Hard Apple Cider (page 195)
Wyeast Belgian Lambic Blend 3278	A combo of all the bacteria that make Lambics great; *Brettanomycese, Lactobacillus,* and *Pediococcus*	No equivalent	Lambic, Flanders Red Ale, Gueuze, Lambic	Fruity Faux Lambic (page 271)

INDEX

ABOUT THE AUTHORS

The Beer Chicks are **Christina Perozzi** and **Hallie Beaune**, beer sommeliers, consultants, and authors based in Los Angeles. Their first book, *The Naked Pint: An Unadulterated Guide to Craft Beer*, was released in 2009 to wide acclaim. They are nationally featured experts in the world of beer and have recently appeared on FOX's *Hell's Kitchen*, the Cooking Channel's *Food(ography)*, and on their own one-hour special combining their love of beer, food, and spirits on the Cooking Channel called *Eat This, Drink That*.

They've also appeared numerous times as beer experts on radio and in print, including KCRW's *Good Food*, *Gourmet* magazine, and *Everyday with Rachael Ray*. Together they curate the beers for the L.A. Craft Beer Crawl, an annual downtown Los Angeles beer festival featuring craft and artisanal beers from some of the world's finest breweries. Christina and Hallie have consulted on some of the best beer lists in Los Angeles, creating a unique selection of craft beer at each venue, and training staff on the intricacies of beer.

Christina and Hallie continue to spread the good word of beer through their website www.thebeerchicks.com. They are avid homebrewers and devoted home cooks.

They live by the motto Beer Is Good.